THE THIRD DOCTOR
SOURCEBOOK

CREDITS

LINE DEVELOPER: Gareth Ryder-Hanrahan

WRITING: Walt Ciechanowski and Graham Walmsley

EDITING: Andrew Kenrick and Dominic McDowall

COVER: Paul Bourne

GRAPHIC DESIGN AND LAYOUT: Paul Bourne

CREATIVE DIRECTOR: Dominic McDowall

ART DIRECTOR: Jon Hodgson

SPECIAL THANKS: Georgie Britton and the BBC Team for all their help.

"My Third is Reversed In The Neutron Flow"

The Third Doctor Sourcebook is published by Cubicle 7 Entertainment Ltd (UK reg. no.6036414).

Find out more about us and our games at www.cubicle7.co.uk

◎ CONTENTS

INTRODUCTION

'Oh, dear. Oh, I can't have changed that much, surely?'

For a Time Lord, the Earth is a prison.

Once able to travel throughout time and space, the Doctor found himself exiled to a single place and time. His TARDIS was disabled and, for the first time, the Doctor had to rely on friends to aid and shelter him. Fortunately, he was able to convince Brigadier Lethbridge-Stewart of UNIT that he was the same man as the short, clownish, cosmic hobo that had helped defeat the Yeti and the Cybermen months before and was appointed Scientific Advisor.

It would prove to be a fortuitous relationship. From the moment the Doctor fell out of his TARDIS, Earth was besieged by alien races, including the Nestene Consciousness, the Silurians, the Axons, and even the Daleks. The Doctor even found a worthy adversary in the Master, a fellow Time Lord. Once granted his freedom for dealing with the renegade Time Lord Omega, the Doctor once again roamed time and space, while occasionally returning to Earth to continue in his role as Scientific Advisor.

Welcome to the **Third Doctor Sourcebook**, a resource for Gamemasters which covers the adventures of the Doctor in his third incarnation. Herein you have everything at your fingertips to recreate this era or to add vintage spice to your current **Doctor Who: Adventures in Time And Space** campaign. You'll find complete information on the Second Doctor, his companions, his enemies, and his adventures.

HOW TO USE THIS BOOK

The Third Doctor Sourcebook is primarily a Gamemaster's resource for running adventures either with or in the style of the Third Doctor. While players will certainly benefit from the background information on the Doctor and his Companions, all of the rules needed to create or portray the Third Doctor's Companions are found in the **Player's Guide**.

This book is designed to be a primer on capturing the feel of the Third Doctor's era and incorporating it into your adventures. **Chapter One: The Third Doctor and Companions** provides information on the Doctor's third incarnation as well his companions and extended UNIT family. **Chapter Two: Tools of the Trade** offers advice for creating characters for this campaign pack as well as new traits and gadgets. **Chapter Three: Enemies** looks at the various opponents that the Doctor faced during his exile and beyond while **Chapter Four: Designing Third Doctor Adventures** offers advice on crafting your own Third Doctor adventures as well as alternative ways to use the material in this book. **Chapters Five to Twelve** describe the Third Doctor's adventures.

Each adventure has the following sections:

- **Synopsis:** This section summarises the key events of the adventure as experienced by the Third Doctor and his companions.

- **Running this Adventure:** Next, we discuss how to run the adventure. We get into the nuts and bolts of plotting and gamemastering, how to adapt the adventure to different groups of player characters, and how to use bits and pieces of the adventure in your own games.

- **Characters, Monsters & Gadgets:** If there are important non-player characters, interesting monsters, or shiny new gadgets in the adventure, you'll find them here. Sometimes, we'll give you full statistics for a character. At other times, when their Attributes and Skills are obvious or irrelevant, we'll just list their key Traits.

- **Further Adventures:** So, what happens after the Doctor leaves? (Or what happened before he arrived?) These further adventure seeds give ideas on spinoffs, sequels and alternate histories that expand on the Doctor's initial adventures.

There are lots of ways to use these adventures. You can use our suggestions for Further Adventures, or build your own adventures using the material provided. In fact, if your players aren't familiar with these classic stories, then you can substitute your player characters for the Third Doctor and his companions and 'rerun' the adventures. Maybe your player characters will take other paths and make different decisions!

'What you need, Doctor, as Miss Shaw herself so often remarked, is someone to pass you your test tubes and to tell you how brilliant you are.'

WHO IS THE DOCTOR?

When the Doctor regenerated for the first time, it was almost as if time simply rolled back the clock; the old man, with help from the TARDIS, peeled back the years and transformed into a younger self, one that was a bit more clownish and anti-authoritarian. Whereas the older Doctor relied on companions to overcome his physical limitations he didn't particularly want the companionship (primarily because he knew that the TARDIS, in its own way, was a prison), the 'younger' Doctor enjoyed the company and actively invited people to join him for the fun of exploring the universe. It's worth noting that the Second Doctor chose teenagers as companions (Ben and Polly were holdovers) whose thirst for adventure matched his. It really was as if, as he agreed, he'd been renewed.

By contrast, the Third Doctor is less a renewal and more of a reboot. He is an active crusader against evil, utilising not only his wits but his martial skills as well. Neither of his previous incarnations took the fight to his enemies so directly. The Third Doctor also has a flair for fashion and a love of gadgets, particularly vehicles. He is not a reluctant hero or an underestimated schemer; he's an action hero. And while he initially distrusts authority, the Third Doctor's position on it softens with time, especially for UNIT. He even refers to the royal family as 'charming.' In spite of his crusade, the Third Doctor rails against being trapped on Earth in a single time and desperately tries to escape at the earliest opportunity, spending most of his free time trying to get the TARDIS working. He even traps the Master, a renegade Time Lord, on Earth for the opportunity to use components from his TARDIS. Once the Doctor's sentence is lifted, however, the Third Doctor finds it difficult to leave his new home entirely, frequently returning to battle the evils that plague it.

PLAYING THE THIRD DOCTOR

During his exile period, the Third Doctor is frustrated. He realises that he is more 'evolved' than those around him and presumes to lead, but is forced to balance that against his genuine need for the people and resources around him. He is at his best when he has a crusade to distract him and enthusiastically embraces scientists over soldiers. He distrusts the military and does his best to influence their decisions, knowing that left to their own devices the military has a tendency to blow things up rather than reason with its enemies.

This Doctor tends to confront his enemies head-on and often volunteers to investigate or meet and negotiate with potential adversaries. He relies on his wits and his Venusian Aikido to survive, utilising gadgets when neither is enough. The Doctor sees himself as an independent negotiator, relying on his own alien status to convince an enemy that he can be impartial over being merely a tool of the Earth authorities. Unfortunately, his efforts tend to be undermined by both sides.

Remember that the Doctor is always looking to escape Earth first and foremost. In his first adventure he almost abandons his work against the Nestene for the opportunity to escape and the closest person he has to a friend, the Brigadier, believes without question that if the TARDIS dematerialised he wouldn't see the Doctor again, at least not quickly enough to resolve the current crisis. Nor does the Doctor ease that concern when the TARDIS doesn't work, admitting that the temptation to travel the universe was too strong.

As the Doctor spends more time on Earth his desire to escape, while still strong, softens. He tried to repair his dematerialisation circuit which may or may not work (it's hinted that the Time Lords are behind at least some of these journeys) but always promises his current companion, Jo Grant, that he'll return to Earth. That said, he does take every opportunity to explore new planets.

If you're playing the Doctor toward the end of this era, especially when Sarah Jane Smith becomes his companion, he's mellowed to the point of treating the Brigadier as a friend rather than an authority figure and returns to UNIT-era Earth because he wants to. He is still as much a crusader against evil as he has always been and ends up giving his life (or at least his current incarnation) in order to save the Earth.

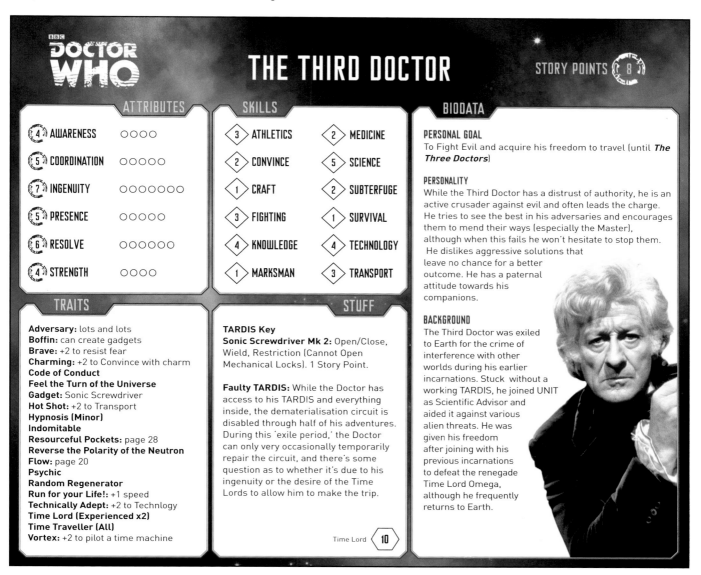

❂ THE DOCTOR'S COMPANIONS

In the beginning the Doctor didn't have Companions in the traditional sense; exiled to Earth, the Doctor lacked the capacity to have anyone join him on journeys through time and space. Instead, Companions are recruited out of professional need and are generally referred to as 'assistants'. Such Companions could come and go as they pleased and they continued to live in their own homes and maintained normal lives outside of the occasional alien invasion.

It was during this period that the Doctor realised he needed Companions, even when he wasn't going anywhere. While Liz Shaw was recruited specifically for her scientific skills, both she and the Doctor soon realised that he didn't need a laboratory assistant; he needed someone to explain things to and stroke his ego. Thus while Jo Grant and Sarah Jane Smith had useful skills outside of the laboratory, they became more the Doctor's confidante than assistant.

Of special note are UNIT members. Strictly speaking, the Brigadier, Captain Yates, and Sergeant Benton aren't Companions in the traditional sense, but they are usually part of the Doctor's inner circle when the Earth is threatened. If the Gamemaster is running an Exile campaign, then these characters would certainly qualify as playable Companions.

BRIGADIER ALISTAIR GORDON LETHBRIDGE-STEWART

Brigadier Alistair Gordon Lethbridge-Stewart, generally known simply as 'the Brigadier', first met the Doctor in his second incarnation while the Yeti invaded London. He was a Colonel then, but government worry over the incident led to the creation of the United Nations Intelligence Taskforce, or UNIT, with Lethbridge-Stewart promoted to Brigadier and offered command of the British division.

The Brigadier met the Doctor again when the Cybermen invaded London and, thanks to the Doctor and Zoe's help, was able to thwart it. It was this incident that convinced the Brigadier that weapons and manpower weren't enough; if he wanted to combat aliens with superior technologies then he needed scientists on his staff. He recruited Elizabeth Shaw, albeit rather ham-fistedly (perhaps reflecting on the Doctor, he relied on her curiosity to be enough to take the job), although during her interview the Brigadier learned that the Doctor had returned.

At first, the Brigadier could not believe that the Third Doctor was the same man as the Second in spite of the obvious evidence. Still, he took a chance and recruited the Third Doctor into UNIT as his Scientific Advisor. The Doctor aided UNIT in repelling many alien invasions and spoiling the plans of the renegade Time Lord known as the Master. When the Doctor regained his freedom the Brigadier took it in stride, although whenever the Doctor returned the Brigadier treated him as a member of UNIT.

The Brigadier is the epitome of the stiff-upper-lipped military officer, a combination of devotion to duty and a healthy respect for discipline. His authoritative demeanour and maintenance of secrecy regarding UNIT's activities has put a mortal strain on his personal life. Indeed, the Brigadier transfers some of his frustrations onto the Doctor, often dismissing his Scientific Advisor's contrary points of view and fearing that the Doctor will abandon him at the earliest opportunity. As their association continues the Brigadier comes to terms with his personal life and begins to consider the Doctor as a friend.

In spite of sometimes being at loggerheads, the Brigadier and the Doctor have a healthy respect for each other which

blossoms into true friendship. While the Brigadier always puts his duty first, he is a devoted friend who can be counted on when necessary. Even when he has to act contrary to the Doctor's wishes (such as blowing up the Silurian caves), the Brigadier is sensitive to his feelings.

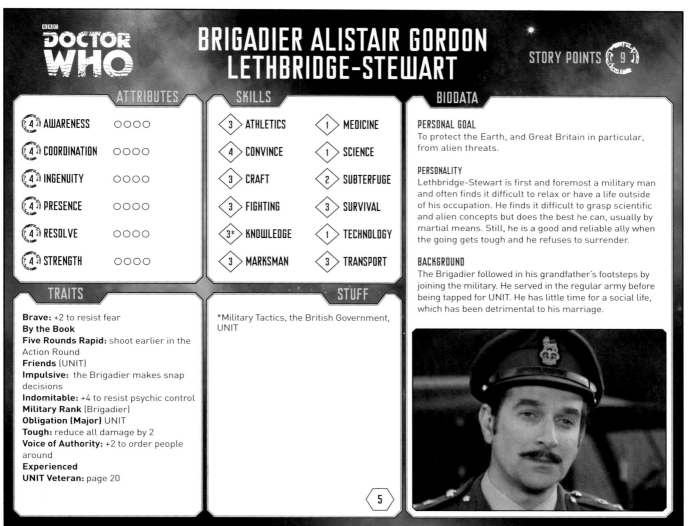

BRIGADIER ALISTAIR GORDON LETHBRIDGE-STEWART

STORY POINTS 9

ATTRIBUTES

- (4) AWARENESS ○○○○
- (4) COORDINATION ○○○○
- (4) INGENUITY ○○○○
- (4) PRESENCE ○○○○
- (4) RESOLVE ○○○○
- (4) STRENGTH ○○○○

SKILLS

- 3 ATHLETICS
- 4 CONVINCE
- 3 CRAFT
- 3 FIGHTING
- 3* KNOWLEDGE
- 3 MARKSMAN
- 1 MEDICINE
- 1 SCIENCE
- 2 SUBTERFUGE
- 3 SURVIVAL
- 1 TECHNOLOGY
- 3 TRANSPORT

TRAITS

Brave: +2 to resist fear
By the Book
Five Rounds Rapid: shoot earlier in the Action Round
Friends (UNIT)
Impulsive: the Brigadier makes snap decisions
Indomitable: +4 to resist psychic control
Military Rank (Brigadier)
Obligation (Major) UNIT
Tough: reduce all damage by 2
Voice of Authority: +2 to order people around
Experienced
UNIT Veteran: page 20

STUFF

*Military Tactics, the British Government, UNIT

BIODATA

PERSONAL GOAL
To protect the Earth, and Great Britain in particular, from alien threats.

PERSONALITY
Lethbridge-Stewart is first and foremost a military man and often finds it difficult to relax or have a life outside of his occupation. He finds it difficult to grasp scientific and alien concepts but does the best he can, usually by martial means. Still, he is a good and reliable ally when the going gets tough and he refuses to surrender.

BACKGROUND
The Brigadier followed in his grandfather's footsteps by joining the military. He served in the regular army before being tapped for UNIT. He has little time for a social life, which has been detrimental to his marriage.

5

ELIZABETH 'LIZ' SHAW

Elizabeth 'Liz' Shaw was recruited by the Brigadier to join the fledgling UNIT as its Scientific Advisor based on her extensive scientific knowledge in a broad range of fields. Liz was not happy with the enforced recruitment, as she was busy researching for her Doctorate at Cambridge (this may not be her first Doctorate). Still, the mystery of several meteorites intrigued her, as well as the announcement that an alien with which the Brigadier was familiar, the Doctor, had resurfaced.

The Doctor took to her immediately, as Liz reminded him of an older Zoe Heriot, one of his former Companions whom he'd lost as the result of his trial. Liz filled a similar role, being more partner than assistant to the Doctor in the laboratory. Still, she longed to return to her studies and felt that her role as Scientific Advisor was becoming more of an honorific as her fellow Scientific Advisor, the Doctor, far outstripped her capabilities. Soon after

helping save the world one last time, from the Inferno Project, Liz submitted her resignation and returned to Cambridge to finish her studies. Liz has a wry manner and wants nothing to do with military or espionage work, although as a scientist she finds alien life and technologies fascinating. She softens considerably when in her element and she genuinely enjoys her work at UNIT while learning from the Doctor. The Doctor even relies on her scientific expertise on occasion...

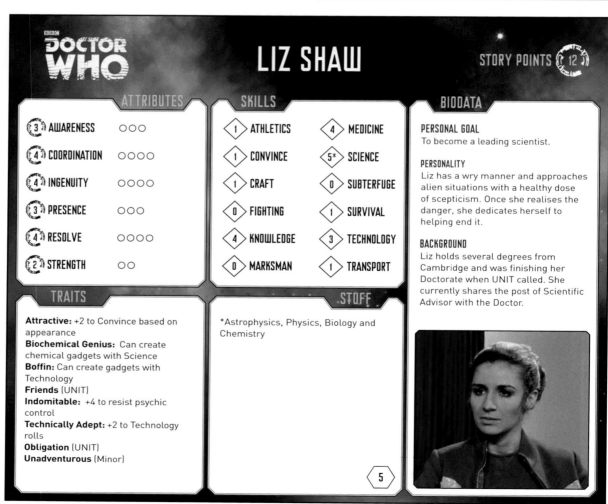

LIZ SHAW

STORY POINTS 12

ATTRIBUTES

3	AWARENESS	○○○
4	COORDINATION	○○○○
4	INGENUITY	○○○○
3	PRESENCE	○○○
4	RESOLVE	○○○○
2	STRENGTH	○○

SKILLS

1	ATHLETICS		4	MEDICINE
1	CONVINCE		5*	SCIENCE
1	CRAFT		0	SUBTERFUGE
0	FIGHTING		1	SURVIVAL
4	KNOWLEDGE		3	TECHNOLOGY
0	MARKSMAN		1	TRANSPORT

BIODATA

PERSONAL GOAL
To become a leading scientist.

PERSONALITY
Liz has a wry manner and approaches alien situations with a healthy dose of scepticism. Once she realises the danger, she dedicates herself to helping end it.

BACKGROUND
Liz holds several degrees from Cambridge and was finishing her Doctorate when UNIT called. She currently shares the post of Scientific Advisor with the Doctor.

TRAITS

Attractive: +2 to Convince based on appearance
Biochemical Genius: Can create chemical gadgets with Science
Boffin: Can create gadgets with Technology
Friends (UNIT)
Indomitable: +4 to resist psychic control
Technically Adept: +2 to Technology rolls
Obligation (UNIT)
Unadventurous (Minor)

STUFF

*Astrophysics, Physics, Biology and Chemistry

5

SERGEANT JOHN BENTON

Sergeant John Benton is a dedicated and reliable UNIT NCO. He rose through the ranks on merit; while he was a corporal during the Cybermen invasion he'd attained the rank of Sergeant prior to the loss of Mars Probe 7. The Brigadier prefers to keep Benton close and often hands him the most delicate assignments, particularly ones in which the Doctor is involved.

Benton grows close to the Doctor and his companions, treating them more like his friends or family than workmates. He's protective of them and not above disobeying an order (often with plausible deniability) when necessary to help them.

He trusts that the Doctor always has everyone's best interests at hand, even when he doesn't understand the full nature of what's happening (a not unfamiliar circumstance for an NCO).

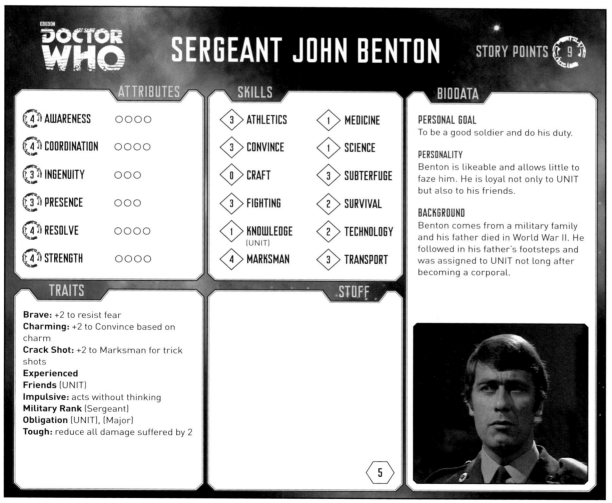

SERGEANT JOHN BENTON

STORY POINTS 9

ATTRIBUTES

4 AWARENESS	OOOO
4 COORDINATION	OOOO
3 INGENUITY	OOO
3 PRESENCE	OOO
4 RESOLVE	OOOO
4 STRENGTH	OOOO

SKILLS

3	ATHLETICS	1	MEDICINE
3	CONVINCE	1	SCIENCE
0	CRAFT	3	SUBTERFUGE
3	FIGHTING	2	SURVIVAL
1	KNOWLEDGE (UNIT)	2	TECHNOLOGY
4	MARKSMAN	3	TRANSPORT

BIODATA

PERSONAL GOAL
To be a good soldier and do his duty.

PERSONALITY
Benton is likeable and allows little to faze him. He is loyal not only to UNIT but also to his friends.

BACKGROUND
Benton comes from a military family and his father died in World War II. He followed in his father's footsteps and was assigned to UNIT not long after becoming a corporal.

TRAITS

Brave: +2 to resist fear
Charming: +2 to Convince based on charm
Crack Shot: +2 to Marksman for trick shots
Experienced
Friends (UNIT)
Impulsive: acts without thinking
Military Rank (Sergeant)
Obligation (UNIT), (Major)
Tough: reduce all damage suffered by 2

STUFF

5

CAPTAIN MICHAEL 'MIKE' YATES

Mike Yates was a dedicated sergeant recruited by the Brigadier to join UNIT after the Silurian incident. Mike was soon promoted to Captain and became heavily involved with the most sensitive missions, generally serving as the Brigadier's second-in-command. Mike quickly established a rapport with the Doctor and occasionally dated Jo Grant, although he was confused about his feelings for her, treating her more like a sister than a girlfriend.

Mike's dedication was broken during BOSS's attempted takeover of Earth, during which the artificial intelligence brainwashed him. As BOSS was running Global Chemicals and destroying the environment, Mike had a mental breakdown and believed that the only way to save the Earth was to thoroughly cleanse it. His psychiatric evaluator after that incident recruited Mike into Operation Golden Age and Mike turned traitor to UNIT to help the group effectively destroy the world in order to save it.

Following Operation Golden Age's defeat the Brigadier allowed Mike to quietly resign and seek help. Mike joined a Buddhist Meditation Centre that was the focus of an alien invasion. Realising that UNIT wouldn't trust him, Mike gave the information to Sarah Jane Smith knowing that the Doctor would investigate. He aided them both in preventing the Eight-Legs invasion.

Mike displays a bit of an upper middle-class air but enjoys a good relationship with his men, especially Sergeant Benton whom he teases on occasion. He genuinely tries to do what he believes is right, even when he turns traitor. It is this compassion that saves him from a psychic attack during the Eight-Legs' invasion.

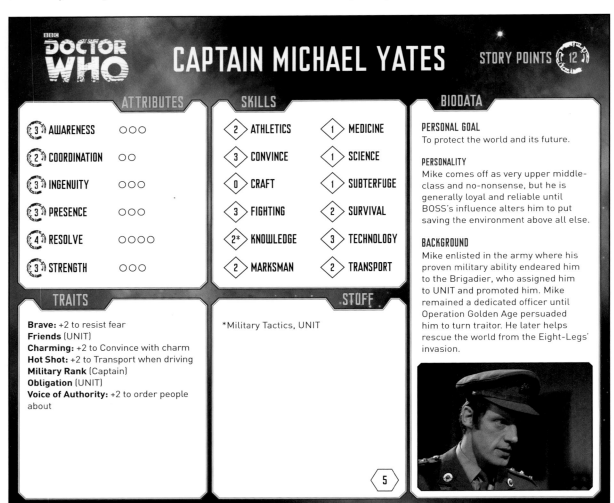

CAPTAIN MICHAEL YATES

STORY POINTS 12

ATTRIBUTES

- **3** AWARENESS ○○○
- **2** COORDINATION ○○
- **3** INGENUITY ○○○
- **3** PRESENCE ○○○
- **4** RESOLVE ○○○○
- **3** STRENGTH ○○○

SKILLS

2 ATHLETICS	**1** MEDICINE
3 CONVINCE	**1** SCIENCE
0 CRAFT	**1** SUBTERFUGE
3 FIGHTING	**2** SURVIVAL
2* KNOWLEDGE	**3** TECHNOLOGY
2 MARKSMAN	**2** TRANSPORT

BIODATA

PERSONAL GOAL
To protect the world and its future.

PERSONALITY
Mike comes off as very upper middle-class and no-nonsense, but he is generally loyal and reliable until BOSS's influence alters him to put saving the environment above all else.

BACKGROUND
Mike enlisted in the army where his proven military ability endeared him to the Brigadier, who assigned him to UNIT and promoted him. Mike remained a dedicated officer until Operation Golden Age persuaded him to turn traitor. He later helps rescue the world from the Eight-Legs' invasion.

TRAITS

Brave: +2 to resist fear
Friends (UNIT)
Charming: +2 to Convince with charm
Hot Shot: +2 to Transport when driving
Military Rank (Captain)
Obligation (UNIT)
Voice of Authority: +2 to order people about

STUFF

*Military Tactics, UNIT

5

JOSEPHINE 'JO' GRANT

When the Doctor needed a new assistant, the Brigadier decided that what he really needed was someone to tell him how brilliant he was. Luckily for the Doctor, Jo Grant could do much more than that.

Jo was trained in escapology and was never without her skeleton keys. She escaped from captivity many times and even sneaked into prisons to rescue the Doctor. There was a tough side to Jo, too: while she wasn't physically strong, she could handle a gun, and sometimes stole one from her captors to secure her escape. The Doctor, in turn, rescued Jo when she was trapped. As Jo spent time with the Doctor, she became more and more effective. At first, she was prone to screaming when she encountered an alien, but later she helped disable a Dalek. Similarly, the first time she met the Master, he hypnotised her, but the last time they met, she successfully resisted his hypnosis, by reciting nursery rhymes.

While other assistants saw the Doctor as a colleague or boss, Jo saw him as a friend. His attitude to her was paternal, even patronising – "Do stop wiffling, Jo", he once said – but she took this as good-natured teasing. In time, the Doctor grew to like Jo in return, telling her about his childhood on Gallifrey. The Doctor wasn't the only person with affection for Jo. In her travels throughout the galaxy, she frequently gained male admirers. Two men even asked her to stay, but she refused. She was always firm about her desire to return home. For, although Jo enjoyed travelling with the Doctor, she was happiest on Earth. When she finally returned there, to marry a man who much resembled the Doctor, the Doctor was visibly sad.

In *Defending the Earth: The UNIT Sourcebook*, you'll find statistics for Jo as the Doctor's assistant, as she accompanies him on his Earth-bound adventures with UNIT. These statistics represent Jo as she travelled with the Doctor as his companion.

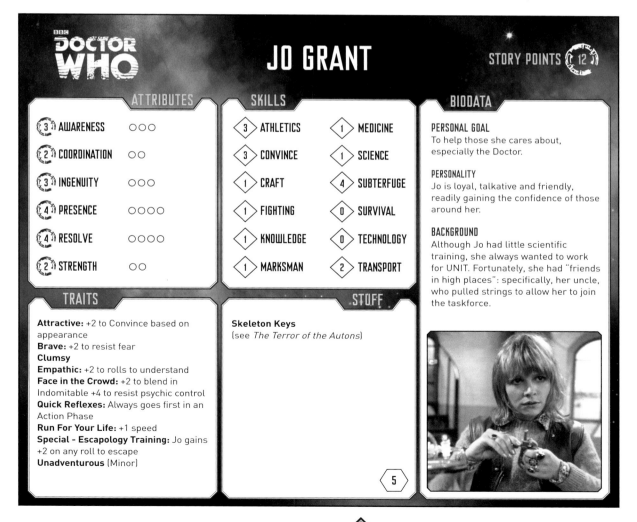

JO GRANT

STORY POINTS 12

ATTRIBUTES

3	AWARENESS	○○○
2	COORDINATION	○○
3	INGENUITY	○○○
4	PRESENCE	○○○○
4	RESOLVE	○○○○
2	STRENGTH	○○

SKILLS

3	ATHLETICS		1	MEDICINE
3	CONVINCE		1	SCIENCE
1	CRAFT		4	SUBTERFUGE
1	FIGHTING		0	SURVIVAL
1	KNOWLEDGE		0	TECHNOLOGY
1	MARKSMAN		2	TRANSPORT

BIODATA

PERSONAL GOAL
To help those she cares about, especially the Doctor.

PERSONALITY
Jo is loyal, talkative and friendly, readily gaining the confidence of those around her.

BACKGROUND
Although Jo had little scientific training, she always wanted to work for UNIT. Fortunately, she had "friends in high places": specifically, her uncle, who pulled strings to allow her to join the taskforce.

TRAITS

Attractive: +2 to Convince based on appearance
Brave: +2 to resist fear
Clumsy
Empathic: +2 to rolls to understand
Face in the Crowd: +2 to blend in
Indomitable +4 to resist psychic control
Quick Reflexes: Always goes first in an Action Phase
Run For Your Life: +1 speed
Special - Escapology Training: Jo gains +2 on any roll to escape
Unadventurous (Minor)

STUFF

Skeleton Keys
(see *The Terror of the Autons*)

5

SARAH JANE SMITH

Sarah Jane Smith was an investigative journalist who was raised by her Aunt Lavinia after her parents died in a car accident. Lavinia Smith was a famous virologist and thus part of the Brigadier's 'net' when he tried to bring all of Britain's most noted scientists under protective custody. Sensing a story, Sarah Jane pretended to be her aunt in order to gain access. While the Doctor wasn't fooled he found her amusing enough to keep her secret. Believing the Doctor to be behind the kidnappings, Sarah Jane stowed away on the TARDIS and, after finding herself in medieval England, finally joined the Doctor to stop the Sontaran Lynx from altering history. She became his Companion both while he was on Earth and in the TARDIS. She is with the Doctor when he regenerates and remains with the Fourth Doctor for a time.

Sarah Jane is confident, curious, and a staunch supporter of gender equality. She sees the Doctor as a kindred spirit and enjoys solving mysteries as much as exploring the universe.

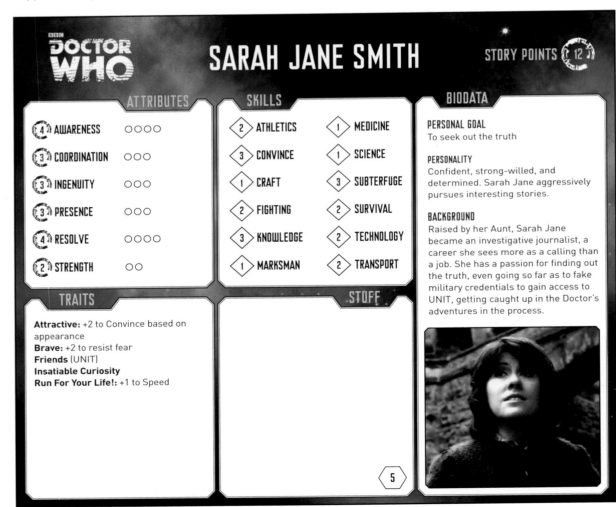

DOCTOR WHO

SARAH JANE SMITH

STORY POINTS 12

ATTRIBUTES

4	AWARENESS	○○○○
3	COORDINATION	○○○
3	INGENUITY	○○○
3	PRESENCE	○○○
4	RESOLVE	○○○○
2	STRENGTH	○○

SKILLS

2	ATHLETICS		1	MEDICINE
3	CONVINCE		1	SCIENCE
1	CRAFT		3	SUBTERFUGE
2	FIGHTING		2	SURVIVAL
3	KNOWLEDGE		2	TECHNOLOGY
1	MARKSMAN		2	TRANSPORT

BIODATA

PERSONAL GOAL
To seek out the truth

PERSONALITY
Confident, strong-willed, and determined. Sarah Jane aggressively pursues interesting stories.

BACKGROUND
Raised by her Aunt, Sarah Jane became an investigative journalist, a career she sees more as a calling than a job. She has a passion for finding out the truth, even going so far as to fake military credentials to gain access to UNIT, getting caught up in the Doctor's adventures in the process.

TRAITS

Attractive: +2 to Convince based on appearance
Brave: +2 to resist fear
Friends (UNIT)
Insatiable Curiosity
Run For Your Life!: +1 to Speed

STUFF

5

⊙ THE THIRD DOCTOR'S TARDIS

The TARDIS spent most of the Third Doctor's tenure in a rather ignominious state – sitting in a UNIT shed, partially disassembled. The Doctor removed the console from the main body of the ship so he could continue to work on the dematerialisation circuits and overcome the blocks in his memory. During this period, the TARDIS was largely non-functional as a travel machine, but it could still be used for other purposes like scanning for temporal anomalies.

With a large expenditure of Story Points (6+), the Doctor can get the TARDIS (or just the console) into flight, but his chances of success are slim. In game terms, no matter how well the Doctor rolls, he cannot exceed an average (Yes, But) success. Something will always go wrong. Of course, this doesn't apply to other Time Lords, who can use the TARDIS without any problems (beyond the usual drawbacks associated with a stubborn Type 40).

By the time his exile was lifted, the combination of a new dematerialisation circuit, the removal of his memory blocks, and his extensive repair of the TARDIS console ushered in a new era of more accurate time travel for the Doctor. From this point in his career onwards, the Doctor was increasingly able to steer the TARDIS accurately.

For more information on TARDIS systems and time travel, take a look at **The Time Traveller's Companion**.

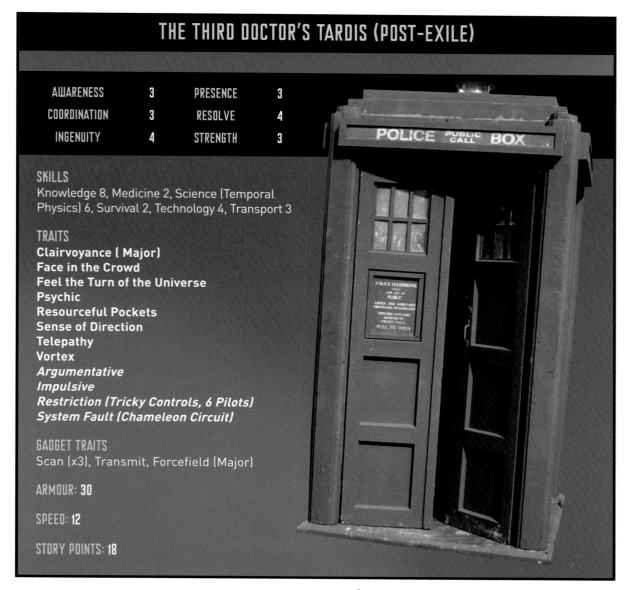

THE THIRD DOCTOR'S TARDIS (POST-EXILE)

AWARENESS	3	PRESENCE	3
COORDINATION	3	RESOLVE	4
INGENUITY	4	STRENGTH	3

SKILLS
Knowledge 8, Medicine 2, Science (Temporal Physics) 6, Survival 2, Technology 4, Transport 3

TRAITS
Clairvoyance (Major)
Face in the Crowd
Feel the Turn of the Universe
Psychic
Resourceful Pockets
Sense of Direction
Telepathy
Vortex
Argumentative
Impulsive
Restriction (Tricky Controls, 6 Pilots)
System Fault (Chameleon Circuit)

GADGET TRAITS
Scan (x3), Transmit, Forcefield (Major)

ARMOUR: 30

SPEED: 12

STORY POINTS: 18

"The Time Lords! Look, they've sent me a new dematerialisation circuit. And my knowledge of time travel law and all the dematerialisation codes, they've all come back. They've forgiven me. They've given me back my freedom!"

⊙ NEW CHARACTERS

The Third Doctor Sourcebook assumes that you'll be using the Third Doctor, his companions, and possibly the UNIT regulars as the player characters in your campaign, but this need not be the case. Your players may wish to use a different incarnation of the Doctor (with his particular companions), a different UNIT commander, or even original characters.

Due to the dangers inherent in the UNIT era and beyond, there may also be times when players need new characters. While everything you need is in the core box set, this section offers guidance on the types of characters best suited for adventures taking place during the Doctor's exile and immediate post-exile.

NEW COMPANIONS

The Third Doctor's Companions (we'll include the UNIT regulars in this) fell into three types: assistants, travelling companions, and support. Assistants are UNIT personnel assigned to the Doctor to assist him

in his work and basically keep him happily working for UNIT. Liz Shaw was a scientist in her own right and Jo Grant, while having many useful abilities, was primarily assigned to the Doctor to stroke his ego.

Travelling companions are characters hand-picked by the Doctor to continue travelling with him once he got the TARDIS working again. The first of these was assistant-turned-companion Jo Grant, while Sarah Jane Smith was the first full-fledged travelling companion and not beholden to UNIT.

Support includes the UNIT regulars, primarily the Brigadier, Captain Yates, and Sergeant Benton. During the Doctor's exile UNIT was often assigned an investigation or duty that invariably needed the Doctor's assistance to resolve, and he needed their manpower and military/espionage skills to help him do so.

One important change from his predecessors is that the Third Doctor is surrounded by adults; there are no teenagers that need mentoring or a father figure (although Jo Grant comes close at times). His companions are capable people with careers of their own that are interrupted by their choice to travel with the Doctor. Both Liz Shaw and Jo Grant leave when they decide to turn the page to the next chapter of their lives.

While a player should feel completely free to create any companion during the UNIT era, companions in the 'Third Doctor mould' would likely be UNIT soldiers or civilians with skills useful to UNIT investigations.

After the Doctor is granted his freedom, he's likely to continue travelling with young adults rather than naïve teenagers (although Tommy from **Planet of the Spiders** could make an excellent companion).

NEW TIME LORD

While the Third Doctor's era is characterised by his relationship with UNIT, there is no reason why his other incarnations can't do the same. It was, after all, the Doctor's previous incarnation that established a relationship with Brigadier Lethbridge-Stewart and UNIT, and later incarnations of the Doctor have worked with UNIT on several occasions. In fact, UNIT

(or even Torchwood) makes it easy for any Time Lord to become embroiled in their adventures. Perhaps the Time Lord is also a renegade stranded on Earth, or she may be an agent from the Celestial Intervention Agency ensuring that history maintains its proper course. The Time Lord may simply be a 'visitor,' having lost her TARDIS in the future and biding her time until it finally arrives.

OTHER GROUPS

Because he spent so much time in a single era, most of the Third Doctor's adventures lend themselves well to player characters that never leave that era. UNIT or a Torchwood team could certainly make do without a Time Lord's assistance and independent investigators, such as Sarah Jane Smith in her post-Doctor years, could note the warning signs of alien invasions and try to resolve them on their own.

A FEW STEPS FORWARD: NEAR-FUTURE UNIT

UNIT dating has always caused a bit of controversy; even the Doctor, no doubt due to the Time War, has trouble remembering exactly when Brigadier Lethbridge-Stewart ran UNIT (he only remembers that it was the 1970s, or the 1980s). From a roleplaying perspective, designing a UNIT campaign set in the near future (such as when Kate Lethbridge-Stewart is running things) offers a unique opportunity.

The early 21st century sees many changes, from other nations rising to challenge the Western World's dominance to smart phones and computer tablets networking humanity almost all of the time. The world economy is on shaky ground and arguments rage over the necessity of environmental protection measures. Setting a UNIT campaign a few years into the future allows the Gamemaster to create a setting that is still familiar to the players but also incorporates predictions about where the world is headed.

On one end of the scale, the world may not be all that unfamiliar. Many of the post-Time War companions have gotten to experience the world a few years later and it really isn't all that different save for the odd piece of new tech (like completely replacing televisions with computers). In this case, the near future setting merely enables the Gamemaster to warn the players that there's a chance a botched adventure could kill a world leader, spark a war, or enable an alien invasion to succeed.

At the other end, the world could be completely different. Perhaps Mother Nature has had enough and global warming is hitting full force while Great Britain's economy collapses. How much support would the Axons have if they offered a solution to food supply while food riots were paralysing London? What if a Silurian colony woke up and actually began working with certain nations? What if World War III was raging? In a setting where your campaign is not likely to last long, you can have a lot of fun turning the world on its head (and if you go too far, don't worry – the Daleks will wipe it out in a hundred years anyway!).

NEW TRAITS

The following new traits were used in designing characters for the **Third Doctor Sourcebook** and are available for general use. Some of these traits can also be found in **Defending the Earth** and the **Time Traveller's Companion**.

BIOCHEMICAL GENIUS (MAJOR, GOOD TRAIT)

The character is a dab hand with chemistry and biology and has a natural 'feel' for the way the two combine.

Effects: The character gains Areas of Expertise for the Science Skill in Biology and Chemistry and may create biological or chemical 'Gadgets' using the Jiggery-Pokery rules, using the Science Skill instead of Technology for all relevant rolls.

CRACK SHOT (MINOR GOOD TRAIT)

A special knack for hitting things from distance. They might have fired weapons for sport or just had a particular gift for accuracy, but it means that they rarely miss, and can literally shoot the wings off a giant insect mutated by chemical slime.

Effect: Crack Shot is a Minor Good Trait, and characters with this gain +2 to their roll when using Marksman for trick shots, like shooting a gun out of an enemy's hand or firing at a Sontaran's probic vent.

FIVE ROUNDS, RAPID (MAJOR GOOD TRAIT)

The Brigadier's favourite solution to any problem: "Five rounds, rapid!" Characters with this Trait have an unsettling tendency to shoot first and ask questions later, but at least they're exceptionally good at shooting first!

Effect: Five Rounds, Rapid is a Major Good Trait that allows characters to shoot earlier. Instead of having to wait until the 'Fighters' part of an extended Conflict (see page 45 of the **Gamemaster's Guide**), they can opt to open fire earlier and use their actions in the 'Runners' or 'Doers' phases. 'Talkers' still go first. This can be a good thing, as the soldiers are able to open fire earlier, but it can also be a disadvantage – trigger-happy troops rarely leave anyone alive to answer questions or point them in the right direction to disarm that doomsday device.

HOT SHOT (MINOR GOOD TRAIT)

Some people are a natural when it comes to most forms of transport. They can fly planes through the harshest of thunderstorms or drive cars at high speeds without crashing. They are the best of the best when it comes to piloting vehicles.

Effect: Hot Shot is a Minor Good Trait providing the character with a +2 bonus to all Transport rolls. This bonus is especially effective when used to push the speed of a vehicle, as they can get the best performance from the craft.

MILITARY RANK* (MINOR, MAJOR OR SPECIAL GOOD TRAIT)

The character has a military rank, with all the privileges and responsibilities that entails. Characters that belong to UNIT but do not have this Trait are considered to be regular enlisted men (Privates or Corporals). As a Minor Trait, the character is a Sergeant. As a Major Trait, the character is a Lieutenant. With the permission of the Gamemaster, the character can begin higher than a Lieutenant, with good back story justification and by purchasing the Trait additional times. The table below summarises ranks. The Special version of this trait also gives the Friends (Government and Military) Trait to represent the officer's political and military connections.

RANK TRAIT	RANKS
None	Private or Corporal (player's choice)
Minor	Sergeant
Major	Lieutenant
Major x2	Captain
Major x3	Lieutenant Colonel or Major
Special (6 CP, 1SP)	Brigadier

REVERSE THE POLARITY OF THE NEUTRON FLOW (MAJOR GOOD TRAIT)

Those with a particular genius for science have an innate understanding of the ebb and flow of energy and can make intuitive leaps that allow them to solve scientific and technological problems through unusual applications of that energy.

Effect: A PC with this trait may use it once per adventure. After they have failed a roll using the Science or Technology skill, they may immediately declare they are "Reversing the polarity of the neutron flow" and turn the result into an automatic Fantastic Success.

UNIT VETERAN (SPECIAL GOOD TRAIT)

UNIT Veteran is a special trait, costing 4 Character Points. You've been part of UNIT for many years, and have seen things that you can't quite believe. Dalek attack-ships hanging in the skies over Earth, plastic duplicates, time-travelling dinosaurs, dimensional rips, and a madman in a blue box. You've seen it all. You've got the benefits of Brave and Voice of Authority, plus you can take either Five Rounds Rapid or Rank (Major). Furthermore, your experience with past alien encounters gives you an edge in the field.

Once per game, you may describe how you faced a similar situation back in the day to gain the benefits of a Story Point without having to spend one. For example, when punching a Orgon in the face, you could describe how this is just like that time you punched a Zygon, and get an extra two dice to your Fighting roll as if you'd spent a story point. The downside is that you've got a bit of a history. Take one of the following Bad Traits – Adversary (Minor),By The Book, Dark Secret (Minor), Eccentric (Minor) or Phobia (Minor).

⚙ NEW VEHICLES

The following are common vehicles used during the Doctor's time with UNIT. Some vehicles have a Story Point cost; this is only to activate the traits. Presuming that the driver knows how to start and steer the vehicle, it costs no Story Points to use as a vehicle.

BESSIE

This yellow Edwardian roadster was bought for the Doctor by UNIT as a condition of his employment. It is a four-seater and has a collapsible roof, although in light rain a passenger may simply open an umbrella rather than having the driver go through the hassle of pulling the roof up. Thanks to the Doctor's tinkering, Bessie is surprisingly durable; when using the Fast trait the driver can brake to a complete stop without throwing the occupants from the vehicle.

Armour: 4   **Hit Capacity:** 10   **Speed:** 8

Traits: Anti-Theft Force Field*, Fast, Restriction (Fast only works when the percolator is poured into the gas tank, Transmit is for remote control only), Transmit
Cost: 3 Story Points

*The Anti-Theft Force Field activates whenever an unauthorised user tries to use Bessie. The initial Strength of the force field is 4; the victim may resist with a Strength roll. If the victim fails, he is held until the force field is shut off; this could be a matter of minutes or hours depending on how long the Doctor set it for. The victim may make multiple attempts to escape, but each failed attempt after the first costs a point of Resolve or Strength from fatigue (this is stun damage, so at 0 the victim merely falls unconscious).

THE 'WHOMOBILE'

The 'Whomobile' is a hovercraft that the Doctor built sometime after Jo Grant left UNIT. It has a futuristic design that makes it look like a small spacecraft.

While the only known trait of the Doctor's Car is its ability to fly, it's possible that it has the same trait package as Bessie. In this case, the Doctor's Car costs 5 Story Points and has all of the traits Bessie has in addition to Flight.

Armour: 6   *Hit Capacity:* 15   *Speed:* 10

Traits: Flight
Cost: 2 Story Points

UNIT JEEP

This is the most common mode of travel for UNIT soldiers during the Doctor's tenure as Scientific Advisor.

Armour: 6   *Hit Capacity:* 14   *Speed:* 8

⊘ NEW GADGETS

SONIC SCREWDRIVER MARK 2 AND MARK 3

After being exiled to Earth, the Doctor made enough modifications to his original sonic screwdriver that it is considered a 'Mark 2'. As with the Mark 1, the Mark 2 sonic screwdriver can turn normal screws. The Weld ability also enables it to make a spark, which can ignite gas or set flammable materials ablaze. The Third Doctor made more modifications to the sonic screwdriver towards the end of his adventures, including adding a magnet to make opening bolted doors easier.

Traits: Hypnosis (minor), Indomitable, Open/Close, Restriction (Cannot open bolted doors – Mark 2 only) or Deadlock Seals, Indomitable against hypnosis only, Tricky Controls), Scan, Transmit, Weld.
Cost: 3 Story Points (Mark 2), 4 Story Points (Mark 3)

TARDIS LOCATOR

This wrist-strapped gadget homes in on the location of the TARDIS.

Traits: Scan
Cost: 1 Story Point

TEMPORARY GADGETS

There are some gadgets that player characters may only use occasionally – Bessie, for example, is only used by the Third Doctor in slightly half of his adventures and the sonic screwdriver was only used sporadically prior to the lifting of the Doctor's exile. It may seem a bit draconian (pun intended) to make the player characters pay for something that they are only going to use on occasion rather than as a regular tool. To simulate semi-regular use, the Gamemaster may allow for 'temporary gadgets'.

In essence, a temporary gadget is a gadget that is considered 'broken' until a player character pays the Story Point cost to activate it. Once the cost is paid, the player character may use the gadget for the rest of the adventure. At the conclusion of the adventure, the story points spent to activate the gadget are refunded to the player character.

One specific use of a temporary gadget is the Doctor's work on the detached TARDIS console.

'I only need two things: your submission and your obedience to my will!'

The Doctor meets many enemies both during his exile on Earth and throughout time and space. He meets a time-threatening Sontaran, the scheming Axons, and the displaced Silurians. He also meets a worthy adversary in the Master and needs to team up with his other incarnations in order to stop an even more dangerous Time Lord, Omega. The Doctor uses his wits and his Venusian aikido to overcome all of these challenges.

This chapter is a rogues' gallery of the many enemies that the Third Doctor has faced in his travels. Individual aliens and adversaries are offered first, followed by a set of generic stock character types that can be used to model the minor characters in the Third Doctor's adventures.

⊙ DALEKS

The Third Doctor encountered the Daleks three times.

He last encountered them on Exxilon, a planet rich in the chemical parrinium, which was needed to cure a plague that was ravaging the galaxy. The Daleks planned to take the parrinium and hold it for ransom, but their expedition was hindered by the Great City, which drained all electrical power. These Daleks ran on psychokinetic energy, which was drawn from the Kaled brain inside the transport unit, but the brain only had sufficient power to move the Dalek and utilise its various sensors; the Exterminator required a separate power pack which was drained.

The Daleks were forced to ally themselves with the Doctor and an Earth expedition to shut down the city, but soon regained command by designing a chemically-powered bullet gun. They forced the native Exxilons to mine the parrinium for them and planned to destroy the planet once they left. Quick thinking by Sarah Jane Smith and some of the expedition members caused the Dalek ship to explode as it took off, saving everyone.

DALEK VARIANTS

The Daleks on Exxilon lost the use of their exterminators due to the energy drain on Exxilon. To compensate, the Daleks made a gunpowder substitute. When using this weapon, the Daleks do (3/7/10) damage.

DALEK

AWARENESS	3	PRESENCE	4
COORDINATION	2	RESOLVE	4
INGENUITY	4	STRENGTH	7*

SKILLS
Convince 4, Fighting 4, Marksman 3, Medicine 3, Science 8, Subterfuge 3, Survival 4, Technology 8

TRAITS
Traits: Armour (Major): The Dalekanium casing reduces damage by 10. This reduces the Dalek's Coordination to 2 (already accommodated in the Attributes).
Cyborg
Environmental: Daleks are able to survive in the vacuum of space or underwater.
Fear Factor (3): Once you realise how deadly the Daleks are, they are terrifying, getting a +6 to rolls when actively scaring someone.
Flight: Daleks are able to fly. When hovering their Speed is effectively 1, when in open skies or space they have a Speed of 6. Note that Daleks rarely fly during the Third Doctor's adventures so this trait costs a story point to use.
Natural Weapon – Exterminator: The legendary Dalek weapon usually kills with a single shot – 4/L/L.
Technically Adept: Daleks are brilliant at using and adapting technology.

TECH LEVEL: 8 **STORY POINTS: 5-8**

*The Dalek mutant inside has different attributes when removed from the Dalekanium casing. Of course, movement outside of the armour is incredibly limited (Speed 1) and they do not usually survive very long. If the mutant is exposed at any time, damage inflicted to the Dalek may bypass the armour.

AWARENESS	3	PRESENCE	3
COORDINATION	3	RESOLVE	4
INGENUITY	4	STRENGTH	5

⚙ THE MASTER

They grew up together in the fields of Gallifrey. One chose to be called Doctor, while the other chose the name Master. Throughout their schooling, the Master's achievements surpassed those of the Doctor. Yet the major difference between them was the Time Vortex: at an early age, the Master had stared into it. It had sent him mad.

When the Third Doctor knew him, the Master was a Machiavellian schemer, whose plans took years to prepare. Often, he worked alongside alien races, to help them rule the Earth. He enjoyed taking on new identities, with disguises, pseudonyms and false credentials. Yet, as the Doctor knew, his weakness was vanity: he would often give a name that, in another language, meant 'Master'.

This Master was not just a schemer, but a fighter. Perfectly at ease with weapons, from guns and swords to lasers and smoke bombs, he once fought a duel with the Doctor that ended when he threw a knife. He also was an expert hypnotist and, once, influenced Jo Grant to arm a bomb. He was almost impossible to capture. At the end of the Doctor's adventures, he would often escape.

What did the Master want? Sometimes, he wanted to destroy or humiliate the Doctor; sometimes, to rule the Earth or the Universe; sometimes, to destroy humanity or the Earth; but all the while his grander goal was always plain: power! Chaos allowed him to gain control, destruction to stand tall amidst the rubble.

THE MASTER

AWARENESS	3	PRESENCE	6
COORDINATION	4	RESOLVE	6
INGENUITY	9	STRENGTH	4

SKILLS
Athletics 3, Convince 6, Craft 2, Fighting 4, Knowledge 6, Marksman 3, Science 5, Subterfuge 5, Technology 4, Transport 3

TRAITS
Attractive: Not only was the Master charming, but he could form romantic alliances. He gains +2 to rolls involving his looks.

Boffin: His skill with electronics was equal to that of the Doctor. Thus, he can create gadgets through Jiggery-Pokery.

Charming: The Master's charm is legendary.

Feel the Turn of the Universe: Having stared into the Time Vortex, the Master instinctively feels the terror and magnificence of the universe.

Hypnosis (Special): An expert hypnotist, the Master would gaze at others and tell them to obey him.

Indomitable: The Master is resistant to hypnosis and similar attacks.

Quick Reflexes: Often, the Master would catch the Doctor by surprise with sudden moves.

Special (Disguise): The Master gains +2 on rolls to disguise himself.

Technically Adept: The Master was as happy in the laboratory as the Doctor.

Time Lord (Experienced): In his years since Gallifrey, the Master has learned much.

Time Traveller: The Master had not just travelled through time, but had a deep understanding of it.

Voice of Authority: Few could resist listening to the Master.

Vortex: The Master has stared into it.

Adversary: The Doctor.

Code of Conduct: In waiting for a particularly satisfying, personal or elegant way to destroy the Doctor, the Master sometimes missed chances to simply kill him.

Outcast: The Master is a renegade Time Lord.

TECH LEVEL: 10   STORY POINTS: 8

OGRONS

Ogrons are ape-like humanoids who possess immense physical strength. On their home planet, they live in scattered communities that worship and fear a huge and bulbous monster that roams the surface.

Simple, honest and loyal, the Ogrons are often exploited by more intelligent races. For those races, the Ogrons' obedience, together with their skill with weapons, makes them ideal mercenaries and policemen. When the Third Doctor encountered Ogrons, they were working either for the Daleks or the Master.

OGRONS

AWARENESS	2	PRESENCE	3
COORDINATION	2	RESOLVE	3
INGENUITY	1	STRENGTH	6

SKILLS
Fighting 3, Marksman 1

TRAITS
Armour (Minor): Hide reduces injury by five levels.
Enslaved: Ogrons are an honest and simple race, who are easily exploited by those more devious than them.

TECH LEVEL: 4   **STORY POINTS:** 2-3

SILURIANS

The Silurians are an ancient race, perhaps the first intelligent race on Earth. Their civilisation flourished through prehistory, although the exact era is a matter of conjecture (the Silurian period is too early; since the Silurians call themselves by this name, it's likely a translation coincidence). Silurian civilisation probably began in the mid-to-late Mesozoic era and waxed and waned until the Eocene era, when

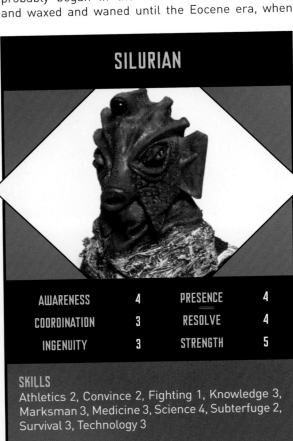

SILURIAN

AWARENESS	4	PRESENCE	4
COORDINATION	3	RESOLVE	4
INGENUITY	3	STRENGTH	5

SKILLS
Athletics 2, Convince 2, Fighting 1, Knowledge 3, Marksman 3, Medicine 3, Science 4, Subterfuge 2, Survival 3, Technology 3

TRAITS
Alien
Alien Appearance
Armour (5)
Environmental: A Silurian suffers no ill effects from extreme heat.
Special – Third Eye: Can use its third eye to Stun (S/S/S), cause injury (4/L/L), weld (as gadget), operate Silurian technology via remote control and even to open up tunnels (as the Burrowing trait). It can also send commands to the Cave Monster.
Weakness: -2 to rolls when operating in cold conditions.

TECH LEVEL: 6   **STORY POINTS:** 3-5

proto-hominids became a pest to them and they used an engineered plague to wipe them out (this is earlier than hominids are generally thought to have appeared; these proto-hominids were perhaps the first attempts by the Fendahl to 'evolve' humanity). Eventually the Silurians went into hibernation to survive a planetoid impact (given the span of Silurian civilisation and climate fluctuations they'd probably hibernated before). Unfortunately, the planetoid was captured by the Earth's gravity and became the moon. As this negated the impact, the Silurians kept sleeping while humanity finally evolved and took over the planet.

When a colony of Silurians awoke in the late 20th century, they found that the 'ape-primitives' had taken over. There was a dispute whether to try and live with this race or wipe them out as they had before; the Doctor attempted to persuade them to do the former.

CAVE MONSTER

AWARENESS	3	PRESENCE	4
COORDINATION	4	RESOLVE	3
INGENUITY	1	STRENGTH	12

SKILLS
Athletics 4, Fighting 3, Survival 4

TRAITS
Armour: Reduce damage by 5.
Fear Factor (2): Grants a +4 bonus to inspire fear.
Huge (Major)
Natural Weapons: Teeth that do Strength +2 damage.

STORY POINTS: 3-5

Unfortunately, distrust and envy won the day and a Silurian leader released the plague. The Doctor and Liz Shaw came up with the cure, while the Brigadier, on orders from the government, destroyed the entrance to the colony, possibly wiping it out in the process.

While the Silurians had knowledge of the dinosaurs, it is unknown whether the Cave Monster is a natural dinosaur or a scientifically-altered creature. The fact that the Silurians can control it remotely lends credence to the latter. In any case, it appears to be a theropod.

THE NESTENE CONSCIOUSNESS

The Nestene Consciousness is a psychic gestalt of the intelligences born on its home world (similar to the Portuguese man-o-war of Earth). It could separate itself into constituent pieces that travelled through the universe in spherical plastic energy units, find appropriate worlds for colonisation and crash on them as meteorites. Once reassembled, the Nestene Consciousness would manifest in a form suited for the world it wanted to conquer. In the case of Earth, this was apparently a cephalopod with a giant eye ...and later a huge energy creature.

The Nestene Consciousness has a special affinity for plastic and uses local plastic factories to fashion servants, the Autons, to help collect the energy units and protect the Nestene Consciousness as it manifests. In the late 20th century, the Nestenes came to Earth and used the Auto Plastics company to manufacture the Autons. It also created a series of Auton facsimilies designed to replace key government and military officials to aid in their invasion.

As the Nestene Consciousness relied on psychic energy, enough of an electrical jolt could force it off the planet and back into space. The Doctor was able to construct a device to do just that. Once the Nestene Consciousness was gone the Autons collapsed, powerless.

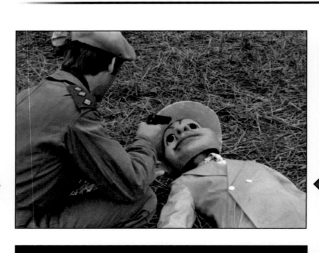

NESTENE CONSCIOUSNESS

AWARENESS	3	PRESENCE	4
COORDINATION	2	RESOLVE	4
INGENUITY	6	STRENGTH	5

SKILLS
Convince 3, Fighting 2, Knowledge 6, Science 2

TRAITS
Alien
Alien Appearance
Fear Factor (1): It's a large eye and tentacles! +2 on rolls to actively scare people.
Hypnosis (Major): It can mesmerise and control agents.
Immunity (All Ballistic Weapons): Guns, bullets and explosives do nothing to it. It's a pool of living plastic, though it can form tentacles and limbs that can be harmed or severed.
Natural Weapons (Tentacles): The Nestene can produce tentacles that can crush and bash their target (Minor Trait, Strength +2 damage (7(3/7/10)).
Psychic: It communicates and controls with a powerful telepathic signal amplified through conventional technology. Without the boost, it can still control the weak willed within its presence to create agents to do its bidding.
Slow (Major): The Nestene is hardly able to move, rolling as a boiling mass with a Speed of slightly above 0.

TECH LEVEL: 7   **STORY POINTS: 8-10**

AUTON

AWARENESS	2	PRESENCE	1
COORDINATION	2	RESOLVE	2
INGENUITY	1	STRENGTH	5

SKILLS
Fighting 2, Marksman 2,
Subterfuge (disguise as shop dummy) 1

TRAITS
Alien
Armour (Minor): Its tough plastic outer protects it from a lot of damage, damage is reduced by 5.
Fear Factor (1): Walking shop dummies can be scary, +2 on rolls to actively scare.
Immunity (Bullets): Any bullets are effectively useless unless it takes a lot of damage at once. Bullets hit it and the Auton either absorbs them into the plastic or they go straight through.
Natural Weapon (Blaster): The Auton's right hand opens to reveal a blaster that can do Lethal damage (4/L/L).
Networked (Minor): The Autons are all aware of each other but are controlled by the Nestene Consciousness. They have no independent thought.
Slow (Minor): The Auton's plastic legs make them slow to move around. Their Speed is effectively halved (to 1).
Weakness (Major): If the controlling signal from the Nestene Consciousness is blocked or severed, the Auton becomes useless plastic and is immobilised.

STORY POINTS: 1-2

' Doctor, slow down. It's not safe to drive so quickly!'

The Third Doctor brought a splash of colour to time and space. His adventures were packed with excitement: heart-stopping chases, giant explosions, daring escapes. He was a fighting Doctor, rushing through gun battles to disable his opponents with Venusian aikido.

Put simply: if something was cool, then it appeared in the Third Doctor's adventures. Yet the Doctor's ideas of excitement seemed to have been influenced by his time on Earth, in the 1970s or thereabouts. So let's put it another way: if something was cool in the 1970s, then it appeared in his adventures. Hovercraft, lasers, remote control, robots, karate, spacecraft: the Third Doctor would drive, fire, operate, defeat, fight with and pilot them all.

Yet, alongside the excitement, there was a serious side to the Third Doctor. His adventures featured fights, chases and escapes, but also diplomacy, bureaucracy and ethical dilemmas. The Third Doctor might spend an entire adventure fighting an oppressive government (**The Mutants**), investigating an environmental disaster (**The Green Death**) or negotiating between two superpowers (**Frontier In Space**).

As he did all this, the Third Doctor took a moral stance. He always stood for ordinary people – whether they were human or alien – against exploitative governments and corporations. Beneath all the excitement, his adventures were often about human greed, stupidity or aggression.

When you run adventures for the Third Doctor, then, balance excitement with a sense of morality. Pack your adventures with explosions, chases and prisons. But base them on topics that could save or destroy the world: a peace conference, a greedy corporation, a danger to the environment, an ill-considered scientific experiment.

In your adventures with the Third Doctor, here are some topics and themes to include.

THE SETTING

For the Third Doctor's adventures, you have two main settings to choose from. The first is Britain in the era of UNIT: that is, the 1970s or thereabouts. When an adventure is set here, it is often based around UNIT, with the Brigadier, Yates and Benton taking significant roles. The Doctor, meanwhile, takes the role of Scientific Advisor. Such adventures might end somewhere else – such as the alien ship in **The Ambassadors of Death** or Atlantis in **The Time Monster** – but they begin on Earth.

The second setting is an alien planet in the future. On the planet, the Doctor often finds a society of humans – or human-like creatures, such as Solonians –

with a problem he must solve. These adventures rarely involve time travel. Once the Doctor has arrived somewhere, he generally stays there until the adventure is finished: you might even put the TARDIS out of reach to ensure this (as we'll discuss under *The Curse of Peladon*). Additionally, there are variations on the alien planet setting: the Doctor might alternatively arrive on a starship or space station in the future.

Here is a curious trick. Whichever setting you use, emphasise the obvious aspects of the other one. When the Doctor is on Earth, put spaceships, lasers and alien invasions into your game. When the Doctor is on an alien planet, emphasise the human element instead: base the adventure around war, agriculture or corporate exploitation. (In fact, as we'll see in *The Mutants*, when the Third Doctor visited an alien planet, it often resembled a specific period of Earth's history).

The Third Doctor rarely visited Earth's past. Unless you count Atlantis, the only real example was when he travelled to medieval England (in *The Time Monster*). However, that doesn't stop you setting an adventure in the past. As we'll discuss under *The Carnival of Monsters*, the Third Doctor fits remarkably well into historical adventures.

To fully capture the flavour of the Third Doctor, however, focus on the present and the future. Perhaps more than any other incarnation, he was a very modern Doctor.

PROLOGUE

To start your adventure, try using a prologue (see *The Gamemaster's Guide*). This is a short scene, in which your players, rather than playing their main characters, play ordinary people.

In this scene, the characters are going about their everyday lives. Suddenly, however, something strange happens. People discover something odd. Or perhaps someone dies, terrified and screaming (see *The Green Death*).

Whatever happens, this is the first hint of the problems the Doctor will face in this adventure. It might even be the first encounter with the adventure's main adversary. But keep it mysterious. Don't describe anything that will spoil the surprise for later. In particular, don't describe the adversary: if someone dies, describe their reaction rather than the thing attacking them.

THE BEGINNING

Now, it's time for the Doctor to start his adventure. In the Third Doctor's time, there were three main sources of adventure: UNIT intelligence, Time Lord missions or the Doctor getting lost.

When an adventure begins with UNIT intelligence, it starts at UNIT headquarters. Begin with the Doctor fiddling with something technical: either the TARDIS or a Gadget (which will likely solve a problem later in the adventure). Put his current companion there, too: they are probably asking what the Doctor is doing. Then introduce a member of UNIT personnel – either the Brigadier, Benton or, if both those characters are controlled by players, then a low-level functionary – with a report of something strange that needs investigating. From there, the adventure begins.

You can vary this. For example, *The Mind of Evil* begins when the Doctor, as UNIT's scientific advisor, attends a scientific demonstration. *The Daemons* begins when he realises that a televised archaeological dig is extremely dangerous. But keep to the basic formula: the Doctor, when on UNIT business, investigates something odd.

When an adventure begins with the Time Lords, they are sending the Doctor on a mission. Sometimes, they simply intercept the TARDIS and send it somewhere (*Colony In Space*). Sometimes, they send him something: in *The Mutants*, it's a capsule for him to deliver, while in *The Three Doctors*, it's the Second Doctor.

When you start the mission this way, then the Doctor won't understand the mission. He'll simply arrive somewhere or receive something. He'll almost certainly realise the Time Lords are involved (without a roll), then begin exploring.

When an adventure begins with the Doctor getting lost, then he is trying to travel somewhere in the TARDIS. Often, in the Third Doctor's time, this planet is Metebelis 3. However, he lands somewhere else instead and begins exploring.

In fact, these adventures are remarkably similar to the Time Lord adventures above: the Doctor lands on a strange planet and must explore it. Here is a guideline: if your adventure occurs before **The Three Doctors** (*see page 106*), then the Time Lords have sent the Doctor to the planet. If it occurs afterwards, then the TARDIS has landed there by mistake. (Later in the Doctor's timeline, we might wonder whether the TARDIS itself has decided to take the Doctor somewhere. However, in the Third Doctor's time, it looks like a mistake.)

Use any of these beginnings to start your adventure or invent your own. What really matters is that the Doctor discovers something strange. Whatever the problem is, he must investigate and stop it.

WHO STARTED IT?

So who started all this? Who is responsible for the problem that, in the adventure, the Doctor must solve? That's where it gets complicated.

In the Third Doctor's travels, he rarely met evil aliens, wreaking havoc simply because they could. Firstly, in his adventures, the aliens weren't necessarily evil. Whatever they did, they had a reason for it. Secondly, they weren't necessarily aliens. In the Third Doctor's time, the problems could be created either by aliens or humans.

When your adventure is about aliens, there are broadly two things they might be doing: invading Earth or creating trouble somewhere else. If they are invading Earth, don't just make them evil. Give them a motive for invading. For example, The Silurians and Sea Devils both wanted their land back. The Axons wanted resources. The Autons, having colonised other planets, now intended to colonise Earth, just as humans colonised other planets. Whatever the motive, make it something your players can understand and even empathise with.

If they are creating trouble elsewhere, then also give them an understandable motive. Omega, in **The Three Doctors**, felt betrayed by the Time Lords and wanted to escape his antimatter universe. Lynx, in **The Time Warrior**, had crash-landed on Earth and wanted to return home. Even the Eight-Legs, in **Planet of the Spiders**, had simply reversed their situation, ruling humans who once had power over them. Whatever harm they are doing, give them a reason to do it.

When your adventure is about humans, they have let their baser instincts out of control and the Doctor must put things right. Generally speaking, there are three root causes.

The first is **aggression**. In his adventures, the Third Doctor often met humans who believed that violence was the best solution. General Carrington (**The Ambassadors of Death**) and the Marshal (**The Mutants**) were most dangerous, but General Williams (**Frontier In Space**) wasn't much better. On one occasion, the Doctor complained "I've got to stop this senseless killing".

The second is **profit**. Often, the Third Doctor found corporations willing to risk lives for the sake of money. The Interplanetary Mining Company (**Colony In Space**) were willing to kill human colonists, while Global Chemicals (**The Green Death**) pumped toxic waste into the earth, creating monsters as they did so.

The third is **hubris**. While the Third Doctor loved science, he knew its dangers, and often met humans who pushed things too far. In search of great things, these people pushed science to dangerous limits. Professor Stahlman (*Inferno*) promised unlimited energy, by drilling into the Earth's core, while Professor Kettering (*The Mind of Evil*) promised to cure criminals.

There were other motives too. Hepesh (*The Curse Of Peladon*) wanted to uphold tradition, by keeping the planet of Peladon out of the Galactic Federation. The Marshal (*The Mutants*) wants to colonise the planet Solos, by making the atmosphere poisonous to Solonians. Vorg (*Carnival of Monsters*) simply wants to make a living, with a machine that captures other creatures.

Whether the adventure's main problem was started by aliens or humans, give them an understandable motive for doing what they did. But here is the twist: they might not be the adventure's main adversary.

THE ADVERSARY

In his adventures, the Third Doctor faced some great villains. Yet things got complicated here too. Sometimes, the main villain didn't create the problem that needed solving. Sometimes, there was more than one villain. And, sometimes, there wasn't really a villain at all.

For a simple adventure, make the villain, whether they are alien or human, the cause of all the trouble. Thus, in *The Three Doctors*, Omega is the main villain: he wanted to trap the Doctors in an antimatter universe. In *The Mutants*, the Marshal is the villain: he wanted to kill the Solonians. To keep things even simpler: choose any alien and let them invade the Earth. That way, they both cause a problem, which the Doctor must solve, and become his main adversary.

If you like things more complicated – and the Third Doctor did – then play around with the villain's role. Try an adventure in which humans start trouble, then aliens take advantage. For example, in *Day of the Daleks*, humans create a time paradox, which lets the Daleks invade Earth.

Try using multiple villains. Often, the Third Doctor discovered that, behind whoever *seemed* to be the villain, the *real* villain was lurking in the background. For example, in *The Green Death*, the main adversary seemed to be Stevens, who was in charge of Global Chemicals. Yet, as the Doctor discovered, he was under the control of BOSS, who really ran Global Chemicals.

Or try an adventure without a clear villain. In *Carnival of Monsters*, Vorg collected creatures in a machine, including the Doctor and Jo Grant. Yet the adventure didn't really have a villain. It simply pitted the Doctor against the other people and creatures in the collection.

Best of all, keep your monsters – that is, your frightening creatures, who threaten the Doctor – separate from your villains. When the Third Doctor met something scary, it often wasn't the adventure's main villain. For example, in *Carnival of Monsters*, the Drashig is simply a carnivore, while in *The Green Death*, the giant maggots are a byproduct of Global Chemical's toxic waste. Try using monsters that, while they are initially terrifying, are actually benign. Aggedor, in *The Curse of Peladon*, turns gentle when the Doctor sings to him, while the mutated insect-people, in *The Mutants*, are actually evolving Solonians.

What does all this mean for your adventure? It means: in the Third Doctor's time, don't worry too much about who the adversary is. Simply pack the story with villains to defeat, people to outwit and monsters to fight.

NO REAL VILLAINS

In fact, the Third Doctor rarely met anybody who was truly evil. So, when you run an adventure with the Third Doctor, find ways to make the villain less villainous.

Try giving them an understandable motive, as mentioned above. Try suggesting they are controlled by someone else, as Stevens was by BOSS (in *The Green Death*). Or, when the Doctor finally defeats them, try giving them a sympathetic death scene.

This is what happens to Stevens, who finally sacrifices himself, or Hepesh (**The Curse of Peladon**), who wonders, as he dies, whether he was wrong.

If your villains are an alien race or human group, try making one of them friendly. For example, Wester (**Planet of the Daleks**) is a friendly Spiridon, who heals Jo. Caldwell (**Colony In Space**) is a friendly member of the IMC, who eventually helps the colonists. An even better idea is to make your characters neither straightforwardly good nor evil. Let them sometimes side with the Doctor, sometimes with the villain. Caldwell is a good example, as is General Williams (**Frontier In Space**) and the Controller (**Day of the Daleks**). Even the Brigadier often fits this pattern. Keep your players guessing whose side they are on.

Paint your characters, not black or white, but in shades of grey. We'll come back to this, in **Colony In Space** and **The Time Warrior**.

THE MASTER

So, if the Master turns up in the adventure, what is his role? Surely he is simply evil, without any redeeming motives? In fact, the Master is the most complex villain of all.

When he appears in the Third Doctor's adventures, he takes various roles. Sometimes, as in **The Time Monster**, he is the ultimate cause of the problem. Sometimes, as in **Terror of the Autons**, he leads other alien races; sometimes, as in **Planet of the Daleks**, he is employed by them; sometimes, as in **The Claws of Axos**, he works alongside them.

The Master is a catalyst: when trouble is brewing, he gives it a helping hand. He summons dangerous creatures. He makes pacts with alien races. He plays on human motives: most prominently in **Frontier In Space**, where he fuels human and Draconian xenophobia, by fabricating a conflict between them that becomes real. Certainly, as outlined above, his motives could change on a whim.

Taken as a whole, the Master exudes a kind of chaotic evil. He rarely creates new problems. He is an expert, however, at inviting existing ones in or making them worse.

THE WORLD

Now put some big themes into your adventure. The Third Doctor wrestled with huge moral topics: war, peace, assassination, the environment, the British Empire, the future of humanity. Two themes were particularly important.

The first is **diplomacy**. In his travels, the Third Doctor met humans and aliens on the brink of war. Like his other incarnations, he preferred talking to fighting, and was particularly fond of diplomatic negotiations. He could scarcely get through an adventure without a peace conference: in **Day of the Daleks**, humans bombed a summit intended to prevent World War Three; in **The Mutants**, a leading diplomat was assassinated; in **Frontier In Space**, the Doctor himself intervened between humans and Draconians.

So, whenever the Third Doctor is pitted against aliens, give him a chance to negotiate with them. He probably won't succeed (which we'll discuss under **Frontier In Space**). Often, something will interrupt his diplomacy and the fighting will start. But let him try.

The second theme is the **environment**. In the Third Doctor's view, the Earth's resources were gradually being depleted. Whenever he described Earth's future, he portrayed it bleakly: "Grey cities linked by grey highways across a grey desert". When he described groundbreaking technology, he often mentioned the vast amounts of energy it consumed.

Yet, in his adventures, he often found people that offered a solution. Professor Stahlmann (**Inferno**) offered unlimited energy. The Axons (**The Claws of Axos**) offered both unlimited food and power. Professor Jones, in **The Green Death**, wants to find a food source that could be mass cultivated to end the world's food shortage. People were always searching for new resources: it seemed that, wherever the Third Doctor went, he found a mine.

Play on these themes in your adventures. You might base an adventure around diplomacy (like *Frontier In Space*) or the environment (like *The Green Death*). If you don't, then at least refer to these themes. Remember, for example, that the Silurians didn't simply invade, but negotiated with the Doctor (diplomacy), then tried to pollute the atmosphere (the environment). For the Third Doctor, the Earth was threatened not just by aliens, but by war and pollution.

THE GOVERNMENT AND THE MILITARY

If you want to make things worse, bring in the government. Wherever the Third Doctor goes, he finds a government that is bureaucratic, incompetent and sometimes corrupt. Whatever the problem, they will double it.

When the Third Doctor was in Britain in the UNIT era, he found the government consisted of pompous men in suits. These people were always unpleasant – when Walker, the Parliamentary Private Secretary in *The Sea Devils*, arrives he orders a Navy officer to bring him breakfast – and the Doctor was scathing in return. Sometimes, he simply found such people bureaucratic: as when Chinn, in *The Claws of Axos*, insisted the Doctor's information be properly filed. Sometimes, he found them dangerous, as when Chinn later organised the worldwide distribution of Axonite. Even the Prime Minister, in *The Green Death*, ordered the Brigadier to cease investigating Global Chemicals.

When the Third Doctor travelled to the future, he found Earth's government equally bureaucratic. Everyone and every spaceship needed credentials: when the Master arrested the Doctor, in *Frontier In Space*, his alleged crimes included piloting a spaceship without tax and insurance. Even the Daleks, in an alternative Earth future, set productivity targets for their human underlings. On other worlds, governments were equally pedantic, and the Galactic Federation was no better.

If you want to make things worse still, bring in the military. They have one solution to everything: blow it up. It never works and always makes the situation worse. When the Navy attacks the Sea Devils' base, they disrupt the Doctor's peace negotiations. When the Brigadier orders an airstrike on giant maggots (*The Green Death*), they simply crawl to the surface.

In any adventure, you can bring in a bureaucratic government or a trigger-happy military. They give the Doctor another problem to deal with. We'll discuss this further in *Terror of the Autons*.

By now, you have a complex and human adventure. But perhaps it feels too serious. Let's liven it up.

VEHICLES!

Fill each adventure with vehicles. Use as many different types as possible: a jet, a submarine, a motorised tricycle.

In particular, whenever the Doctor needs to travel, have a vehicle nearby. If it's Bessie, consider adding something to make her even better, like the remote control in *The Daemons*. If not, make it something exciting, which you've never used in an adventure before.

Ensure that, when the Doctor confronts a villain, they flee in a vehicle. This means that the Doctor must grab a vehicle, too, and chase them. (We'll talk about transport, more, in *The Sea Devils*.)

ESCAPES!

Put the Doctor in prison, then let him escape. Or put him in prison, then let his companion come to rescue him. Or switch that around: imprison the companion, sending the Doctor to the rescue.

The Third Doctor's adventures are full of daring escapes. Yet his imprisonment never stopped the adventure: instead, it often allowed him to meet his captors. We'll discuss this more in *Frontier In Space*.

TRAVELS IN SPACE!

Put a spaceship in your adventure (and not just the TARDIS). If your adventure is on Earth, try an alien spaceship. If it's elsewhere, try a human spaceship: either a cargo ship (*Frontier In Space*), a space station (*The Mutants*) or simply a one-man craft (*Colony In Space*).

In **Frontier In Space**, we'll see much more of space. For now, put a spaceship into your story and see where it takes you.

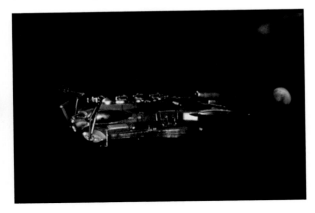

TRAVELS IN TIME!

For the Third Doctor, time wasn't just something to travel in. It was something that could go wrong. In **The Claws of Axos**, he put the Axons into a time loop. In **The Time Monster**, he witnessed both slowed and frozen time. In both **The Time Warrior** and **Carnival of Monsters**, people were kidnapped through time.

So, in the Third Doctor's adventures, play tricks with time. We'll come back to this in **Day of the Daleks**.

DISGUISE!

In the Third Doctor's adventures, things weren't always what they seemed. Deadly creatures turned out to be hallucinations. Villains wore disguises. In fact, whole worlds could be different from how they appeared.

In **Carnival of Monsters**, we'll list all the ways that appearances could deceive the Doctor.

TECHNOLOGY!

The Third Doctor loved science. Again, his ideas of technology seemed influenced by his time on 1970s Earth, when everything was big, white and boxy. He even liked the interior of his TARDIS that way. So fill your adventures with technology, especially if it resembles things that were exciting in the 1970s: robots, oscilloscopes, remote controls, reel-to-reel tape recorders and computers the size of a room.

Try using scientist characters, too. When the Third Doctor met scientists, he generally found them to be as unpleasant as the bureaucrats. He reacted, in turn, by criticising their knowledge. Fill your

scientist characters with hubris (as above): give them grandiose plans, without the knowledge to achieve them. Finally, put laboratories throughout your adventures.

FIGHTS!

The Third Doctor often found himself surrounded by violence. Especially towards the end of each adventure, there was often a gun battle. When UNIT were available, this was their job: they arrived with guns and began shooting alien creatures. When they weren't, someone else always had guns or lasers.

There is a protocol to this. The Doctor and his companions don't join in the gunfight. While the military types are shooting, they are elsewhere. This often works as follows: outside a building, UNIT shoot aliens; inside the building, the Doctor is solving the problem. Importantly, as we'll discuss under **The Daemons**, the battle never stops anyone getting where they want to go or doing what they need to do.

Equally importantly, the Doctor isn't part of the gun battle. He preferred Venusian aikido: an extraordinary martial art, with which he fought crowds of assailants. He did, occasionally fire a gun, but this was very rare and very much not part of his character. This Doctor still abhorred guns. He was never seen hunkered down with UNIT, firing a machine gun from cover. He had better things to do.

GET DOWN, EVERYONE!

Finally, when the Third Doctor is around, things blow up. His adventures often featured explosions, especially from bombs: both the kind you drop from the sky and the kind you need to defuse.

At the end of the Doctor's adventure, a building often blows up. There are many different reasons for this: Irongron's castle explodes when Lynx's spacecraft fails to take off (**The Time Warrior**); the Primitive's city goes bang when their Doomsday Weapon self-destructs (**Colony In Space**); Global Chemicals blows up when Stevens sacrifices himself to destroy BOSS (**The Green Death**). In any case, the Third Doctor's adventures often end with a bang.

HERE, LET ME SHOW YOU.

That, then, is the Third Doctor. His numerous adventures combined weighty themes with high-speed excitement. And they started like this.

SPEARHEAD FROM SPACE

'We have been colonising other planets for a thousand million years. Now we have come to colonise Earth.'

SYNOPSIS

England, UNIT era

Fifty meteorites landed in Essex in the same area where a handful fell six months before. UNIT investigated the matter while Brigadier Lethbridge-Stewart recruited Cambridge researcher Liz Shaw to join as Scientific Advisor. The TARDIS arrived in the same area, with the newly regenerated Doctor collapsing and being taken to the local hospital. The Brigadier and Liz visited him and, while the Brigadier didn't recognise him, the Doctor called him by name. These events were observed by Channing, an Auton facsimile that took over Auto Plastics by hypnotising the owner, Hibbert. He attempted to kidnap the Doctor, but the Doctor escaped.

Several Autons were dispatched by the Auto Plastics factory to collect the meteors, which were actually energy units containing parts of the Nestene Consciousness. UNIT took the TARDIS to its London headquarters and the Doctor, using his TARDIS Locator, escaped from the hospital and offered his services to the Brigadier. Meanwhile, a former Auto Plastics employee, Ransome, investigated the happenings at his old job and was almost killed by an Auton. He escaped to UNIT, where he reported his findings before an Auton secretly killed him. UNIT managed to capture the last meteor, 'the Swarm Leader', in spite of Auton interference.

The Brigadier tried to get General Scobie to assist in investigating the factory, but Scobie was replaced by an Auton Facsimile which rejected the request. After hearing that the waxworks museum had recently made a model of Scobie, the Doctor and Liz went to Madame Tussauds and discovered that many government leaders and military officers had been replicated in plastic. He also discovered that Scobie's 'replica' was actually the real Scobie in suspended animation, kept alive to mask the psychic signal and ensure the duplicate went undetected. The Doctor and Liz observed Channing and Hibbert animate the replicas in order to replace the originals.

The Scobie replica took the Swarm Leader from UNIT and merged it with the rest of the Nestene Consciousness manifesting in the factory. Autons that had been placed as shop window dummies all over London animated and started killing people. Using what he'd learned from analysing the Swarm Leader, the Doctor created a Scrambler to force the Nestene Consciousness from Earth.

Hibbert finally realised what was going on and tried to destroy the Nestene, but Channing stopped him and ordered the Autons to kill him. The Doctor and UNIT arrived at the factory only to be intercepted by Scobie and his troops. The Doctor used his device on Scobie and revealed that he was a replica. UNIT soldiers entered the base and held off the Autons while the Doctor confronted the Nestene Consciousness. The Nestene Scrambler stopped working and the Doctor struggled against the tentacled horror the Consciousness had created for itself as a body until Liz fixed a broken connection in the Scrambler's wiring, forcing the Nestene to retreat back into space and deactivating the Autons. The Doctor, needing a place to repair the TARDIS, accepted the Brigadier's offer to remain with UNIT and adopted the alias of Dr John Smith.

CONTINUITY

The Doctor emerges from the TARDIS wearing his previous incarnation's clothes. Later, in hospital, he speaks like his previous self. Both suggest that this takes place just after his trial in **The War Games**. That said, he has a TARDIS Locator wristwatch, something his previous incarnation lacked (this may be a Time Lord gift).

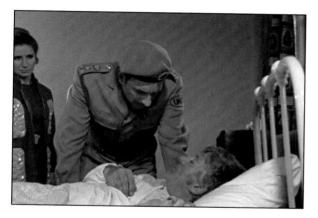

UNIT makes its second appearance in the Doctor's life. Brigadier Lethbridge-Stewart is still in charge and the events of **The Invasion** took place months before.

⊘ RUNNING THE ADVENTURE

Spearhead from Space is a great example of how to begin a **Doctor Who: Adventures in Time and Space** campaign. There is a newly regenerated Time Lord, a new companion with a scientific skill set, and a military character in a position of authority but with enough bureaucracy hanging over his head to rein him in when he gets too trigger-happy. There is no baggage left from the previous campaign, enabling a fresh start.

In addition, both the Time Lord's circumstances and the basic plot showcases the direction of the campaign moving forward. The Doctor is stranded on Earth and becomes UNIT's scientific advisor against alien threats to the planet. Not only does this allow for more character development (as NPCs don't get left behind at the end of adventures) but it also enables a Gamesmaster to develop a single campaign era where all of the adventures will take place.

The plot itself is a relatively straight-forward invasion story that draws a lot of parallels with the previous Earth invasion story, **The Invasion**. Both involved taking over a private corporation and using it to build an invasion force complete with 'meteorite sightings' that fed the sense of threat. The foot soldiers were then placed throughout London in order to start the invasion when the time was right. Finally, it takes a bit of jiggery-pokery to put an end to the invasion.

The plot also plays on the prevalence of plastic in modern society as well as the inherent creepiness of shop window mannequins. Both are symbols of a consumerist culture that produces more and more mass-produced items without worrying about the consequences. Here, plastic threatens to choke and replace that culture with a faceless one; the fact that the Auto Plastics factory could run 'fully automated' suggests that there is no room for humanity in a Nestene world. Worse, it appears humanity will only be replaced by yet another race that would consume the planet even more quickly before moving on.

There are also parallels to be drawn with cold war paranoia and concerns over sleeper agents. The targeted government and military personnel are 'activated' (in this case by replacement with an Auton facsimile) and then secretly work against the interests of their country. It's interesting that the Nestene need to keep the replaced person alive. This makes it a great plot device to use in your game. You can replace a long-standing recurring character with a facsimile – it doesn't kill them off, and as they are not responsible for their actions they can continue in their role after the adventure.

FROM TRAVEL MACHINE TO TOOL SHED?

This adventure marks the beginning of the Doctor's exile. As such, the TARDIS is no longer capable of travelling through time and space. Instead, it is more of a trans-dimensional closet or locker. The Doctor is often seen tinkering with some gadget or gizmo found within the TARDIS, and the Gamemaster can expect the same of his player characters, who, deprived of the primary use of their transport, would certainly try to find an alternative use for it in their adventures.

The easiest way to handle this is by enforcing the Gadget rules; the player characters can have anything they want so long as they pay for them. The TARDIS itself is hobbled by the Time Lords so the player characters may only have access to a few things. Alternatively, the player characters, and even the TARDIS, may spend a story point or three to use something from the TARDIS during the course of an adventure.

BUT WE DON'T WANT TO CHANGE CHARACTERS!

While the Doctor has little control over when he regenerates and his companions come and go regularly, player characters have a way of sticking around as long as their players want to play them. Thus, even if the Gamemaster anticipates a regeneration or change of cast, the players may resist this. Alternatively, the Gamemaster may wish to use an adventure designed with a particular cast in mind, only to have to run it with the cast at hand. The main consideration when adapting an adventure to a particular cast of characters is to make sure that they have between them the abilities needed to succeed.

What if the Time Lords allowed the Doctor to go into exile with his current companions and not force him to regenerate? In terms of ability mix, it's not difficult to match up to the capabilities of the Third Doctor's team. The Second Doctor was the incarnation that the Brigadier was familiar with, so that's no problem. Zoe Heriot could easily step into the shoes of Liz Shaw.

With slightly more work even Jamie fits, as the Third Doctor was more physical, this aspect would simply be transferred to the Highlander companion.

Removing the exile scenario entirely, **Spearhead from Space** could easily be reconfigured for other Doctors or groups. The First Doctor would have to convince the Brigadier of his identity; while later Doctors may have to double-up and fill Liz Shaw's role too if his companions aren't suitable (one could easily see Romana, Adric, Nyssa, or Martha filling the role). It's also easy to extrapolate how this would run as a UNIT or Torchwood adventure. Prior to meeting the Doctor, the Brigadier recruits Liz Shaw to be his scientific advisor and intends for UNIT to solve the mystery alone. All they would need is Ransome to come to them with information about the plastic factory. It's likely that Channing would send an Auton to silence him, deepening the mystery.

UNIT LIAISONS

General Scobie was the liaison officer between UNIT and the conventional British Army. In cases where UNIT needed more manpower or other resources, the request would go through Scobie's office. This position gave Scobie considerable influence over UNIT operations in the United Kingdom. Scobie presumably worked closely with Sir Charles Grover (see **Invasion of the Dinosaurs**), as both were involved in government oversight of unexpected problems. Presumably, if the Nestene failed to control Scobie, then Sir Charles was their next target.

In a UNIT-based game, the UNIT Liaison is a recurring character. You can make them comic relief, showing how the conventional troops are completely overwhelmed and confused by alien invasions, or obstacles to overcome in order to get needed resources. Or, of course, you can just have them replaced by Rutan spies or some other shape-shifting monster from space.

VILLAINS GET STORY POINTS TOO!

Bad guys and monsters also have Story Points, and can use them in just the same ways as player characters. They can spend Story Points to get extra dice, to reduce the margin of failure, or to ignore the effects of damage. They can build gadgets, if they've got the right skills and traits. They can even give Story Points to one another – an Auton might jump in the way of an energy blast meant for the Nestene Consciousness, spending its own Story Points to protect its master.

Villains can also spend Story Points to alter the story and introduce plot twists. Now, as Gamemaster, you've got full control over the Story. You can put in any plot twist you want. You can ignore dice rolls. For that matter, you could say that your villains have millions of Story Points. You can do all those things – but you shouldn't. It's much more fun to 'play the villain' fairly.

When it comes to villainous plans and plot twists, you don't need to spend Story Points for everything. Villain Story Points are *reactive* – only use them when the villain acts to foil the plans of the player characters. Things that the villain was going to do anyway, or things that are part of the plot whether or not the player characters get involved, are free.

For example, say you come up with an adventure in which the Autons take over a nice little seaside town by turning all the living statue performers on the pier into, well, living statues. You decide that in addition to the street performers, the Nestene Consciousness has also made plastic duplicates of various key figures in town, like the mayor and the police chief. Meanwhile, in the funfair at the end of the pier, the Autons work on building a rollercoaster that's also a hyperspatial accelerator, so they can start shipping human victims off to some distant world. None of that costs the Nestene any Story Points.

However, let's say that during the game, the player characters try talking to the night watchman at the pier. You didn't include any such character in your original notes, but it's a perfectly plausible course of action, so you agree they can find such a watchman... and then, secretly, you spend one of the Nestene's Story Points. That night watchman was a duplicate all along! Now, as Gamemaster, you're perfectly entitled to do that without spending a Story Point, but putting a limit on the Nestene's resources forces you to reuse what assets you have. Later on in the game, instead of creating another Auton, you might find yourself reusing the night watchman. Deliberately limiting yourself will, paradoxically, make for a more exciting game.

The other thing to remember is: *spend your villain's Story Points!* There's no point in hoarding them all until the end of the scenario. Just keep a few back to boost rolls, and spend the rest on nasty plot twists and villainous plans.

THIS PLANET IS DEFENDED

This is the first of many adventures in which the Third Doctor helped thwart an alien invasion of Earth (and more importantly, England). These alien invasions mostly follow the same pattern, and you can use that as a model for your own tales of doom from the stars!

First, *the aliens arrive*. This may take the form of a classic flying saucer landing, but the aliens could arrive in other forms (such as the meteorites used by the Autons) or arrive at other times (the Daemons landed long ago). The arrival is always noticeable, and may attract the notice of the player characters.

Next, *the invaders recruit allies*. The invaders either convince a human to work with them, or take over some human institution like a corporation or a church, or replace humans with mind-controlled slaves. Around the same time, *the invaders deploy servants*. The invaders usually have a lesser type of alien serving them. The Nestene have their Autons; the Daemons had gargoyles; the Daleks have Robomen or Ogrons.

The aliens then use their human allies to *establish a base*. They take over some human structure and make it into a stronghold, or hide their alien vessels within this structure. The aliens always have a base on Earth; the Doctor or UNIT will inevitably blow up this base at the end.

Over the course of the adventure, the player characters will *encounter the servants* and be *deceived by the aliens' allies*. Encountering the servants puts the characters in physical peril, forcing them to flee or fight the simple-minded servant creatures. Being deceived by the alien's allies is even more dangerous, and often results in the characters being captured.

Note that together, the alien's servants and alien allies act as layers of a mystery. The characters only encounter the invaders towards the end of the adventure; most of the time, the invaders remain shadowy presences in the background, working through their allies and servants.

Often through being captured, the characters *discover the aliens' invasion plan*. There should always be some impending doom to provide both a target and a time limit for the player characters' actions. Maybe the aliens are about to release a deadly plague into Earth's atmosphere, or seize control of all our planet's nuclear weapons, or activate a beacon to summon the rest of their forces. If the characters can stop this plan in time, the whole invasion will be thwarted.

AUTON FACSIMILE MK 1

AWARENESS	2	PRESENCE	2
COORDINATION	3	RESOLVE	2
INGENUITY	3	STRENGTH	5

SKILLS
Facsimiles have the same skills as the individual they're duplicating, plus a Convince score of at least 3.

TRAITS
Armour (Minor): Tough plastic skin protects it from a lot of damage, any taken is reduced by 5.
Dependency (Minor): Without the original subject being held by the Nestene, the copy cannot mimic their mannerisms and knowledge. If the subject escapes, the copy reverts to normal Auton intelligence.
Immunity (Bullets): Any bullets are effectively useless unless it takes a lot of damage at once. Bullets hit it and the Auton either absorbs them into the plastic or they go through. Also works on bottle corks too!
Natural Weapon (Blaster): The copy's right hand opens to reveal a blaster that can do Lethal damage (4/L/L).
Weakness (Major): If the controlling signal from the Nestene Consciousness is blocked or severed, the facsimile becomes useless plastic and is immobilised.

STORY POINTS: 3-5

NEW GADGET – TARDIS LOCATOR
This wristwatch homes in on the TARDIS' location.

Traits: Scan (locates TARDIS)
Cost: 1 Story Point

NEW GADGET – NESTENE DISRUPTOR
This suitcase-sized device can disrupt a Nestene signal to incapacitate Autons and prevent the Nestene Consciousness from fully manifesting.

Traits: Delete (Restriction – Delete only shuts down Autons; if Nestene Consciousness is deleted, all Autons cease to function)
Cost: 1 Story Point

FURTHER ADVENTURES

- This adventure worked so well that it was used again twice. Both **Terror of the Autons** and **Rose** utilise the same basic plot, complete with jiggery-pokery forming the solution. There's no reason why it couldn't be used a third time, perhaps on a different world or near-future setting. Just come up with a twist on a plastic factory (Orbital zero-g plastic factories! 3-D printers in every home! Plastic prosthetic parts for war amputees!) and have the Autons arrive.

- For a Torchwood, UNIT, or other conspiratorially-minded group, the Nestene could have already placed duplicates in key places; they are now pushing the world into World War III, ensuring that enough of the planet is left for them to consume. The characters have to expose the conspiracy before it is too late.

- A starving Nestene running out of time crashes on a backwards world (possibly historical Earth) and influences an alchemist to develop plastics technology for its purpose. The characters need to convince the alchemist that he is working for evil – if he hasn't already been replaced.

DOCTOR WHO AND THE SILURIANS

'But that's murder. They were intelligent alien beings. A whole race of them. And he's just wiped them out.'

⊘ SYNOPSIS

England, UNIT era

Strange losses of power have plagued a nuclear research centre in Wenley Moor. In addition, psychiatric illnesses amongst the staff are at an all-time high, and at least one worker was killed by what looked like an animal attack in the caves beneath the centre. UNIT was asked to investigate and the Doctor and Liz arrived in the Doctor's new car, Bessie. The Doctor discovered that not only was there a dinosaur in the caves, but also evidence of intelligent humanoid reptiles. One of these intelligent reptiles, or Silurians, was wounded by the centre's security chief Major Baker and escaped to the moor.

The Deputy Director of the centre, Quinn, had secretly conspired with the Silurians, granting them power from the facility in return for scientific secrets. Quinn was dissatisfied with the agreement and, when the Silurians sent him after their wounded companion, Quinn decided to use the situation to his advantage. He imprisoned the wounded Silurian in his cottage, where he tried to force secrets from him. The Silurian escaped and killed Quinn.

Baker investigated the caves again and was captured by the Silurians. The Doctor and Liz followed and discovered that the Silurians were using the power from the research centre to revive their race; the Silurians weren't aliens at all, but the former masters of Earth! The Doctor and Liz returned to the facility and tried to convince the authorities to peacefully negotiate but, due to Quinn's death, Permanent Undersecretary Masters (the government official in charge) refused.

The Doctor went to the Silurians on his own, partly to warn them and partly to try and get them to negotiate. The Silurian leader was willing to listen, but another Silurian Triad member infected Baker with a bacteriological weapon they once used to eliminate the 'apes' that infested their farms, and released him. When the leader discovered this, he gave the Doctor a vial of the disease so that he could find a cure. When the rebellious Silurian learned of this he killed the leader and took power.

Baker returned to the centre and succumbed to the bacteria, but not before infecting Masters, who returned to London. The Doctor and Liz inoculated the centre staff with antibiotics to stave off the bacteria until the Doctor could find a cure. The plague spread through London and got as far as France when the Doctor was captured by the Silurians, to prevent him from completing his medical research. Luckily, Liz found the Doctor's notes and was able to produce the cure.

Undeterred, the Silurians decided to change the Earth's atmosphere to make it hostile to humans but perfect for Silurians. They forced the Doctor to help by using the reactor to power their weapon, but the Doctor overloaded it, irradiating the area. The new leader attacked the Doctor but was killed by the Brigadier. The Silurians had no choice but to return to their hibernation chambers until the radiation had dispersed. The Doctor hoped to revive them for further negotiations, but after sending the Doctor away the Brigadier blew up the caves, sealing in the Silurians for good.

⊘ RUNNING THE ADVENTURE

The heart of this adventure is a very complex political question that has flummoxed humanity for thousands of years: how should we handle two groups vying over the same piece of real estate? There are no good guys or bad guys in this adventure; at least there are no exclusively good guys and bad guys. Both sides have good claims on the world; the Silurians see the humans as squatters while the humans think of the Silurians as 'aliens' given their abandonment of the Earth so long ago. Those that are considered 'bad' simply distrust the intentions of the other side, which they see as ugly creatures incapable of rational thought. These Silurians can't see that the humans have evolved beyond their primitive roots and the 'bad' humans see the Silurians as bug-eyed monsters.

The plot itself is relatively straightforward. A nuclear research station inadvertently creates the conditions necessary to thaw the Silurians, who go about corrupting a human scientist by promising him great secrets. Upon learning that the world is full of humans, the Silurians are given the choice of trying to peacefully co-exist or exterminating the 'apes'. Unfortunately, one of the Silurians decides that the 'primitives' can't be reasoned with and unleashes a plague. The characters need to find a cure while placing the Silurians back into hibernation, whereupon the human government decides that the Silurians are too dangerous and blows up their caves.

ARE THEY 'SILURIANS?'

There seems to be some question as to the name of the species that ruled the Earth before man. Only once does a member of this race use the term 'Silurian' and that is in reference to the 'Silurian Triad', making it just as likely a political term as a biological one. More curious is the fact that 'Silurian' is a human designation for a particular geological period. The Doctor has used at least three names for this race, including Silurian, Eocene, and Homo Reptilia. The prior two names are human in origin and both are problematic for the Silurians, as there were no terrestrial fauna in the Silurian period and the dinosaurs are long gone by the Eocene, which also predates any hominids (both of which the Silurians are familiar with).

Considering the possibility of dinosaur preservation and a proto-hominid race appearing early, the Silurian civilisation is likely late Cretaceous to early Eocene. Thus, 'Eocene' would be the proper term ('Homo Reptilia' seems more an appellation to equate Silurians with Humans, as the designation implies that the Silurians are descended from mammalian hominids). The persistence of 'Silurian' suggests that it is indeed the name for the race in the Silurian tongue that just happens to sound like a human English word.

PRIMORDIAL FLASHBACKS

Humans who encounter the Silurians may suffer from a primal, atavistic terror as racial memories reawaken. In game terms, this is a special form of being scared. While Silurians are too human-like to have a Fear Factor, it's still alarming to run into one in a dark cave! A Silurian can roll Resolve + Presence against a human's Resolve + Ingenuity to scare the monkey. If the human fails Disastrously (9 or more below the Silurian's total), he's scared *and* he gains the temporary Minor Bad Trait (Eccentric – Primordial Flashbacks).

A character suffering from Primordial Flashbacks cannot say what he saw, and can only express himself through primitive scrawlings like cave paintings. Basically, some un-evolved bit of the brain gets activated by the sight of a Silurian, and the character can only describe Silurians in a way that makes sense to that caveman brain.

SILURIANS OF MONDAS?

Mondas is Earth's twin, complete with similar landmasses and a sister human race; perhaps a sister race of Silurians developed there as well. This begs the question: was it a bit more than an erratic orbit that advanced Mondasian technology beyond that of Earth? Perhaps they received help from the Mondasian Silurians.

The comparison is closer than one might think. The jug-head look of the Cybermen imitates the head of a Silurian, complete with a 'third eye' set in the forehead. The Cybermen have hypnotic powers, similar to those of the Silurians, and some Cybermen models use their 'third eyes' as weapons. It's also interesting to note that two Cybermen models had three-fingered digits like the Silurians, and that the Silurians themselves seem to be 'upgraded' with mechanical implants (this is evident in the powers of their third eye and even more obvious in *Warriors from the Deep*).

The possibilities are endless. Perhaps a failsafe in the Silurians' hibernation system woke them when Mondas broke free of its orbit. Perhaps the Mondasian humans discovered the Silurians first and stole their technology, destroying them in the process. Or perhaps the two races worked together to ensure their survival. This final possibility is even more intriguing, as the conversion to Cybermen eliminated any lingering differences between the two races. It's also possible that some Cybermen models are primarily Silurian, while others are human (although cyber-conversion can be done on any roughly humanoid race).

SILURIAN PLAGUE

The Silurian Plague is an extremely potent bacteria that is capable of wiping out millions of human beings. Should a character become infected then she loses 1 Resolve point per hour until she dies (this can be temporarily resisted with a TN 18 Resolve and Strength roll) and anyone that comes in contact with her becomes infected.

Creating a cure requires a TN 21 Ingenuity and Science roll.

FURTHER ADVENTURES

- The characters arrive in caves as a spelunking expedition is about to uncover a Silurian base. They soon discover that they are on Mondas, not Earth, and the spelunkers come from a community that moved underground after the atmosphere was torn away. The fusion of Silurian technology and human flesh is destined to give rise to a new and more dangerous form of Cyberman...

- You can have a Silurian adventure without any Silurians. What if an archaeological expedition stumbles across a buried Silurian base? The characters need to convince the archaeologists to leave before they awaken the sleepers. Flavour the adventure with, say, Egyptology or 19th dinosaur bone hunters, add in a guardian monster and a few stubborn NPCs, and you're good to go.

- The premise is sound without involving Silurians. The characters arrive on Earth in the far future, where mankind has gone into hibernation to escape the solar flares. Unfortunately, another animal race adapts to the flare-seared environment and evolves in mankind's place. The humans awaken and want their world back, as the world's resources were depleted under man's rule and can't sustain both races.

EDWARD MASTERS

AWARENESS	2	PRESENCE	3
COORDINATION	2	RESOLVE	4
INGENUITY	3	STRENGTH	2

Edward Masters was the Permanent Under-Secretary at the Ministry of Defence. He went to the nuclear research centre to investigate the mental breakdowns and suspicious power drains. He died after being infected by the Silurian virus and inadvertently bringing it with him to London.

SKILLS

Convince 3, Knowledge (bureaucracy, politics) 4, Science 2, Subterfuge 2, Technology 1, Transport 2

TRAITS

By the Book: Masters must be convinced to act against procedure.
Friends (Major): Masters can call upon the British Government for aid.
Obligation: Masters puts the government's needs first.
Voice of Authority: +2 bonus to Presence and Convince rolls.

TECH LEVEL: 5   **STORY POINTS: 4**

MAJOR BAKER

AWARENESS	3	PRESENCE	4
COORDINATION	3	RESOLVE	3
INGENUITY	2	STRENGTH	3

Major Baker was in charge of security at the nuclear research centre. He was quick to neutralise any threats, real or imaginary; he made a mistake once, long ago, that cost him dearly, so he was doubly determined to ensure the safety of the facility. His paranoia led to him being captured by the Silurians, and his aggression convinced the younger Silurians that the surface apes could not be reasoned with. He was the first victim of the Silurian plague.

SKILLS
Athletics 3, Convince 2, Craft 1, Fighting 4, Knowledge 2, Marksman 4, Medicine 1, Survival 3, Technology (security) 3, Transport 2

TRAITS
Argumentative: Baker doesn't tolerate opposing points of view.
Impulsive: Major Baker doesn't think things through before acting.
Voice of Authority: +2 bonus to Presence and Convince rolls.

EQUIPMENT
Hard Hat with flashlight, assault rifle 3/7/10

TECH LEVEL: 5   **STORY POINTS: 6**

DR JOHN QUINN

AWARENESS	3	PRESENCE	2
COORDINATION	2	RESOLVE	4
INGENUITY	4	STRENGTH	2

Dr Quinn met the Silurians and agreed to provide them with power in return for their technological secrets. He had the foresight to realise that the Silurians were centuries in advance of humanity, and that a partnership between the races could benefit both sides. Unfortunately, he got antsy when the secrets aren't revealed fast enough and overplayed his hand. His attempt to take a Silurian hostage resulted in his death.

SKILLS
Athletics 1, Convince 2, Craft 1, Fighting 1, Knowledge 3, Medicine 1, Science 4, Subterfuge 2, Survival 1, Technology 4, Transport 2

TRAITS
Boffin: Allows the character to create Gadgets.
Insatiable Curiosity: Character will investigate anything that sparks their curiosity unless they pass a Resolve or Ingenuity roll at a -2 penalty.
Technically Adept: +2 to any Technology roll to fix a broken or faulty device.

EQUIPMENT
Scientific tools

TECH LEVEL: 5   **STORY POINTS: 6**

THE AMBASSADORS OF DEATH

'No, you saw three spacesuits. I don't know what came down in Recovery 7, but it certainly wasn't human.'

SYNOPSIS

England, UNIT era

The British Space Programme hadn't received any communication from the three crew-members of its Mars Probe 7 vessel in seven months, since it left Mars for the return journey to Earth. A rescue ship, *Recovery 7*, was sent to investigate but contact was lost when the ship docked with the probe. The ship was broadcasting a live feed as it neared the probe, and just before the loss of contact there was an ear-splitting sound. The Doctor believed the noise was a coded message and, as UNIT were providing security for the British Space Programme, he travelled to the Space Centre to help. He then discovered that a reply to the message was sent from a warehouse in England.

UNIT investigated, getting into a firefight with troops defending the warehouse. Meanwhile back at Space Control, a conspiracy became apparent as scientist Taltalian threatened the Doctor and Liz before fleeing.

Embarrassingly for UNIT, *Recovery 7* was stolen soon after its arrival back on Earth, but the Doctor helped find it again. Voices of the astronauts could be heard within the ship, but they turned out to be a recording – the vessel was empty and awash with radiation.

The Minister for Technology, Sir James Quinlan, tried to cover up what was going on, saying that the astronauts were dangerously contaminated by the radiation, and that he had ordered General Carrington to secretly remove them to quarantine without causing public alarm. When Carrington took the Doctor and Liz to see the astronauts, they discovered that the spacefarers had been taken and the personnel at the base slaughtered.

Liz was captured by Reegan, the criminal who had abducted the astronauts. But it wasn't astronauts that had been in the ship – it was three aliens, and Reegan needed Liz to help keep them alive. The Doctor had also deduced that aliens had been onboard the *Recovery 7*, as the radiation in the capsule would have killed humans. He found out that Taltalian had been ordered by Carrington to sabotage equipment, after which Reegan threatened to kill Liz if the Doctor didn't stop his investigation.

Reegan decided to make sure that the Doctor couldn't cause further trouble, and sent Taltalian to plant a bomb that would kill him. The explosion injured the

Doctor, but killed Taltalian. Shortly afterwards, many of the staff at the Space Centre, including Sir James Quinlan, were killed when the aliens attacked.

The Doctor piloted the *Recovery 7* back to the probe and encountered an alien vessel. The aliens brought him onto their ship, and revealed that a treaty between them and Earth had been violated when their ambassadors were abducted. The aliens had the human astronauts on board as insurance and warned that they'd declare war if their ambassadors weren't returned. The Doctor promised to resolve the situation and was released.

On his return, the Doctor was kidnapped by Reegan and taken to Carrington, who revealed himself as the architect of the conspiracy. Aliens had killed his co-pilot when Carrington was an astronaut piloting the *Mars Probe 6*, convincing him of their nefarious intentions. He had signed the peace treaty with them in order to lure the ambassadors to Earth, where he could manipulate events to reveal their true nature and turn public opinion in favour of war. Carrington had been using Reegan for muscle, and had the backing of Sir James Quinlan before the General had him killed so that he couldn't get cold feet and reveal the plan.

Reegan recognized the Doctor's scientific skills, and convinced Carrington to put him to work instead of killing him. Carrington departed to enact the final part of his plan – a public broadcast of the ambassadors confessing to their murderous intentions. However, the Doctor and Liz used the equipment at Carrington's base to secretly contact UNIT, who swooped to the rescue and stopped the general from starting an interstellar war. Leaving Liz behind to make sure that the alien ambassadors were exchanged for the astronauts, the Doctor headed back to the TARDIS to continue his repairs.

CONTINUITY

The TARDIS control console can be removed from the TARDIS and operate independently of it.

The Time Vector Generator makes an appearance. This time it's deactivated and the Doctor tries to get it working. It projects the Doctor and Liz a few seconds into the future.

The British Space Programme is fully operational and has fielded seven missions to Mars.

The Doctor refers to the fate of the Silurians from his previous adventure.

⊙ RUNNING THE ADVENTURE

This adventure is a government conspiracy with the leader of a public programme manipulating an interplanetary mission for what he believes is for the good of humanity. Like all good conspiracies, there are no 'bad guys'; each side is doing what they believe is necessary to protect their own, even when it includes killing. Carrington can't get past the accident that killed his fellow astronaut, while the aliens, indignant at the apparent betrayal of a diplomatic offer, are willing to destroy the Earth and its ambassadors along with it if they don't get their way. The Ambassadors themselves are being tortured to do Carrington's dirty work and 'prove' to be the threat he's guarding against.

The set-up is simple. There are problems with the space programme and UNIT is sent to investigate. Once the characters notice enough irregularities then Carrington steps in to assure them that the subterfuge was necessary, but his explanation is still full of holes. The kidnapping of someone close to the characters is the next move, followed by killing anyone involved in the conspiracy that may be having second thoughts. Eventually the characters meet the aliens and discover the truth, resulting in a climax that involves exposing the conspiracy while exchanging the alien ambassadors and the human astronauts.

TIMING THE SPACE RACE

Given that the Third Doctor's UNIT stories take place in the early 1970s (Brigadier Lethbridge-Stewart retires in 1976 and this adventure takes place towards the beginning of his tenure), it seems odd that the British Space Programme would have flown manned missions to Mars at this point.

Each Mars mission seems to take about a year; assuming mission overlap, that would make the length of time between Mars Probe 1 and Mars Probe 7 between 5-6 years, or well before Apollo 11 landed on the moon. This seems unreasonable, especially since it takes another 80+ years to found a colony on Mars.

One way to neatly sidestep this issue is to simply change the destination from Mars to the Moon. The aliens aren't indigenous to Mars anyway and little of the adventure has to do with Mars. Similarly, as Apollo 11 has already made history in this respect, further lunar missions would be increasingly seen as routine and would only be newsworthy if, as happened in this adventure, the mission went awry.

Alternatively, perhaps the British Space Programme was a casualty of the Great Time War, or the Cracks

in Time – it represents a better, more optimistic future for Britain that never actually had a chance to bloom.

AMBASSADORS

The Alien Ambassadors from Mars are never given a name but it is obvious that they aren't originally from Mars. Given the state of their appearance as well as their need for radiation (and the ability to emit it), it's possible that they are survivors of a nuclear war on their own planet.

As a result they've dedicated themselves to peace, although their previous, war-like proclivities are in evidence when they determine that the loss of three ambassadors (in spite of their accidental killing of a human astronaut) is worth destroying the Earth, possibly at the cost of the captured ambassadors' lives.

The ambassadors detailed here are diplomats, rather than martial members of their species. Nevertheless they have trouble communicating with humans, as the ambassadors speak via radio waves (again, whether this is natural or due to irradiation is unknown).

AMBASSADOR

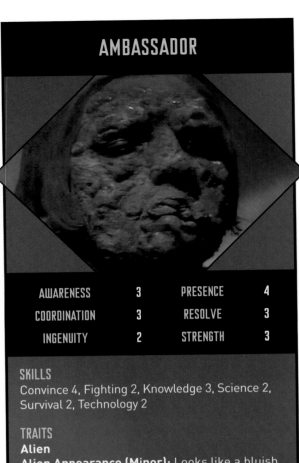

AWARENESS	3	PRESENCE	4
COORDINATION	3	RESOLVE	3
INGENUITY	2	STRENGTH	3

SKILLS
Convince 4, Fighting 2, Knowledge 3, Science 2, Survival 2, Technology 2

TRAITS
Alien
Alien Appearance (Minor): Looks like a bluish, irradiated humanoid.
Alien Senses: +4 to Awareness when using radio waves to speak.
Dependency (Major): Suffers -4 to all rolls if denied radiation for a few hours.
Immunity (Bullets): Takes no damage from bullets due to a radiation field.
Immunity (Radiation): Ambassadors need radiation to survive and are thus immune to its harmful effects.
Natural Weapon – Radioactive Touch: Can touch someone and cause (4/L/L) damage; if the ambassador touches a conductive material that someone else is holding (such as a metal bar), then the victim takes (3/5/7) damage.

TECH LEVEL: 6 **STORY POINTS: 5-7**

ALIENS ON MARS?
Very little is known about the aliens save that they've been on Mars for over a year. What were they doing there? They can't have set up a colony, as the mother ship is still in orbit. Were they looking for Ice Warrior technology or perhaps even working with the remaining Ice Warriors on Mars? There is the suggestion that the aliens were victims of a nuclear holocaust and, like the Daleks, became dependent on the radiation.

In keeping with the radiation theme, it's possible that the aliens came to warn Earthlings of the dangers of nuclear holocaust before the Cold War exploded into a hot nuclear conflict. As this is a mission of mercy, it's easy to see how quickly the aliens would sour on warnings once their ambassadors were kidnapped and used as killing machines. The aliens likely wrote Earth off as a civilization that would destroy itself in short order before it had a chance to join the civilized races of the galaxy.

Given their similar history, it's possible that the aliens and the Chameleons are the same race, with the Chameleons simply being too irradiated to evolve into the aliens of this adventure. Perhaps they didn't want to merely survive with the radiation scars and chose instead to use humans as models. As the events of **The Faceless Ones** and this adventure are less than a decade apart, it's possible that the aliens came to see just who it was that defeated their brethren.

TORCHWOOD CONNECTION?
It is very possible to view the events of **The Ambassadors of Death** as a power struggle between Torchwood and UNIT. Carrington's xenophobia, the hush-up of what happened on his mission, the creation of a British Space Security Department

(as opposed to letting international UNIT handle alien contacts), and the manipulation of a credible alien threat have all the hallmarks of a Torchwood power-grab. This being the case, it's no wonder that Torchwood had to lie low for a couple of decades; its upper ranks were probably purged after Carrington's plot was discovered.

Conspiracy theorists can take this fight a step back further by tying the events of **The Invasion** into this power struggle as well. Given the amount of power he had it's likely that Tobias Vaughn was a Torchwood agent, or at least a co-conspirator. Likely Torchwood hoped to dupe the Cybermen into being their alien threat when Vaughn's own ambitions mucked it up. Between Vaughn and Carrington, Her Majesty probably restricted Torchwood's affairs to artefact-collecting for the immediate future.

The strange absence of further references to the Space Security Department could also be tied to Torchwood. Maybe a resurgent Torchwood had the space programme covered up and ret-conned out of memory after one too many missions went wrong.

FURTHER ADVENTURES

- The characters arrive on Mars and discover a Martian (Ice Warrior) tomb that is heavily irradiated. The aliens, who are looking for something, are pumping the radiation in. What secret did the Ice Warriors hold that is worth all the trouble?

- The aliens aren't waiting for a solution to present itself; they have sent a team of alien commandoes to rescue their ambassadors. You could run an adventure that plays out in parallel to the events of **The Ambassadors of Death**,

where the player characters have to find and detain these invaders before they start a war.

- Carrington's hatred of the Ambassadors comes from a previous encounter with the creatures during the *Mars Probe 6* expedition, where they accidentally killed one of his team with a lethal touch. What happened during that encounter? What happens if the characters arrive on Mars at the same time as the probe?

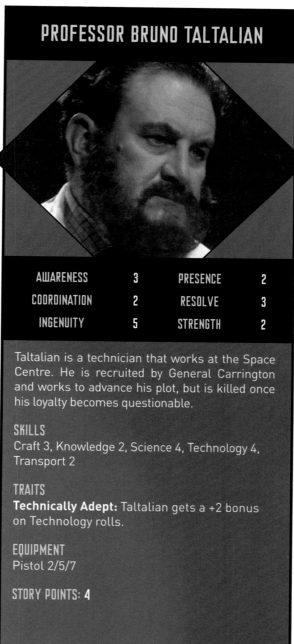

PROFESSOR BRUNO TALTALIAN

AWARENESS	3	PRESENCE	2
COORDINATION	2	RESOLVE	3
INGENUITY	5	STRENGTH	2

Taltalian is a technician that works at the Space Centre. He is recruited by General Carrington and works to advance his plot, but is killed once his loyalty becomes questionable.

SKILLS
Craft 3, Knowledge 2, Science 4, Technology 4, Transport 2

TRAITS
Technically Adept: Taltalian gets a +2 bonus on Technology rolls.

EQUIPMENT
Pistol 2/5/7

STORY POINTS: 4

REEGAN

AWARENESS	3	PRESENCE	4
COORDINATION	3	RESOLVE	4
INGENUITY	3	STRENGTH	3

Reegan is a criminal drafted by Carrington to carry out his plans. An opportunist, Reegan sees the potential in using the aliens to perform bank robberies. When captured, Reegan gives UNIT the idea of using the aliens to stop Carrington's broadcast in the hope that it will garner special consideration when he is sentenced.

Reegan's lorry can be treated like a minor gadget, as it can change its license plate and markings but retains its overall shape and colour.

SKILLS
Athletics 2, Convince 3, Fighting 3, Knowledge 2, Marksman 3, Subterfuge 4, Survival 3, Technology 3, Transport 3

TRAITS
Selfish: Reegan puts his own needs first.
Tough: Reduce total damage by 2.

EQUIPMENT
Pistol 2/5/7

TECH LEVEL: 5   STORY POINTS: 8

GENERAL CHARLES CARRINGTON

AWARENESS	3	PRESENCE	4
COORDINATION	4	RESOLVE	4
INGENUITY	4	STRENGTH	3

Carrington is a former astronaut and the head of the British Space Security Department. He met the aliens when his fellow astronaut was accidentally killed and believes that the aliens are preparing an invasion. In order to gain support for his cause he kidnaps the alien ambassadors and makes them do the horrible things he's accusing their race of planning.

SKILLS
Athletics 3, Convince 4, Fighting 3, Knowledge 3, Marksman 4, Medicine 2, Science 3, Subterfuge 4, Survival 4, Technology 2, Transport 2

TRAITS
Friends (Major): Carrington has friends in high levels of government .
Military Rank: General.
Obligation (Major Bad): Space Security Department.
Obsession (Major): Carrington wants the alien 'invasion fleet' destroyed.
Voice of Authority): +2 bonus to Presence and Convince rolls.

EQUIPMENT
Pistol 2/5/7

TECH LEVEL: 5   STORY POINTS: 8

INFERNO

'An infinity of universes, ergo an infinite number of choices. So free will is not an illusion after all. The pattern can be changed.'

SYNOPSIS

England, UNIT era

Professor Stahlman created a project to penetrate the Earth's crust and gain access to 'Stahlman's gas', a source of unlimited energy. UNIT provided security for the project and the Doctor was using the on-site nuclear reactor to fix his TARDIS. Unfortunately, the drilling brought small amounts of toxic slime to the surface, which infected a worker and turned him into an atavistic monster – a Primord. The mutation was contagious, and began to spread...

Upset by the distractions, Stahlman accidentally touched the green slime, burning his hand. After sabotaging the computer to stop its alerts that the project was becoming dangerous and should be stopped, the Professor diverted all power from the facility to accelerate the drilling. Unfortunately, the Doctor was working on the TARDIS when his power was cut and the console, the Doctor and Bessie were propelled into a parallel universe.

The Doctor realized that something was awry when Benton and a group of soldiers opened fire at him, and he was soon captured by 'Section Leader Elizabeth Shaw', who was a soldier rather than a scientist. He learned that this world's Britain was a fascist republic and that Lethbridge-Stewart was Brigade Leader of the Republican Security Forces.

In spite of the differences, the Doctor discovered that very similar events were taking place on this world, albeit at an accelerated pace. The Inferno Project was out of control, and Professor Stahlman was mutated here as well.

An RSF soldier-turned-Primord sabotaged the project and green slime bursts through the pipes. Stahlman fully mutated into a Primord and infected several workers as the project cracked the Earth's crust. This caused earthquakes throughout the world and the Doctor lamented that it was too late; the pressure being released would destroy the world. With the help of some of the project team (and after Section Leader Shaw gunned down the Brigade Leader who tried to stop them), the Doctor managed to power his console long enough to escape back to his home reality.

The Doctor initially appeared in a coma, but recovered in time to recognise that he had a chance to stop the project before it destroyed this world as well. With Liz's help, he got the project computer to recommend shutting down the project, information Stahlman had tried to conceal. Stahlman mutated into a Primord, but was stopped from restarting the project. The Doctor recommended to the authorities that they fill in the drill shaft and abandon the project for good.

CONTINUITY

This is the second time a scientist attempts to crack through the Earth's crust (the first was Professor Zaroff in **The Underwater Menace** – see **The Second Doctor Sourcebook**).

The Doctor slips into a parallel universe for the first time.

The Doctor first displays Venusian Aikido.

RUNNING THE ADVENTURE

This adventure is actually two adventures in one. The characters arrive at the Inferno project and assess the situation, but before they can solve the problem they are whisked away into a parallel universe. After seeing the catastrophe that the drilling leads to, they return to their original universe and try to prevent it. It's worth noting that this adventure could be run without the alternate universe complication; the threat of everyone turning into a Primord should be enough of an impetus to shut down the project.

A clever Gamemaster could use the parallel Earth to show players a different side of their characters. Take a look at their traits – is there something you could flip or exaggerate? Or would a character that chose life aboard a TARDIS find her counterpart well-settled and happy? Would a player that always threatens violence as a solution see what happens when there is no one to hold him back?

THE REPUBLIC OF GREAT BRITAIN

The Republic of Great Britain seems like a hybrid of Nazi Germany and the Soviet Union. The regime executed its royal family like the Bolsheviks, presents its leader as a 'Big Brother' figure, and its army uses fascist-sounding new ranks such as 'Platoon Under Leader' and 'Brigade Leader'.

In this parallel universe, the Inferno Project is referred to by the Doctor as a 'scientific slave-labour camp', and there's evidence of a 'central register' of citizens, suggesting that daily life in the Republic is extremely restricted and controlled by the oppressive central government.

One possible cause of this temporal divergence could come from World War I. If America joined the German Empire, then it's likely that Britain and France could have surrendered while Russia collapsed into revolution. Therefore it is Great Britain and not Germany that is forced to pay the war debt while suffering humiliating terms of surrender, leading to a fascist movement within England. The Royal Family might be considered the figureheads of the 'capitulation' and an obstacle to a strong Britain.

The new Soviet Union would need a counterbalance against a strong German Empire and thus aided Great Britain in its own revolution as America, returning to isolationism, was content to watch. Fearing an invasion from the German Empire, Britain passed the Defence of the Republic Act, cementing its alliance with the Soviet Union. Needless to say, there is no United Nations and therefore no UNIT.

A WORD OF CAUTION: THE IMPOSSIBLE ADVENTURE

One of the things about this adventure likely to frustrate the players is 'the impossible adventure', or the feeling that the ending is pre-ordained. The Republic is doomed and there is nothing that the characters can do about it except survive long enough to fix the real world. Or is it? There is no real reason why the characters can't succeed in the Republic universe, and then return to their own to implement the field-tested plan.

Good advice is evident in **Inferno**. The Doctor arrives and is put through imprisonment and interrogation while the Inferno project cracks the crust. It is also

HEY, WHERE ARE THE RULES FOR VENUSIAN AIKIDO?

As a great many karate-chopped goons know, the Third Doctor is a master of many martial arts, including Venusian Aikido. In the game, this works as a form of Fighting – the player can describe his attacks however he likes. The Doctor uses flips and joint locks, Leela uses kicks and stabs with her Janis thorns, and Rory the Roman has an excellent right hook. They all do damage equal to the character's Strength...

...assuming they're trying to do damage. Remember, reducing your opponent's Attributes is just one possible outcome of a Physical Contest.

If you beat a foe's Strength + Fighting with your roll, you could punch him, or you could knock him down, or pin him against a wall, or steal his hat. The outcome has to be a reasonable one – you can't, say, declare that just because the Dalek lost a single Physical Contest with you, it explodes (unless, of course there happens to be a handy hyper-furnace to push it into).

By combining a successful Physical Contest with Story Points, you can do all sorts of clever things. For example, it might cost you six Story Points to declare that the guard outside the enemy base is asleep – but if you punch the guard and spend a Story Point, then a kind Gamemaster might agree that's enough to knock him out.

evident that the project is moving faster in this timeline. Thus, through no fault of the Doctor, the world is doomed. In an RPG campaign, so long as you make it evident up front that the characters aren't expected to save the world, they are more likely to roll with it and use their time in the doomed world to learn lessons for their own.

HAVEN'T WE SEEN THIS BEFORE?

Professor Stahlman is attempting to crack the Earth's crust to provide a source of unlimited power. At approximately the same time (the dates are subjective), Professor Zaroff is in Atlantis also trying to break through the crust (see **The Underwater Menace** in **The Second Doctor Sourcebook**). Unlike Stahlman, Zaroff has no illusions about the consequences; he expects the world to be destroyed and, in the alternate universe, that is exactly what happens.

It is possible that Zaroff and Stahlman were colleagues; their ages are approximately the same and they may have even gone to school together or worked on various projects together. Perhaps they learned about the properties of Stahlman's Gas by studying some long-forgotten Atlantean texts. Obviously, Zaroff disappeared before he discovered the folly of drilling through the Earth's crust; Stahlman never learned that lesson.

OOPS

One of the problems in roleplaying game campaigns is that, when the stakes are high, it's tough for the Gamemaster to let the characters fail. Just look at the track record of the first four adventures of the Third Doctor. Losing means that the Nestenes take over and purge the Earth of Humanity, the Silurians do the same, the Ambassadors turn it into a burning cinder, and the Inferno Project utterly destroys it. It's difficult to see where an earthbound campaign would move forward from any of these apocalyptic climaxes.

This adventure provides a solution. If the characters are going astray, then 'punt' them into a parallel universe. Unlike the Republic of Great Britain, this new universe may not be very different from theirs; in fact, the characters may only become aware of the differences when an impossible event occurs, such as a television reference to the 'Confederate States of America' or 'the King of Great Britain'. After this, the characters are free to fail, but the knowledge they take with them can help them in the normal timeline (after they work out how to get back).

PRIMORDS

The Primords aren't a true race, but rather the alteration of a human being that has come into contact with the green goo accompanying Stahlman's gas. At first, the contact causes a green discolouration on the skin which rapidly spreads across the body. At this point the human ceases to exist and becomes a Primord, a bestial creature that may be an evolutionary throwback or mutation. She develops bestial features and gains incredible strength.

PRIMORD

AWARENESS	3	PRESENCE	1
COORDINATION	4	RESOLVE	3
INGENUITY	1	STRENGTH	5

SKILLS
Athletics 3, Fighting 3, Survival 2

TRAITS
Alien Appearance: Primords look like green bestial humans.
Environmental: A Primord suffers no ill effects from extreme heat.
Immunity: A Primord takes no damage from bullets.
Infection (Special): If the Primord does damage to an opponent they are infected with green goo and become a Primord as well. A character struck by a Primord must roll Strength + Resolve against a Difficulty of 15 or become infected. See the *Infection sidebar*.
Natural Weapons: A Primord can use its teeth or claws to add +1 damage.
Special: Primords radiate heat. Merely touching a Primord inflicts 2 damage on the character, and a Primord inflicts an extra +2 damage when making a physical attack. This extra damage is in addition to the Primord's claws, so a Primord could hit for 4/8/12 damage!
Weakness: -2 to rolls when operating in cold conditions.
Weakness: Fire Extinguishers do 4 levels of damage to a Primord.

STORY POINTS: 3-5

At higher temperatures this transformation may take only seconds and the bestial features become more pronounced, resulting in Primords that look like green werewolves. Primords have a pack mentality and try to expose normal humans to the green goo, thereby creating more Primords. This presumes at least an animal's cunning, but whether the Primords are capable of higher intelligence is unknown. They certainly seemed unconcerned with the world's impending doom.

INFECTED CHARACTERS

Primords are just one in a long line of monsters that can infect their victims with some icky plague or radiation or nanotechnology that slowly turns the infected victim into another monster. The usual way to handle this is to give the infected character a chance to resist the initial attack – usually with a Strength + Resolve test – and then drain Resolve or Strength over time if the character does get infected.

There are different ways to drain Resolve, each of which gives the infection a different 'flavour'.

- **The player rolls Strength + Resolve again every so often to resist damage:** This shows the character struggling against the infection. It does involve a lot of dice rolling, and can be unpredictable – someone with high Attributes or lucky dice rolling might remain unaffected for the whole adventure, but an unlucky person might succumb quickly.

- **The character automatically loses Resolve:** This is the scariest alternative – there's nothing the character can do to stop the progress of the infection. The character's doomed unless she finds a cure in the next few hours or days, like Spectrox Bat Milk or something equally exotic.

- **The character swaps Resolve for Story Points:** This puts control of the disease into the hands of the player. Some players don't want to see their characters infected; others like the thrill of risking their lives. If the player gains a Story Point each time she loses Resolve, then that sets the player up for some thrilling heroics (or, more likely, a dramatic sacrifice).

Non-player characters should *mostly* follow the same rules as player characters, except when you want someone to turn especially quickly!

There are also a few other concerns to keep in mind when you introduce a vampiric creature like the Primords.

- **Is it too dangerous?** If a disease drains Attributes, then it can stop the player characters' investigating and exploring. Imagine a disease that drains, say, Resolve, and the victims loose 1 point of Resolve every thirty minutes. Most player characters have only 2 to 4 Resolve – can a cure be found within an hour of play?

- **Can you use Story Points to reduce damage?** Spending a Story Point restores lost Attributes (see *It was just a Scratch*). If player characters can reduce damage from an infection, they can avoid being turned into a monster for a very, very long time if they've got the Story Points to spend.

- **What does Medicine do?** Can Medicine be used to cure or slow the progress of a disease? Finding a full cure is probably better left for the end of an adventure, but maybe medicine can find a way to stop the disease from spreading.

PRIMORD INFECTION

The Primord infection is a particularly nasty one. It's an automatic loss of Resolve at the rate of one point every hour. Instead of losing Resolve, a character can choose to gain the Alien Appearance or Weakness traits (all the nice traits, like Immunity and Natural Weapons, happen when the character hits Resolve 0 and becomes a Primord).

PROFESSOR STAHLMAN

AWARENESS	3	PRESENCE	4
COORDINATION	3	RESOLVE	4
INGENUITY	5	STRENGTH	2

In both universes, Professor Stahlman is passionate about completing his project and providing unlimited energy for Earth. He sports a moustache and goatee in the normal universe and is clean-shaven in the Republic one, thus reversing the polarity of the classic test for evil twins. Stahlman's parallel-universe duplicate may be even more ruthless. He may have arranged for the death of Sir Keith Gold, the overseer of Project Inferno, and he drove the machines onwards to complete the drilling several hours ahead of his counterpart in the 'original' continuum.

SKILLS

Convince 3, Craft 2, Fighting 1, Knowledge 3, Medicine 1, Science 5, Subterfuge 2, Technology 4, Transport 1

TRAITS

Obsession (Major): Stahlman will complete the drilling at all costs.
Argumentative: Stahlman is abrasive and easily annoyed. Anything and anyone that interferes with his project will face the full brunt of his temper.
Technically Adept: Stahlman gets a +2 bonus on Technology rolls.

TECH LEVEL: 5   **STORY POINTS: 10**

SECTION LEADER ELISABETH SHAW

AWARENESS	3	PRESENCE	4
COORDINATION	4	RESOLVE	4
INGENUITY	4	STRENGTH	3

Instead of becoming a scientist, young Liz Shaw joined the Republic Security Forces in this reality after studying Physics at university. She was more flexible in her thinking than many of the other Republic soldiers, and was willing to listen to the Doctor (even though she suspected he was an eccentric free-thinking liberal protestor, not a traveller from an alternate reality).

SKILLS

Athletics 2, Convince 4, Knowledge 4, Marksman 4, Medicine 2, Science 2, Survival 3, Technology 3, Transport 2

TRAITS

Attractive: +2 to rolls based on appearance.
Brave: +2 to resist fear.
Friends: (Republic Security Forces).
Indomitable: +4 to resist psychic control.
Military Rank (Major x2): Section Leader.
Obligation (RSF).
Tough: Reduce all damage taken by 2.
Unadventurous (Minor)
Voice of Authority: +2 to order people about.

EQUIPMENT

Pistol 2/5/7

STORY POINTS: 8

BRIGADE LEADER LETHBRIDGE-STEWART

AWARENESS	4	PRESENCE	4
COORDINATION	4	RESOLVE	4
INGENUITY	4	STRENGTH	4

The Brigade Leader is a parallel of the Brigadier. Like the Brigadier, the Brigade Leader is a devoted military officer, albeit one that's grown up in a dictatorship. This gives the Brigade Leader a harsher edge and, perhaps because of this devotion and ruthlessness, he isn't quite as brave as the Brigadier. Unlike the Brigadier, the Brigade Leader sports an eye-patch and is clean-shaven, causing the Doctor to remark to the Brigadier that he looks better with a moustache.

SKILLS
Athletics 3, Convince 4, Fighting 3, Knowledge 3 (Military Tactics, the British Government, RSF), Marksman 3, Medicine 1, Science 1, Subterfuge 2, Survival 3, Technology 1, Transport 3

TRAITS
By the Book: The Brigadier sticks to the rules.
Five Rounds Rapid: Attack earier in the Action Round.
Friends (Republic Security Forces).
Impulsive: He's quick to act.

Indomitable: +4 to resist psychic control.
Impaired Senses (Minor): Due to poor depth perception, the Brigade Leader suffers -2 to rolls relying on sight.
Military Rank: (Brigade Leader).
Obligation: (Republic Security Forces) .
Tough: Reduce all damage suffered by 2.
Voice of Authority: +2 to ordering people about.

EQUIPMENT
Pistol 2/5/7

STORY POINTS: 6

FURTHER ADVENTURES

- So, where did Stalhman's gas come from? If it's a natural phenomenon, it's a very strange one – it's an incredible source of power, it turns people into monsters, and although no-one's ever drilled deep enough to recover it, Stalhman knows a great deal about its properties. Perhaps the gas was actually produced by some alien race, like the Racnoss, and Stalhman learned about it through some secret contact. Stalhman might actually have been the pawn of this alien race, using him to tap the gas so they can reawaken their buried forces.

- The Republic of Great Britain is doomed. Their world is overrun with Primords, and soon it's going to crack like an egg. However, thanks to the interloping Doctor, they know there's a perfectly good parallel universe next door, full of weak-willed cowards who can easily be conquered. The characters have to stop an invasion of Earth from another Earth – and what happens when Primords start slipping through the gaps in reality?

- The Master claimed that the Valeyard was the Doctor's dark side between his 12th and 13th incarnations, but perhaps he was mistaken or simply lying. The Valeyard is from the alternate universe, where the Doctor, like the other parallel characters, is several shades darker (this makes sense of how the Valeyard tried to acquire the Doctor's remaining regenerations). The characters may be surprised to bump into a 'future incarnation' of the Doctor that is selfish and ruthless, but in a more subtle way than the Master.

TERROR OF THE AUTONS

'I came to warn you. An old acquaintance has arrived on this planet.'

SYNOPSIS

England, UNIT era

The Master arrived on Earth. With his TARDIS taking the form of a horse-box, he travelled to a circus, overpowering the owner, Rossini. He then stole a Nestene energy source from the National Space Museum and, to power it, sabotaged a radio telescope at Beacon Hill. Finally, he hypnotized the manager of a plastics factory and took over its production.

Meanwhile, the Doctor was on his trail, with his new assistant Jo (although he was less than impressed with her qualifications). On arriving at Beacon Hill, a bowler-hatted Time Lord materialized to warn of two things: firstly, that the Master had returned; secondly, that there was a bomb behind the door. The Doctor dived into the room, catching the bomb before it hit the floor. The facility Director told him that two scientists, Gooch and Philips, had disappeared: the Doctor found Gooch miniaturized and trapped in his own lunchbox.

At the plastics factory, Jo attempted to spy on the Master, but he caught and hypnotized her. Under his influence, she used her skeleton keys to try to open a box which UNIT had retrieved from Philips' abandoned car. Just in time, the Doctor realised it was a bomb, and threw it out of the window. Using the living plastic produced at the factory, the Master began killing anyone who questioned him: first a factory manager, with an inflatable plastic chair; secondly, Farrell Senior, to whom he gave a plastic doll which came to life and attacked.

Meanwhile, lured by Philips' abandoned car, the Doctor arrived at the circus. The owner and a strongman captured him, but Jo arrived and smashed a vase over the strongman's head. Philips emerged from the Master's TARDIS with a grenade, but the Doctor broke the Master's influence, and Philips blew himself up. The Doctor stole the dematerialisation circuit from the Master's TARDIS.

A police car arrived to rescue the Doctor and Jo, but the Doctor realised that the driver was an Auton. UNIT arrived and, after a gun battle, rescued the Doctor and Jo. Back at UNIT headquarters, Brownrose from the Ministry brought news of unexplained deaths. The Doctor installed the dematerialization circuit in the TARDIS but his attempt to leave failed – the circuit was the wrong model. Meanwhile, led by the Master, Autons in carnival costumes toured shopping centres giving out plastic daffodils.

Investigating the Master's previous victims, the Doctor found the doll. When he took it back to UNIT headquarters, it attacked Jo. In the plastics factory, a plastic telephone cord attacked the Doctor. Yates shot the doll, while the Brigadier disconnected the telephone cord. At UNIT headquarters, one of the Master's daffodils sprayed Jo's face with plastic. She began to suffocate, but the Doctor rescued her. The Master arrived and, just as he was about to shoot the Doctor, the Doctor told him that the dematerialization circuit would be destroyed.

Instead, the Master tied them up and took them to Beacon Hill. They signaled UNIT, using the car's brake lights, then escaped. As UNIT fought the Autons, the Master used the radio telescope to summon the Nestene. However, the Doctor persuaded him the Nestene would turn against him. At the last minute, the Master joined the Doctor in shutting down the telescope. Finally, he escaped, driving a coach through the UNIT forces.

CONTINUITY

This is Jo Grant's first appearance and the first of many times she rescues the Doctor from imprisonment.

It is also the Master's first appearance and the first of many, many times he avoids capture.
Liz Shaw has gone "back to Cambridge".
UNIT use their call-signs 'Greyhound' and 'Trap One' for the first time.

◯ RUNNING THE ADVENTURE

This is a fast-paced adventure, full of unexpected twists. There is an evil killer chair! An evil killer doll! A bomb, a skeleton key, a gunfight, a fighter plane! The policeman is an Auton! The Master has appeared! Everything moves so fast that it's hard to keep up. It also shows the Master at his most chaotic. In his murder attempts, he shapes living plastic into a bewildering variety of forms: telephones, daffodils, a living doll. We never find how he got into UNIT headquarters. We are never sure why, at the last minute, he abandons his careful plan. He is frightening because he is unpredictable.

Try filling your adventures with surprising twists, horrific set-pieces and amazing events. Don't worry about making sense: if you go fast enough, nobody will care, providing you make some effort to pull everything together. If things seem dull, bring in a killer telephone, doll, chair, daffodil or anything else made of plastic. Best of all; bring in the Master, with his gun pointed at the Doctor.

REPORT FROM ONE OF OUR FIELD SECTIONS, SIR.

Sometimes, in roleplaying games, players get stuck. They don't know what to do next. They know something strange is going on, but they don't know what to do about it. When this happens in **Doctor Who: Adventures in Time and Space**, the players can spend a Story Point to get the next clue. This adventure shows you how, in the era of the Third Doctor, this might work.

When the Doctor and Jo are completely stuck, they go back to UNIT headquarters. Eventually, a UNIT underling simply gives them the next piece of the puzzle. "Some kind of sabotage at a radio telescope", "They found Philip's car abandoned", "A wave of sudden deaths". From that clue, they can continue with their investigation.

Try doing this in your games. When your players are stuck, encourage them to return to UNIT headquarters. Then, if they spend a Story Point, a UNIT underling – or whoever else is available – enters with a report of unusual activity. That report takes everyone to the next location in the plot. Best of all, this takes away the problem of failing an investigation. If someone fails to get a vital piece of information, let them fail. Perhaps they will find another way to get it later. If they don't, you can simply get an underling to give them what they need.

I SHALL OBEY

For a short time, Jo is under the control of the Master, and tries to kill the Doctor by detonating a bomb. It is rare for one of the Doctor's companions to turn against him: later, the Fifth Doctor's companion Turlough would also be ordered to kill him, but would eventually choose loyalty to the Doctor instead.

When a companion turns against the Doctor, it adds something exciting to the adventure, but makes running the game more complex. Your first decision is: will you tell the other players that the companion has turned bad? If you don't, then they get the excitement of making the discovery for themselves at some point during the adventure. However, if you tell them, then everyone can play along, knowing that the traitor will eventually be discovered. Much depends on your players: if you tell them, will they treat the companion in the same way? Or will they turn on them? Often, you will find that they'll play along, which means you can trust everyone with the knowledge that the companion has turned bad. (Of course, if the companion is 'turned' by a Hypnosis roll, then everyone will know what has happened anyway.)

Companions can work against the Doctor for a short time, like Jo, or for a long time, like Turlough. This trick makes for an interesting adventure, but it'll get old if you do it too often. Once you've turned one Companion against the Doctor, don't do it again for the remainder of the campaign. Remember that, the next time the Master tried to hypnotise Jo (**Frontier In Space**), she resisted his powers.

THE MINISTRY AND THE MILITARY

In this adventure, the British government shows itself in two ways: the bluster of the Ministry and the military power of UNIT. When Brownrose from the Ministry arrives, the Third Doctor is patronizing, even pompous. He claims to know Brownrose's superior in a high-class gentleman's club: "Wrong sort of chap is creeping into your lot, Tubby, I said."

In your adventures, the Doctor's player might try this tactic, using a Social Challenge to assume an air of authority. Remember, though, that such people wield extraordinary power: in **The Claws Of Axos**, the equally pompous Chinn orders missiles to be fired at an alien ship, while in **The Sea Devils**, the unbearable Walker threatens a nuclear strike.

Even more threatening, however, is UNIT itself. Towards the end of the adventure, the Brigadier orders an airstrike on Beacon Hill. This serves an important function in the story: it creates a countdown and a sense of urgency. (If, in your adventure, someone plays the Brigadier, it is practically mandatory for them to call in an airstrike.) However, it also shows UNIT's brutal side. Later in the Doctor's timeline, Torchwood would act with similar callousness, when they destroyed a retreating Sycorax ship.

Remember, then, that UNIT isn't all about exciting gun battles. It has a brutal side, too, which sometimes threatens the Doctor's plans. And remember the faceless bureaucrats from the Ministry: ineffectual, pompous, but with hidden power.

HE'S GONE!

At the end of the Third Doctor's adventures, the Master often escapes. This isn't always true – at the end of **The Daemons**, he is captured, only to escape from prison in **The Sea Devils** – but it is an ongoing theme.

You can, of course, play out the Master's escapes by rolling dice. Instead, however, you might offer players a Story Point (for use next time) if they let the Master escape. If they refuse, then he starts the next adventure in prison. Of course, he might not stay there.

BACK TO CAMBRIDGE

During the Third Doctor's travels, two companions left him. The first was Liz Shaw, the second Jo Grant. However, they leave in very different ways.

In this adventure, the Brigadier reveals that Liz Shaw has left. It's a low-key exit: she has simply gone "back to Cambridge". If, in your games, a character leaves unexpectedly, this is a good way to handle it. For example, if a player leaves the game or wants to change character, you can simply explain that their old character has gone back to Cambridge, or wherever is suitable.

Later, in **The Green Death**, Jo Grant gets a whole adventure to say goodbye – more on that later.

FURTHER ADVENTURES

- The night before Christmas, plastic toys come to life under the Christmas tree. At first, the children are delighted. Then the toys meet in the streets and unleash a tide of destruction. The Doctor must discover what is happening and stop it. Why has the Nestene Consciousness returned to Earth? Who has brought it there?

- What other secrets does Rossini's fairground hold? Perhaps, like Vorg in **Carnival of Monsters,** it holds a Miniscope. Perhaps it holds monsters: either old adversaries or ones the Doctor has never seen before. Or perhaps there is a monstrous artifact from the Cybermen, Daleks or the Great Intelligence. Whatever is there, a

mysterious fairground is a wonderful start to an adventure.

- Which other creatures could use Beacon Hill? Perhaps the Cybermen or the Master himself could adapt it for mind control. Perhaps the Silurians or Sontarans see it as a threat. Indeed, Beacon Hill may hold its own secrets. What if, rather than being a radio telescope, it is a weapon developed by UNIT? How would an alien race respond to that?

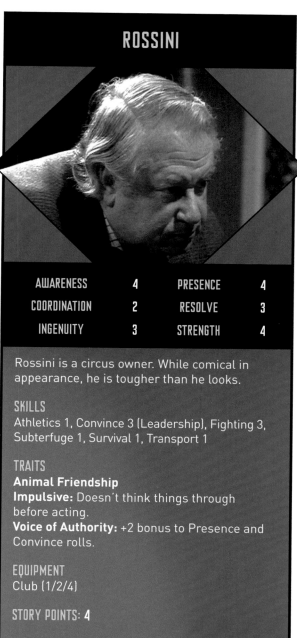

ROSSINI

AWARENESS	4	PRESENCE	4
COORDINATION	2	RESOLVE	3
INGENUITY	3	STRENGTH	4

Rossini is a circus owner. While comical in appearance, he is tougher than he looks.

SKILLS
Athletics 1, Convince 3 (Leadership), Fighting 3, Subterfuge 1, Survival 1, Transport 1

TRAITS
Animal Friendship
Impulsive: Doesn't think things through before acting.
Voice of Authority: +2 bonus to Presence and Convince rolls.

EQUIPMENT
Club (1/2/4)

STORY POINTS: 4

TONY

AWARENESS	3	PRESENCE	3
COORDINATION	3	RESOLVE	3
INGENUITY	1	STRENGTH	5

When Rossini wants to capture the Doctor, he calls on Tony's help. Tony is a strongman, muscular and clad in a loincloth. Despite his size, he follows the Doctor without being spotted.

SKILLS
Athletics 4 (Weightlifting), Convince 1, Fighting 3, Subterfuge 2, Survival 1

TRAITS
Tough: Reduces damage by 2.

STORY POINTS: 3

NEW GADGET –SKELETON KEYS

Jo's Skeleton Keys can open any lock. In adventures, then, they work like the sonic screwdriver, helping Jo to explore or releasing her from captivity. However, while they cannot open electronic locks, the skeleton keys have one advantage over the sonic screwdriver: they can open wooden locks.

Traits: Open / Close, Restriction (Cannot open electronic locks)
Cost: 1 Story Point

NEW GADGET – SONIC SCREWDRIVER

If Jo has her skeleton keys, it is only fair to use this alternative sonic screwdriver for the Doctor, which cannot open wooden locks. Make sure you put wooden locks in your adventure.

Traits: Open / Close, Restriction (Cannot open wooden locks, Tricky controls), Scan, Transmit.
Cost: 2 Story Points

NEW GADGET – FACEMASK

Using his skin-tight facemasks, the Master can impersonate anybody, from a telephone engineer to a general. While it is unlikely that these would fool the Doctor, facemasks are invaluable for fooling the public. They are also essential for ensuring that, at the end of an adventure, the Master escapes.

Traits: One Shot, Disguise (gives +3 to any Subterfuge roll).
Cost: 1 Story Point

THE MIND OF EVIL

'This machine has the power to affect men's minds, Governor, and it's growing stronger'

⬥ SYNOPSIS

England, UNIT era

Emil Keller's ground-breaking invention promised to reform criminals at the flick of a switch, His 'Keller Machine' removed from its subjects' brains the negative emotions which led to criminal behaviour. At Stangmoor Prison, the Doctor and Jo witnessed a demonstration of the machine which did not go according to plan, putting the prisoner, Barnham, into a coma.

Following the demonstration, people at the prison began dying in ways that seemed to mirror their innermost fears: a medical student with a fear of rats was covered in bites; a scientist with a fear of drowning had water in his lungs. In addition, the inmates of the prison seemed to grow restless when the device was used. The Doctor took a closer look at the machine and was assaulted by visions of flames which vanished when Jo interrupted. He realised that the machine worked by bringing a person's deepest fears to life in their mind. Before the Doctor could investigate further, Captain Yates of UNIT arrived

to retrieve him. The Brigadier wanted his Scientific Advisor's assistance at the historic first World Peace Conference.

The conference had started poorly, with the theft of confidential documents from the Chinese delegation closely followed by the Chinese delegate's death. The Doctor charmed his way into the confidence of the Chinese delegation, speaking fluent Hokkien and claiming to have spent time with Mao Zedong on the Long March.

The American delegate was visited by Chinese diplomat, Chin Lee, who appeared to transform into a terrifying dragon. Before he could die from this projected fear, however, the Doctor and Brigadier arrived. When questioned, Chin Lee revealed she had worked with Emil Keller, the inventor of the machine. That man, the Doctor realised, was really the Master.

With the assistance of the Master, who supplied gas grenades and masks, the prisoners took over the prison. When the Doctor arrived, the Master captured him and connected him to the Keller Machine. This time his hallucinations were of the various enemies he had faced, and one of his hearts stopped, before the Master shut down the machine. The Doctor warned his enemy that the machine would soon be too powerful to control. The Master locked the machine in a room, but it then began teleporting around the prison.

The Master demanded the Doctor's help in controlling the machine, and the Doctor developed a coil which restrained it for a while, but it escaped in a flurry of sparks. However, when it appeared near Barnham, it became powerless: the Doctor realised that, because Barnham's evil impulses had been extracted, he neutralized the machine. Meanwhile, UNIT entered the prison and began taking it back, but the Master had escaped. Together with the prisoners, he had captured a nerve gas containing Thunderbolt missile, with which he intended to destroy the peace conference. The Doctor offered to return the TARDIS dematerialization circuit, if the Master agreed to leave the planet.

When the Doctor arrived for this rendezvous, he brought the Keller machine with Barnham acting as its trigger – when the man was close to the device it was inactive; when he stepped away it activated. While the Master writhed in agony, the Doctor enabled the missile's abort function. UNIT aborted the missile, which exploded, destroying the machine. During the excitement, the Master managed not only to escape, but also to grab the dematerialization circuit!

CONTINUITY

There is an alien inside the Keller Machine, that "feeds on the power of the mind", but it is never identified.

The Doctor claims to have met Chairman Mao and Walter Raleigh.

Unusually, it is the Brigadier who wears a disguise, pretending to be a delivery driver when he enters the prison prior to UNIT's assault ("Ere, wait a minute. I've got a week's supply of food in there!").

⊙ RUNNING THE ADVENTURE

If you are tired of adventures in which the Doctor fights monster after monster, this is the story for you. In it, the enemy is a sinister machine that preys on people's fears. There are complex moral issues here too: the Doctor must prevent a World War and stop a dangerous scientific project.

SOMETHING EVIL ABOUT THAT MACHINE

Many of the Doctor's adventures begin with a scientific demonstration. The plot runs like this: the Doctor witnesses the demonstration, which promises great benefits for mankind. While the Doctor realizes something is wrong, he cannot stop it going ahead. During the demonstration, something appears to malfunction. For a moment, everything seems to have worked, but suddenly, it is clear that something has gone terribly wrong. For the rest of the adventure, the Doctor deals with the fallout.

These scientific demonstrations always promise something extraordinary. The Keller Machine promised to cure criminals. The Lazarus Experiment, witnessed by the Tenth Doctor, promised to stop people ageing. Try using the same formula in your adventures. Start with a scientific demonstration that promises something extraordinary: perhaps a cure for disease, hunger or war. Then think how it could go wrong.

Indeed, as we mentioned above, many of the Doctor's adventures involve scientific hubris. In **Inferno**, Professor Stahlman thought he could produce unlimited energy; in **The Claws of Axos**, Axonite promised unlimited power and food. The Tenth Doctor encountered pills that promised extraordinary weight loss, but also caused death. The Eleventh Doctor met a scientist who had invented something to help Britain win World War II. It was a Dalek.

In fact, when the Doctor encounters dangerous science, he often finds an alien influence behind it.

In this adventure the Doctor suspected there was a 'mind parasite' in the Keller Machine. Do these mind parasites exist elsewhere? Could the Doctor meet another in his travels, perhaps on an alien world?

YOU'D NEED AN ARMY TO GET IN THERE

While the Doctor abhors guns, UNIT uses them regularly. As mentioned above, the Third Doctor's adventures often end in a gunfight. While UNIT shoots things, the Doctor runs through the gunfire to do whatever needs doing.

This adventure contains one of UNIT's most spectacular and well-planned battles. They do not simply begin firing. Instead, they have a strategy, which they plan by looking at a map of the prison (which happens to be a former fortress). It is a two-pronged attack. The first prong is a 'Trojan horse': the Brigadier, disguised as a delivery driver, takes a van holding UNIT soldiers into the prison courtyard. The second prong uses a forgotten underground passage, through which more troops enter.

If your players enjoy it, try putting such battles in your adventures. Simply have a fortress or other military building which, at the end of the adventure, UNIT can attack. Prepare a map for this building, with underground passages, secret entrances and structures to provide cover. Let them plan a strategy. Then let the bullets fly. Be ready with all the combat rules from **The Gamemaster's Guide** and **Defending the Earth: The UNIT Sourcebook**, especially Duck And Cover. However, don't let a gunfight stop the Doctor or his companions. Let them dodge through to get wherever they need to go.

WELL, WHAT CAN I DO TO HELP?

In **Terror of the Autons**, the Master joined forces with the Doctor to stop the Nestene Consciousness. In this adventure, they join forces to control the Keller Machine. Whenever the Master and Third Doctor appear in the same adventure, they often find a way of working together.

In your adventures, try encouraging the Master and Doctor to cooperate, especially on scientific projects. There are two ways to do this. Firstly, as in this adventure, the Master can force the Doctor to help. Secondly, the Doctor can persuade the Master to cooperate.

Now, when the Master works with the Doctor, that doesn't mean he is no longer a threat. On the contrary: he only works with the Doctor when something else is threatening them. Indeed, in the early stages of an adventure, the Master rarely works with the Doctor: instead, he works with others, to destroy the world. He only works with the Doctor when his plans go awry. Remember, however, that their cooperation is only temporary. After their collaboration, one of them escapes. Afterwards, they are sworn enemies again.

IT'S HAPPENING AGAIN

One reason the Keller Machine is frightening is because, before it attacks, there is a build-up of events. Firstly, the prisoners become restless. Second, the Machine starts flashing. Third, if the machine has begun teleporting, it appears in the room. Only then does it attack.

You can use this in any adventure. Don't just let a creature attack. Instead, describe threatening omens.

In an adventure with the Cybermen, describe the approaching sound of marching feet.

In an adventure with the Weeping Angels, describe the lights flickering. Your players will associate the omens with the approaching danger.

FEAR

The Keller Machine is frightening because it feeds on fear. It even works on the Doctor and Master. The Master's fear is the Doctor, while the Third Doctor fears a planet destroyed by fire (**Inferno**) and his various adversaries, especially the Daleks.

This isn't the only time that the Doctor faces an adversary that preys on fear. In **The Frontier In Space**, the Master makes Humans and Draconians see their fears, which brings them to the brink of war.

In **The God Complex**, a hotel created rooms containing people's fears. When Amy saw her fear there, it was the fear her seven year-old self had that the Doctor would not return for her

What else in the human mind could the Doctor's adversaries prey on? Might a creature prey on people's prejudice? What about people's anger? Could you write an adventure in which a machine presents people with their worst memory?

FURTHER ADVENTURES

- The Doctor arrives on a world that shows him and his companions their deepest desires. Secretly, however, the world is controlled by a corporation which studies the human mind. Will the companions stay with the Doctor or follow their desires? And what, deep down, does the Doctor really want?

- In a backwater of space, the Doctor finds the Keller Machine's mind parasite. This time, it has taken control of a space station, where it shows the human crew members their deepest fears. How can the Doctor stop it, before the crew members die?

- The Doctor faces one of his most feared adversaries: perhaps the Daleks, the Cybermen or even the Time Lords. However, the creatures are not real, but a collective hallucination. As the Doctor explores, he realizes he is trapped inside a variant of the Keller Machine. How can he escape? Must he face his fears?

THE KELLER MACHINE

The Keller Machine shows people their worst fear and feeds on their terror. It contains an alien parasite, which preys on the human mind. As the machine goes stronger, it can teleport to find more victims. It can be restrained with some Jiggery Pokery, but not for long. Because the Keller Machine is simply a large box, many of the normal attributes do not apply. For example, the Keller Machine does not really have Coordination or Strength. If you must make a roll with these attributes – for example, if someone tries to restrain the machine as it is teleporting – use the figures in brackets.

AWARENESS	6	PRESENCE	N/A (3)
COORDINATION	N/A (3)	RESOLVE	6
INGENUITY	6	STRENGTH	N/A (5)

SKILLS
Convince 6

TRAITS

Empathic: +2 to understand people.
Fear Factor (2*): When striking fear into its victim's hearts, the Keller Machine adds +4 to the attempt.
Hypnosis: +2 to calm or control people.
Immunity: All but the most powerful physical attacks (anything short of a nuclear explosion won't even dent it).
Indomitable: +4 to resist control.
Psychic Training: +2 to resist psychic powers.
Dependency (Major): Feeds on fear.
Weakness (Major): Powerless in the presence of someone whose mind is free from evil.
Psychic (Special): Can read minds.

Teleport: Once the Keller Machine has successfully struck fear into a victim, it can transport itself anywhere within a short range, usually a building.
Special Trait - Their Worst Fear: The Keller Machine can kill by turning its victims worst fears against them. The victim can attempt to resist the attack with a Resolve + Convince roll, but if they fail they suffer damage (2/5/7) to their Resolve. The Keller Machine does not suffer any damage if it loses the conflict. The Keller Machine adds its current Fear Factor to any damage caused by its Their Worst Fear attack. Unlike most mental conflicts, if the victim's Resolve is reduced to 0 by the attack, it is treated as Lethal damage.

*Each time the Keller Machine successfully strikes fear into a victim, or that victim tries and fails to shake off the fear, its Fear Factor increases by one against that victim.

TECH LEVEL: 6   **STORY POINTS: 7**

THE CLAWS OF AXOS

'All things must die, Doctor. Mankind, this planet. Axos merely hastens the process.'

SYNOPSIS

England, UNIT era

An unidentified flying object landed on Earth, sending out a distress call. As it descended, a Ministry of Defense official, Chinn, tried to destroy it with missiles, but it somehow avoided them. When the Doctor and Brigadier went to investigate, they found golden-skinned Axons inside. The Axons explained they had fled their planet and offered a chameleon-like material, Axonite, which promised unlimited food and power. In the bowels of the ship, Jo found a tentacled creature, but the Axons dismissed her claims as a hallucination.

Unknown to the Doctor, the Master was imprisoned on board the ship, along with CIA agent Bill Filer. When they tried to escape, the Axons recaptured them. They cloned Filer, but released the Master, keeping his TARDIS to ensure his compliance.

At the nearby Nuton nuclear power station, the Doctor encountered Dr Winser, who was researching time travel. The cloned Filer arrived, asking the

Doctor to "come to Axos". However, the original Filer, having escaped, entered and fought the clone, which finally died in Dr Winser's light acceleration chamber. When Winser tried to open the chamber, he transformed into a gelatinous blob, which attacked Filer, the Doctor and Jo. Tentacled creatures – the Axons, in their natural form – invaded the laboratory and joined the attack.

The Axons captured the Doctor and Jo, taking them to their ship. There, they explained their plan: Axonite, which preys on human greed, would consume the entire planet. Threatening Jo with an unnatural aging process, they demanded the secret of time travel from the Doctor, and realised it would require the full power of the Nuton Complex. They attacked the complex and an Axon walked into the main reactor. Meanwhile, Chinn had ordered the worldwide distribution of Axonite.

Back at the power station, the Brigadier captured the Master, who had stolen the Doctor's TARDIS and was using the light accelerating chamber to get it working. In return for his release, the Master proposed to defeat the Axons, with a devastating power surge from the TARDIS. However, the Axons reversed the surge. Hardiman, the power station's head, sacrificed his life to save it.

Having escaped the Axon's ship, the Doctor offered to escape with the Master. When Filer tried to stop them, the Doctor shot him with a laser. They left in the TARDIS as the Axons attacked, energising the light accelerator and making the laboratory explode.

However, the Doctor had tricked the Master. The TARDIS materialized inside Axos. There, the Doctor offered the Axons access to time travel through the TARDIS. This, too, was a trick, and the Doctor trapped the Axons in a time loop. The Master and Doctor escaped in their respective TARDISes. However, the Doctor's TARDIS, reprogrammed by the Time Lords, returned to UNIT headquarters.

CONTINUITY

The Doctor shoots someone! Admittedly, it's a laser gun on lower power: it only forces Filer to drop his gun.
The Master's TARDIS looks like a grey box.
The Time Lords have blocked areas of the Doctor's memory. (At the end of **The Three Doctors**, they will release those blocks).

⊙ RUNNING THE ADVENTURE

A mysterious ship lands. That's a great start to an adventure, which you could use for many different creatures. Imagine a Dalek, Ood or Silent ship landing and consider what might happen from there. What if, like the Axons, those races claimed to come in peace? What would happen if they offered a gift to humanity?

A mysterious material, which promises great benefits, is dangerous. That's another great seed for an adventure. Again, it could involve various alien creatures. If the material were plastic, then the Nestene Consciousness might be involved. If it were a metal, then the Cybermen might be responsible. If it were stone, then look no further than the Weeping

Angels. Or perhaps the material could be a form of Flesh, which the Eleventh Doctor saw formed into dopplegangers, and now threatened to create an army.

Aside from those two themes, this adventure uses many themes we've seen before, with startling complexity. The Master helps the Doctor. People go in and out of prison: in a short space of time, the Master escapes from captivity, is recaptured by the Axons and then released. Incompetent government officials and hubristic scientists make dangerous decisions. There are references to human greed and promises of unlimited resources. And, of course, the adventure with a gun battle, followed by a big explosion.

KEEP AN EYE ON MISS GRANT

Why does the Doctor try to stop his companions following him? In this adventure, Jo was kept under guard to stop her following the Doctor. Naturally, she slips away, and sneaked onto the Axon ship. Later in the Doctor's timeline, the Eleventh Doctor told Amy Pond not to follow him under any circumstances. "Will you follow him?" someone asked, after had left. "Of course," she replied.

So why does the Doctor do this? The simple answer is: it makes the story better. When the Doctor leaves, it allows his companion to explore somewhere different. Here, while the Doctor talks to the golden Axons, Jo explores the bowels of the ship and finds a tentacled creature.

Use this in your games. When someone is playing the Doctor, they should regularly tell their companions to wait, while he investigates. Once he has gone, the companions should explore separately. This works with any Doctor, but especially with the protective, paternal Third Doctor.

Unless the current plot revolves around duplicates or mind control or some other paranoid theme, don't worry about the players witnessing scenes that their characters aren't present for. Just remind the players to keep what they know and what their characters know separate, and give them opportunities to inform each other of what happened while they were separated. Later, after they have gone their separate ways, the Doctor and companions will cross paths again. Don't make it hard for the Doctor and companions to reunite: unless, of course, that would make the adventure even better.

Alternatively, you can let players play 'secondary' characters. You could give the Doctor's player a UNIT soldier to play in scenes with Jo. The wonderful thing about these secondary characters is that the player is usually much less invested them. While it lessens the impact of the game if they are used too frivolously, players are likely to be more open to unfortunate events happening to these characters. Conversely, you could see the development of recurring secondary characters that become like members of the family!

THIS IS MY RESPONSIBILITY

When Hardiman tries to stop the plant exploding, he doesn't just die randomly. He sacrifices himself. By going to his death, he saves the Nuton complex and everyone in it.

Here is a rule of thumb for your adventures: if a character sacrifices their life, it should have an impact. If they sacrifice their life to stop a threat, it should usually succeed. At least, it should hold back the enemy for a while.

The Doctor has seen many such sacrifices. In the Tenth Doctor's time, K-9 sacrificed himself to stop the Krillitane. In the Ninth Doctor's era,

Jack Harkness sacrificed himself to hold back the Daleks. Both were later revived, in different ways, but that doesn't always happen: when Harriet Jones gave her life to hold back the Daleks, the sacrifice was permanent. (Admittedly, the Fifth Doctor's companion Adric sacrificed his life in vain against the Cybermen. That was a tragic death, not a heroic sacrifice.)

In your adventures, allow characters to sacrifice themselves to hold back an enemy. Let them accomplish something as they die, spending any remaining Story Points to ensure success (and heroic, self-sacrificing actions should be rewarded with more Story Points to spend). Perhaps the Doctor could sacrifice a regeneration to save someone, as the Ninth Doctor did with Rose.

THAT'S NOT ME IN THERE

One of the best moments in this adventure is when two Bill Filers fight. Fortunately, the real Filer wins. This is interesting for many reasons: Filer must bring himself to punch his replica; nobody can help, because they cannot tell which Filer is which; and, after the fight, the Doctor remains unsure which Filer has won.

Whatever you call such creatures – clones, replicas, dopplegangers, Chameleons – stealing identities is fun. The Third Doctor has already dealt with one replica, Scobie, in **Spearhead from Space**. In **Rose**, the Autons form themselves into a poor replica of Mickey Smith, while in **The Sontaran Stratagem**, the Sontarans, a clone race themselves, clone Martha Jones. The Eleventh Doctor meets his doppelganger in **The Rebel Flesh** and persuades the Teselecta to mimic him in **The Wedding of River Song**.

In your games, try creating replicas of characters, especially the Doctor and his companions. There are many adversaries that might plausibly do this: the Autons, the Sontarans or anything capable of inducing a hallucination. For a challenge, try letting the players play their own clones: until, of course, they meet the original character (or even afterwards – the best way to fool the other players as to which duplicate is real is to have the GM play the true character!).

GET AWAY FROM MY EQUIPMENT!

Finally, in this adventure, there is a laboratory. In fact, there's often a laboratory in the Third Doctor's adventures, even in buildings where you might not expect one. Skybase One (**The Mutants**) had a laboratory. Even Stangmoor Prison, in **The Mind Of Evil**, had a surprisingly sophisticated workshop.

Whenever the Third Doctor needs a laboratory, there is always one available. In your adventures, put laboratories everywhere. Even better, let the Third Doctor pay a Story Point to let him have access to one.

AXONITE

The Axons claimed that Axonite was a 'thinking molecule' that could replicate any other material, given enough energy. It could provide infinite energy by replicating oil, infinite food by replicating meat, and solve any problem that stems from a lack of resources. From this description, Axonite sounds like a form of nanotechnology – it can assemble itself into different forms to mimic other substances. However, Axonite defies analysis – it adapts to any conventional method of scanning or examining it to conceal its secrets.

The Doctor discovered the true nature of Axonite by analyzing it using Dr. Winser's light accelerator. By accelerating the Axonite sample beyond the speed of light, he sent it back in time and fooled it into analyzing itself. He learned that the purpose of Axonite was actually to suck energy from the planet – by distributing samples of Axonite to all the worlds' major governments, Axos spread its claws over the whole world!

AXONS

AWARENESS	3	PRESENCE	6
COORDINATION	3	RESOLVE	4
INGENUITY	4	STRENGTH	4

The Axons are… actually, it might be more accurate to say "Axos is", because the angelic, golden-faced Axons, the tentacled blob-monsters they became, their organic ship and the chunks of Axonite were all parts of the same singular entity, called Axos. In effect, Axos could turn pieces of itself into whatever it needed. When it wanted to travel through space, it shaped part of its structure into a living spacecraft. When it needed to fool the human inhabitants of Earth in order to siphon off the planet's energy, it created pleasing-looking figureheads – the Axons.

Still, these human-scale bits of Axos are the aspect of the creature most likely to be encountered by players. In their 'Angel' forms, Axons look like handsome, gold-skinned humans. They can become blobs with flailing tentacles when they want to fight or intimidate humans.

SKILLS
Convince 3, Fighting 3, Marksman 4 (tentacle)

TRAITS
Alien Appearance
Fear Factor 2 or **Attractive,** depending on their current form.
Natural Weapons (Tentacle, 2/4/6 or S/S/S, Major Good): Axons can use their tentacles to injure, consume or 'de-energise' their victims. By sucking life energy from a target, they temporarily stun the victim.
Networked
Shapeshift

TECH LEVEL: **7** STORY POINTS: **8**

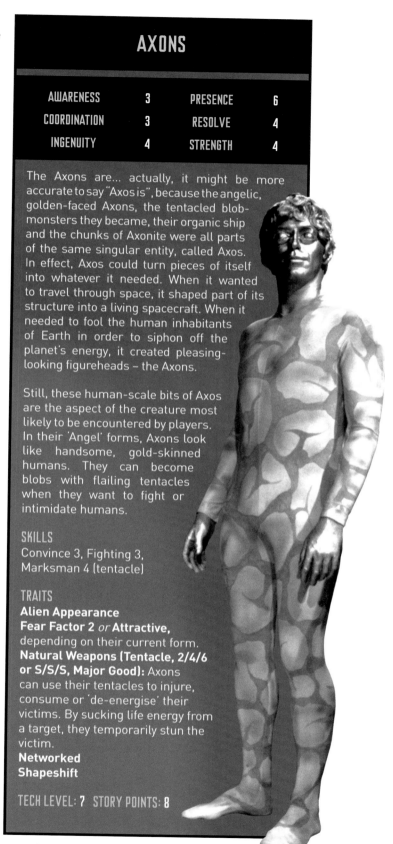

BILL FILER

AWARENESS	3	PRESENCE	4
COORDINATION	4	RESOLVE	4
INGENUITY	4	STRENGTH	4

Filer is an agent from Washington, sent to arrest the Master for his crimes in *Terror of the Autons* and *The Mind of Evil*. It's not clear which agency he works for. If the Master is treated as an international criminal, then he could be from the Federal Bureau of Investigation. If the Master's considered a threat to world security, then Filer may belong to the CIA.

The most sinister interpretation, though, is that Filer was dispatched by the American equivalent of Torchwood, Area 51, to acquire the Master from UNIT. If you go with this option, then Filer may be equipped with some salvaged alien gadgetry on his next mission.

SKILLS
Athletics 3, Convince 3, Fighting 3, Marksman 4, Subterfuge 1, Transport 1

TRAITS
Attractive
Brave
Friends (Washington)
Quick Reflexes
Insatiable Curiosity

EQUIPMENT
9mm Pistol (2/5/7)

STORY POINTS: 9

AXON BLOB

AWARENESS	1	PRESENCE	-
COORDINATION	1	RESOLVE	2
INGENUITY	-	STRENGTH	3

When Winser touched the accelerator containing the Axonite, he became a blob-like creature made of Axonite. The Axonites reacted to this development with alarm. Winser's mutation may have been the result of an automatically triggered defense mechanism – if anyone successfully analyses Axonite, the substance tries to infect and destroy them.

SKILLS
Fighting 2

TRAITS
Alien Appearance
Fear Factor 1
Networked (Minor)
Shapeshift (Minor)

STORY POINTS: 1

FURTHER ADVENTURES

- While Axos tried to trick humanity into accepting its gifts, there are other approaches it could have tried. Chunks of Axonite might fall from the sky as meteorites that 'just happen' to all land close to major power stations...

- The Doctor trapped Axos in a time loop, but Axos can take any form it needs, and may have absorbed the intelligence and memories of Dr. Winser. Given time – and Axos has infinite time in the loop – it could make part of itself into a time machine, and escape the loop in the same way the Doctor did. Axos might arrive anywhere in time and space, to threaten any planet. Worse, it might try to use its mastery of time travel to consume not just individual planets, but the whole universe! All shall become part of Axos!

- What became of Dr. Winser's light accelerator experiments afterwards? You could start a new campaign with a group of UNIT soldiers and scientists who step into the light accelerator – and vanish when they are hurled across time and space...

COLONY IN SPACE

'The exploitation of this planet could make us both rich.'

SYNOPSIS

Uxarieus, a colony and mining planet, 2472

The Time Lords sent the Doctor to a colony planet, which reported failed crops and attacks by giant lizards. The colonists had formed an alliance with the Primitives, a spear-carrying alien race.

However, as the Doctor investigated the attacks, he was attacked by a robot from the Interplanetary Mining Commission, and then captured by their agent, Caldwell. At the IMC base, their leader explained the corporation's plan to mine the planet, displacing the colonists. When the robot attacked again, with lizard-like claws, the Doctor realised what was happening: the IMC was faking the lizard attacks using the robot and a holographic projector.

Looking for evidence against the IMC, Jo and the colonist Winton infiltrated their ship. However, the IMC captured them and chained them within a Primitive dwelling. With Jo's help, Winton escaped and was found by Caldwell, who treated his wounds.

The Primitives captured Jo and took her into their ruins. The Doctor entered the ruins, trying to find her, but was taken prisoner too. From ancient carvings, he deduced that a catastrophe had once nearly destroyed the Primitives' civilization. They were taken to meet an ancient Primitive, the Guardian, who released them from their death sentence.

An Adjudicator from Earth arrived, to decide whether the mining would proceed. The Adjudicator was the Master, who ruled that the colonists must leave. Using a key he had previously stolen, the Doctor infiltrated the Master's TARDIS, but Jo broke an alarm beam and both were knocked out by sleeping gas. When they awoke, the Master held Jo as a hostage and forced the Doctor to take him to the Primitive City.

The colonists assaulted the IMC ship, where they found evidence of the faked lizard attack, then forced the ship to leave. However, the ship landed again secretly, attacked the colony and forced the colonists to leave in their ship, knowing that it would probably not survive the voyage. When the ship took off, it exploded, but only the colony leader Ashe was on board: all the other colonists had secretly disembarked.

Upon reaching the city, the Master revealed the knowledge he had gleaned from the Time Lord files – the controls to a Doomsday Weapon were within the Guardian's chamber – and offered to use it to rule the universe with the Doctor. The Doctor realised that it was the weapon that was poisoning the planet's soil and had caused the decline and fall of the Guardian's people. The Guardian refused to give the Master control of the weapon, instead activating a self-destruct mechanism. The Doctor and the Master fled the crumbling city, and the renegade Time Lord escaped.

CONTINUITY

Jo enters the TARDIS for the first time and travels to an alien world. She doesn't seem to like it.

Jo uses her escapology training to remove her handcuffs.

According to the Master, the current time is a "regimented age", in which permits are necessary for interplanetary travel and the TARDIS.

The Master stole information on the Doomsday Weapon from the Time Lords' files.

The Doctor's TARDIS is still under Time Lord control.

RUNNING THE ADVENTURE

This is a human adventure: the problems in it are created by humans. The Doctor's antagonist is an evil corporation, which exploits ordinary people. There is hardly a monster in it: only the holographic lizard and the Primitives (who, in any case, strongly resemble humans).

The characters in the adventure have complex motivations. Caldwell is sometimes good and sometimes bad (more on him shortly). The colonists are particularly complex: Ashe favours diplomacy, Winton favours fighting, but neither of their solutions is perfect. Only Dent, the IMC's leader, approaches being objectively evil and even he has a strong motivation for his actions: it is profit that drives him to murder.

At heart, the adventure is about land rights: who has the right to the planet, the colonists or the IMC? Fortunately, there is more to the story than simply negotiating this issue: in fact, it's solved in moments, when the Master makes a ruling. In your games, don't spend too much time on diplomacy, even if that's what the story is about. Get to the action.

There are two more things to note. First, when Jo arrives on the planet, she wants to go home. She is a reluctant traveller in time and space. Second, this is one of many times the Third Doctor encounters miners. These themes recur in *The Green Death*. The Doctor will encounter another group of miners, exploited by another unethical corporation, and Jo's homesickness will make her leave the TARDIS.

I'VE GOT TO STOP THIS SENSELESS KILLING

Throughout this adventure, the Doctor keeps trying to stop the fighting. There is barely a moment when a gun isn't being fired: the colonists attack the IMC, the IMC attack the colonists and the Primitives attack anyone who passes.

Fighting is important in this adventure. When a battle is being fought, the Doctor must stop it, and when it isn't, the Doctor must prevent one starting. So, in this kind of adventure, keep introducing the threat of violence. Let the Doctor discover that someone is planning to attack, then see what he does. If he fails to stop it, then a fight breaks out. If he succeeds, then the tensions remain, threatening to break out later. Alternatively, the Doctor might attempt diplomacy between the two warring sides. We'll talk about this in *Frontier In Space*.

IF YOU DON'T HELP US, WE'RE ALL GOING TO DIE!

In this adventure, the most intriguing character is Caldwell. He begins as a bad guy, capturing the Doctor for the IMC. Yet, when he hears colonists are dying, he begins to doubt: he'd happily scare the colonists off the planet, but not commit murder.

When Winton escapes from captivity, he even treats his wounds. So he seems to have become a good guy, like others in the Doctor's adventures who saw the light: for example, the Controller, who worked for the Daleks but ultimately let the Doctor go (*Day of the Daleks*).

But he hasn't. Later, he forces the colonists onto their ship, telling them their engines are fine. Perhaps he hoped they would escape – as they take off, he says "They've made it" – but then the ship blows up. Towards the end of the adventure, he seems to side with the IMC.

CALDWELL

AWARENESS	3	PRESENCE	3
COORDINATION	3	RESOLVE	4
INGENUITY	4	STRENGTH	3

SKILLS
Athletics 2, Convince 4, Craft 2, Fighting 2, Knowledge 4, Marksman 2, Medicine 2, Science 4, Survival 1, Technology 3, Transport 2

TRAITS
Technically Adept
Face in the Crowd
Friends (Minor): Interplanetary Mining.
Obligation (Major): Interplanetary Mining.

EQUIPMENT
Pistol (2/5/7), Medical Scanner (see below).

TECH LEVEL: 6   **STORY POINTS: 8**

PERSONAL GOAL: Use science to benefit people.

Instead, however, Caldwell stays with the colonists, promising to fix their power. He is neither good nor bad nor neutral, but morally ambiguous.

How could you use someone like Caldwell in your adventures? Perhaps the GM could play him as a character. If the Doctor and his companions persuade him, he'll assist. If not, he'll drift over to the bad side, assisting the corporation in their dubious operations.

For a challenge, try letting a player be Caldwell. Throughout the game, there'll be tension between characters, as Caldwell decides whose side he is on. If you do this, then Caldwell will probably assist the corporation occasionally, but mostly be on the Doctor's side. You can imagine Caldwell joining the TARDIS crew, using his scientific knowledge to assist the Doctor.

NEW GADGET – MEDICAL SCANNER

Caldwell's medical scanner is used to scan wounds, before administering medical treatment.

Traits: Scan (Minor Good): +3 to medicine rolls, +1 for scanning anything else.
Cost: 1 Story Point

CHARLIE THE ROBOT

AWARENESS	5	PRESENCE	1
COORDINATION	1	RESOLVE	4
INGENUITY	1	STRENGTH	4

SKILLS
Fighting 5

TRAITS
Robot (Special Good)
Fear Factor (Special Trait): Add +2 when trying to actively scare someone.
Weakness (Major): Can be disabled by grabbing the remote control.

EQUIPMENT
Claws (2/5/7)

STORY POINTS: 3

THE PRIMITIVES

The Primitives were the original inhabitants of Uxarieus. They once possessed a highly advanced civilization, but their own technology poisoned them, resulting in the collapse of their culture. Most of their descendants became the hunter-gatherer tribes of the Primitives. Before their collapse, the Uxarieans used genetic engineering to enhance themselves, and created a splinter race that possessed psychic abilities. These enhanced Uxarieans became a priest-caste that worshipped the machines as gods.

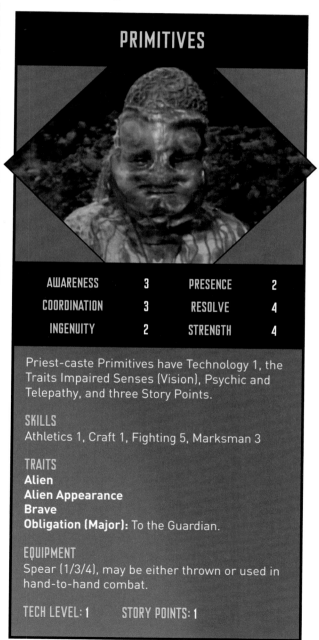

PRIMITIVES

AWARENESS	3	PRESENCE	2
COORDINATION	3	RESOLVE	4
INGENUITY	2	STRENGTH	4

Priest-caste Primitives have Technology 1, the Traits Impaired Senses (Vision), Psychic and Telepathy, and three Story Points.

SKILLS
Athletics 1, Craft 1, Fighting 5, Marksman 3

TRAITS
Alien
Alien Appearance
Brave
Obligation (Major): To the Guardian.

EQUIPMENT
Spear (1/3/4), may be either thrown or used in hand-to-hand combat.

TECH LEVEL: 1   **STORY POINTS: 1**

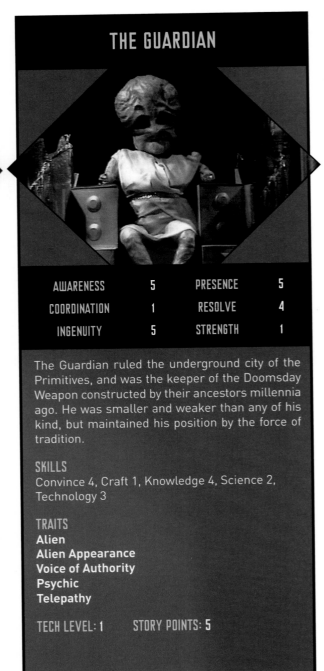

THE GUARDIAN

AWARENESS	5	PRESENCE	5
COORDINATION	1	RESOLVE	4
INGENUITY	5	STRENGTH	1

The Guardian ruled the underground city of the Primitives, and was the keeper of the Doomsday Weapon constructed by their ancestors millennia ago. He was smaller and weaker than any of his kind, but maintained his position by the force of tradition.

SKILLS
Convince 4, Craft 1, Knowledge 4, Science 2, Technology 3

TRAITS
Alien
Alien Appearance
Voice of Authority
Psychic
Telepathy

TECH LEVEL: 1   STORY POINTS: 5

THE DOOMSDAY WEAPON

The ancient ancestors of the Primitives created a Doomsday Weapon – a stellar manipulator that could cause any star to go nova. With this weapon, they could hold the galaxy to ransom, but the radiation from the weapon's power source poisoned their food supply and ruined them before they could use it – a cautionary tale for any would-be doomsday weapon builders.

Nothing livens things up like a Doomsday Weapon. It poses moral dilemmas of its own: who should control it? What should the Doctor do with it? Often, it can create a countdown: can the Doctor stop the weapon before it goes off?

Throughout his adventures, the Doctor has faced many such weapons: the Doomsday Weapon, the Doomsday Bomb, the Z-bomb, the Time Destructor, the Hand of Omega and many others. Sometimes, they destroy planets. Sometimes, they harm time itself.

If you put a Doomsday Weapon in your adventures, it creates a plot around itself. First, the Doctor and his companions will discover it exists. Next, everyone will want the weapon. The Doctor will want it, so it can be destroyed. His adversaries will want it, to hold the universe to ransom or destroy the world.

Often, when an adventure contains a Doomsday Weapon, the story is about the Doctor trying to stop it being used. What *Colony In Space* shows, however, is that Doomsday Weapons can create other sorts of adventures. This Doomsday Weapon poisons the soil, creating a complex story about agriculture and land rights. (And, of course, the Master wants to hold the universe to ransom with it.)

YOU COULD END WARS, SUFFERING, DISEASE...

When the Master discovers the Doomsday Weapon, he offers to rule the universe with the Doctor. He makes a good case for it, too. If the Doctor ruled well, perhaps he could make things better. He could, the Master suggests, do more good by ruling the universe than simply travelling through it.

The Doctor often faces moral dilemmas like this. The Fourth Doctor faced the dilemma: should he destroy the whole Dalek race? He chose not to. The Ninth Doctor faced the dilemma: should he destroy the Daleks, even though that meant destroying the people of Earth? He thought he would, but couldn't bring himself to do it. And the Tenth Doctor faced the dilemma: should he warn the population of Pompeii of their imminent destruction? He chose not to interfere. That, in fact, is a common dilemma for the Doctor: should he interfere with the timeline, even if it would save lives?

The Third Doctor is no exception. One dilemma he continually faces is: should he abandon everybody else and travel the universe? Sometimes, he chooses to travel, and only the Time Lords or a malfunctioning TARDIS bring him back.

THE TIME LORD FILES

The Time Lords sent the Doctor to Uxarieus because the Master stole their records on doomsday weapons – which brings up the interesting question of what the Time Lords were doing with a file on doomsday weapons in the first place.

One possibility is that there isn't a 'Doomsday Archive' per se – the Time Lords collect information on everything, and the Master extracted the information he wanted. The villainous renegade has a history of looking for short cuts to conquest. It's also possible that some secretive branch of the Time Lords do deliberately collect information on potential threats to Gallifrey – maybe there are secret Celestial Intervention Agency agents out there, spying on races like the Daleks or Sontarans who might, one day, pose a problem for the Lords of Time.

For a more sinister interpretation, the Doomsday Archive is a weapon of the Time War. The Gallifreyans are few in number, and prefer to manipulate others into doing their dirty work for them. Maybe the Time Lords have a list of potential assets they can use to deal with major threats throughout time. "So," says one Time Lord to another, "our enemies have travelled back in time 10,000 years, and are in the third belt of Mutter's Spiral? Let's send someone to Uxarieus and borrow their Doomsday Weapon. It'll never be traced back to us..."

Are there more weapons on this list, or did the Master just steal the files related to the Uxariean weapon? Maybe some of the Master's other schemes also stem from these stolen files.

One final thought – a weapon that blows up suns? That sounds rather like the Hand of Omega, the Gallifreyan doomsday weapon that was used to achieve mastery over time. Maybe the Gallifreyans were worried that the Uxarieans were on the verge of discovering the secret of time travel. Could the poisoning of the planet's ecology have been deliberate sabotage?

Put moral dilemmas in your games. Pose them explicitly, in the form of a question: "Should you do this thing or the other thing?" Even if you know the answer – after all, we knew that the Third Doctor wouldn't join the Master to rule the universe – the dilemma makes the adventure more interesting.

FURTHER ADVENTURES

- While the Primitives' civilization is at its height, the Rutans hear of the Doomsday Weapon and determine to capture it. This, the Doctor realizes, is the catastrophic event that causes the fall of the Primitives' civilization. Can the Doctor stop the Doomsday Weapon being detonated? Will he interfere with the timeline and stop the fall of the Primitives?

- In the 26th Century, the once-struggling colony now thrives. The surviving Primitives have established a budding community in caves near their ruined city. However, the colonists insist that the Primitives are poisoning their land and wish to drive them out. Can the Doctor broker a peace between them? How is the soil being poisoned now: are they constructing another Doomsday Weapon?

- Now that the existence of the Primitive's underground city is known, archaeologists and explorers come to Uxarieus to investigate the ruins of the former civilization. What wonders – and horrors – will they find down there?

THE DAEMONS

'Be present at my command and truly do my will. Aba, abara, agarbara, gad, gadoal, galdina!'

SYNOPSIS

Earth, UNIT Era.

In the village of Devil's End, the archaeologist Horner was digging into a mound that had long been a feature of local superstitions. The village had recently suffered high winds, an unexpected death and a constable who appeared possessed. Miss Hawthorne, a self-styled white witch, protested that evil was afoot. As midnight approached, the Master, posing as the local vicar, conducted an occult ceremony beneath the church. Too late, the Doctor arrived to stop the dig and was frozen by a chilling wind as the tunnels collapsed around him.

The village doctor pronounced the Doctor dead. There were more strange omens: red eyes in the darkness, huge hoofmarks and a freak heat wave that revived the Doctor. When the Doctor investigated the archaeological dig, he found a chamber containing an impossibly heavy miniature spaceship. A living gargoyle attacked the Doctor, but he repelled it with cold iron (a trowel) and ominous-sounding words (a Venusian lullaby).

Back in the village, the Doctor deduced that the spaceship belonged to Daemons: an ancient, horned race who treated the Earth as a failed scientific experiment, ripe for destruction. Their spaceship had created the heat wave when it was miniaturised. Meanwhile, the Master had bent the villagers to his will, including Girton, who chased the Doctor in a stolen UNIT helicopter.

In the church, the Master repeated the ceremony to summon the Daemon Azal. When the Master asked to be granted its power, the Daemon promised to return one last time. Under the Master's influence, Morris dancers surrounded the Doctor and tied him to their maypole, ready to be burned. He was rescued by Miss Hawthorne, who addressed him as the wizard Qui Quae Quod. When the Doctor demonstrated his 'wizardry' – which was really Benton, shooting things with a silenced gun, and Bessie, summoned by remote control – the villagers released him.

Since the freak heat wave, the village had been surrounded by a perfectly spherical heat shield, which had left the Brigadier stranded outside. Using a heat exchanger built following the Doctor's instructions, he drove through the heat shield with UNIT troops, and began battling the living gargoyle outside the church – "Jenkins... chap with wings, there. Five rounds rapid."

The Master performed the ceremony for the third time and offered Jo, whom he had captured, as a sacrifice to Azal. Azal offered the Doctor his power, but he refused. Azal threatened to kill him, but Jo moved in front of the Doctor, sacrificing her own life to save him. Azal could not comprehend this act and his own power destroyed him.

The church exploded, the Master was arrested, the Doctor and Jo danced around the maypole and the Brigadier went for a pint.

CONTINUITY

All magic is the 'secret science of the Daemons'. Many mythological creatures, the Doctor suggests, have in fact been based on the horned Daemons. Later, in **The Satan Pit**, the Doctor would give a similar explanation regarding the appearance of the similar-looking Beast.

⊙ RUNNING THE ADVENTURE

In this adventure, the Doctor meets the supernatural. He has a scientific explanation for it, naturally, but this is really a story about dark magic. It begins with omens, continues with occult rituals and ends with a deal with a Daemon. The Doctor's adventures don't get more supernatural than this.

WELL, THAT WOULD BE MAGIC, WOULDN'T IT?

All magic, as the Doctor said, is the secret science of the Daemons. And, with that statement, he showed you how to base your adventures around magic. If you want to put magical rituals, spells and creatures in your game, you can. Simply say that, while it looks like magic, it's actually a secret kind of science. This is the same sentiment as Clarke's Third Law: Any sufficiently advanced technology is indistinguishable from magic.

Despite the Doctor's protestation that "everything must have a scientific explanation," his description of the Secret Science of the Daemons sounds pretty magical. It runs like this: strong emotions, such as fear, hatred or greed, generate a charge of psychokinetic energy. This energy is channelled, by invocations and rituals, to produce effects that seem magical.

If you take away the scientific language from this, it sounds exactly like magic. As Jo says: if something happened and nobody knew the explanation, that would be magic, wouldn't it?

But let's not argue with the Doctor. What matters is: in the Doctor's adventures, the supernatural can be effectively real. Let's say you wanted to run an adventure about witches, fairies or druids. The story might go like this. Start with strange omens. Put in some rituals, which summon a strange creature. The creature creates trouble. Eventually, the Doctor finds a way to banish it. Throughout this kind of adventure, all the supernatural elements are real. They aren't really magical – they are based on a secret type of science – but it works the same as magic.

Sometimes, however, the Doctor faces a different type of supernatural threat. In his next adventure, **Day of the Daleks**, the Doctor investigates a haunted house. However, there is no 'secret science of ghosts' at work: no suggestion that, when someone dies, the energy is channelled into ghostly figures. Instead, the ghosts are actually visitors from the future. Later in his timeline, the Doctor would face many more supernatural threats, including a werewolf and Vampires. Really, however, they were aliens. In this kind of adventure, magic really doesn't work. Everything seems to be supernatural, but it isn't: it's the work of aliens.

To write this type of supernatural adventure, start with strange omens. Put in rumours of supernatural activity or a magical creature. Then let the Doctor discover what's really happening. Whatever is going on, it isn't supernatural. It's an alien creature. And the Doctor must deal with it.

NO, NO, HE CAN'T BE DEAD!

After being frozen by the unnatural wind, the Doctor is unconscious for a long time. This isn't the only time that the Doctor has been close to death. In **The Mind Of Evil**, one of his hearts stopped. Later, both the Fifth and Tenth Doctors

were unconscious after their regenerations. The Eleventh Doctor was nearly assassinated, until River Song gave her regenerations to save him.

How can you use this in your own adventures? You could simply declare that, when the Doctor is hurt badly, he is out of action for a few hours. But that seems unfair: it excludes the Doctor's player from the game. There are better ways to do it than that. In fact, there are three better ways.

Firstly, you can use the rules for Lethal injuries (see Dying or Leaving The TARDIS, **The Gamemaster's Guide**, p46). When a character takes a Lethal hit declare that, instead of dying, the character is knocked unconscious. So here is how the Third Doctor's injury in the dig might work: when hit by the freezing wind, the Doctor takes a Lethal injury. However, the Gamemaster decides, it's too early in the adventure for the Doctor to regenerate. Instead, the Gamemaster suggests that the Doctor be knocked unconscious, and the player agrees.

Secondly, you can use the Healing rules (**The Gamemaster's Guide**, p53), which state that a character heals when they rest for a day or receive medical attention. In this case, when the tunnel collapses the Doctor takes an injury that reduces his Strength to zero. He collapses to the floor and Jo drags him away. Because Jo doesn't have the Medicine Skill, her character asks the Gamemaster whether there is a doctor in the village. The Gamemaster says yes and the Doctor recovers in the care of the village doctor.

Thirdly – and this, for the players, is probably the most fun – try using Story Points. When a character takes an injury, the player or the Gamemaster can suggest the character falls unconscious. When this happens, the character goes out of play and the player receives Story Points. When that character

is needed in the story, they suddenly recover. (In the mean time, that player can play a secondary character, or just sit and watch. Note that even if a player's character isn't present, that player can still spend Story Points to help others or to change the course of the story.)

Injuries like this make the game more interesting, and also give you a little bit more wiggle room beyond the strict application of the damage rules. A pointless death due to a single unlucky dice roll is no fun for anyone!

DOCTOR, WAIT!

Finally, look what happens when UNIT is battling the gargoyle. There's a gunfight in the village and the gargoyle is blocking the church's entrance. However, in the middle of the battle, the Doctor dodges past and enters the church.

How does he do this? Perhaps he is lucky or perhaps, with his Venusian Aikido training, he's simply good at dodging. In any case, it makes the adventure better. UNIT is good at fighting, while the Doctor is better at talking. So it's better if the Doctor dodges inside, to talk to Azal the Daemon, leaving UNIT fighting outside.

Never let gunfights stop characters going where they need to go. Ask for a roll (Awareness + Coordination) or let the player pay a Story Point to dodge through. Then let the adventure continue, with everyone where they want to be.

The battle rules in **Defending the Earth: The UNIT Sourcebook** can be used to great effect providing the background of a clash between allies and enemies while the characters are doing something else. The course of the battle can even be used as a race against time for the group to achieve their goals.

NEW GADGET – REMOTE CONTROL

A remote control operates a particular piece of machinery, such as Charlie the Robot or Bessie, and allows it to be controlled from a distance.

Traits: Transmit (Minor Good)
Cost: 1 Story Point

NEW GADGET – HEAT EXCHANGER

This complex, bulky device creates a tunnel through heat-based defense systems, allowing humans and vehicles to pass through safely. In this form, it can only be used once, before overloading and exploding within the hour. If the Doctor had time, he could probably make a more reliable device. He might even create a similar device that allowed safe passage through other defenses: a Gas Exchanger, a Cold Exchange or a Force-Field Tunneller.

Traits: Forcefield (Major Good), One Shot (Minor Bad).
Cost: 2 Story Points

MISS HAWTHORNE

AWARENESS	5	PRESENCE	4
COORDINATION	2	RESOLVE	4
INGENUITY	4	STRENGTH	1

SKILLS
Convince 4, Craft 2, Knowledge 3, Subterfuge 2

TRAITS
Indomitable
Keen Senses (Minor): Hearing
Lucky
Obsession (Minor): Black Magic
Argumentative
Eccentric (Minor Bad)

STORY POINTS: 8

PERSONAL GOAL: Defend against black magic. (Note: In a campaign, Miss Hawthorne will see any alien threat as black magic)

DAEMON

AWARENESS	3	PRESENCE	6
COORDINATION	1	RESOLVE	5
INGENUITY	3	STRENGTH	7

SKILLS
Convince 2, Fighting 3, Marksman 3, Science 5, Technology 5

TRAITS
Fear Factor (3): Daemons are immensely tall and resemble a mythological creature. They are one of the scariest creatures you are likely to see.
Huge (Major): +4 to Strength and +2 to Speed. +4 to be hit and +8 to be seen. Daemons can also change their size at will, shrinking down to a much more manageable size.
Natural Weapon – Electricity: Daemons cause electricity to play over their victims. They can do this as a threat or they can kill (4/L/L).
Alien Senses: Daemons can sense how powerful those in the vicinity are. This means, of course, that they can detect the presence of Time Lords.
Immortal (Major): Daemons' lifespans are so vast that they watch worlds developing through many stages of civilization.
Weakness (Major) – Sacrifice: Altruism is so alien to the Daemons that, if someone offers to sacrifice themselves, they see it as a logical error. This leads to their power turning inwards: in effect, they defeat themselves.

STORY POINTS: 5-8

GARGOYLE

AWARENESS	2	PRESENCE	2
COORDINATION	1	RESOLVE	3
INGENUITY	1	STRENGTH	5

SKILLS
Fighting 3, Marksman 5

TRAITS
Armour (Special): Gargoyles are very, very tough. Even the Brigadiers favourite "Five rounds rapid" has no effect on them.
Enslaved: Gargoyles are servitors of the alien creature that has animated them.
Fear Factor (1): An animated stone gargoyle might not turn you into a trembling wreck, but it'd scare you.
Immunity (Major): Bullets. Because Gargoyles are immune to bullets, they are particularly useful for guarding doorways. Unlike many other races, they have no specific weakness that allows them to be defeated: your best hope is to destroy them with heavy weaponry, run past them while they are reforming (see below) and defeat whatever is controlling them.
Immortal (Special): Even if you destroy the Gargoyle, using heavy weaponry, the pieces reform ready to attack again.
Natural Weapon – Energy bolt: Gargoyles shoot energy bolts, which cause things to explode (4/L/L).
Phobia (Minor): Gargoyles are afraid of iron.

STORY POINTS: 3

MORRIS DANCERS

AWARENESS	2	PRESENCE	3
COORDINATION	3	RESOLVE	3
INGENUITY	1	STRENGTH	3

SKILLS
Fighting 4

TRAITS
Fear Factor (1): While it may sound comic, being surrounded by a pack of murderous Morris dancers is certainly creepy.
Enslaved: The Morris dancers are controlled through psychic forces.

EQUIPMENT
Stick: 1/3/4

STORY POINTS: 1

FURTHER ADVENTURES

- A popular television show visits Devil's End and invites residents to bring their antiques for valuation. Several villagers bring artifacts which they retrieved after the Daemon's last summoning. When the artifacts and villagers are brought together, the combined psychic energies begin the summoning process again. Winds blow, gargoyles return to life and strange footprints are found in the neighbouring fields.

- On a far-away planet, the Eleventh Doctor finds a colony of humans, who are mysteriously dying in their mines. Deep beneath the planet's surface, the Doctor finds the dying Azal, who regards the colony as a failed experiment ready to be destroyed. Can the Doctor convince the Daemon that humanity is worth saving?

- A young girl sees fairies playing at the bottom of her garden. Nobody believes her, until one day, she meets a mysterious stranger in a blue box, who listens to her stories. The stranger explains the secret science behind fairy magic and the dangers it can bring.

DAY OF THE DALEKS

'It's a very complicated thing, time, Jo. Once you've begun tampering with it, the oddest things start happening.'

SYNOPSIS

Earth, UNIT Era and an alternative 22nd Century.

On the eve of a summit to prevent a Third World War, a ghostly figure tried to kill Sir Reginald Styles. In the grounds of his house, UNIT found an unconscious soldier, a futuristic disintegrator and a crude time-machine. The Doctor and Jo – who had just met identical versions of themselves when the TARDIS malfunctioned – stayed in the apparently haunted house. Nothing happened that night, but in the morning, three more soldiers appeared from a tunnel in the grounds and attacked.

The soldiers, who had come to assassinate Styles, imprisoned the Doctor and Jo in the basement. When they were released, Jo grabbed the time machine and threatened to destroy it, but it catapulted her into the 22nd century. Ogrons, a slave race of the Daleks, attacked the house and the Doctor and the soldiers ran to the tunnel. There, a Dalek appeared, and the time machine sent the Doctor and soldiers into the future. One soldier, Shura, was left behind.

In the 22nd Century, humans were forced to work in mines and factories, as part of the Dalek Empire. The Controller, who worked for the Daleks, had captured Jo, keeping her in luxurious quarters as a 'guest'. The Doctor was also captured and taken to join her. The Daleks, who had not yet met the Third Doctor, used mind analysis to identify him.

Before the Daleks could kill the Doctor, the soldiers rescued him. They explained why they had travelled back in time to assassinate Styles. In the 20th century, the peace summit had been destroyed by a bomb, which toppled the Earth into all-out war, leaving it ripe for Dalek invasion. They wanted to change history, by killing Styles, whom they believed had planted the device. The Doctor realized it had in fact been Shura who planted the explosives in an attempt to complete his mission. The assassination, intended to stop the bomb, was in fact achieved by planting the bomb. The Earth was trapped in a paradox.

The Doctor returned to 20th Century Earth, where Styles' summit was about to start. As UNIT battled Daleks, who were attempting to preserve their version of history, the Doctor persuaded Shura not to kill Styles with the bomb. Once Styles had left, the house began filling with Daleks and Ogrons pursuing the Doctor, but they were destroyed when Shura detonated the explosives.

CONTINUITY

The Doctor mentions the Blinovitch Limitation Effect for the first time.
The Daleks have discovered time travel.
Dalekanium is the only explosive that works against Daleks. (But don't confuse it with the identically-named Dalekanium, the metal of which Dalek casings are made.)

RUNNING THE ADVENTURE

It's time for a paradox. While this adventure starts with a ghost story – indeed, the Doctor and Jo even spend the night in a 'haunted' house – it ends when the Doctor realizes that the whole thing is a mistake.

The guerillas travelled back in time to stop a bomb detonating, but ended up detonating the bomb themselves.

The paradox isn't the whole story. The adventure contains familiar themes: capture, imprisonment and escape; a gunfight and a peace conference; a bleak future and a totalitarian government; the morally-ambiguous Controller and a moral dilemma (is it wrong to kill one person, if it prevents many dying?); and, from Shura, a noble self-sacrifice.

Most of all, however, it is about a paradox.

THIS TIME IT'S GOING TO BE DIFFERENT

At the start of this adventure, the Doctor and Jo met alternative versions of themselves. It was a reminder that, when you tinker with time, strange things happen. As it turned out, the whole future of Earth was an anomaly in time. (Why didn't it attract the Reapers? Perhaps the Daleks continually needed to fight them off.) The adventure ended when the Doctor prevented the event that caused the anomaly.

How can you write time paradoxes into your adventures? Here's a tip: don't try and understand how time works. There is basic guidance in the **Gamemaster's Guide**, lots more in **The Time Traveller's Companion**, but it's much more complicated than that. Unless you're the Doctor – in which case, hello, and we hope you're enjoying reading about your adventures – you won't be able to explain time paradoxes.

Instead, just think of some interesting tricks to play with time. What happens if you save your own father from dying (**Father's Day**)? What happens when you meet someone you've never met, but who has met

you before (**Silence In The Library**)? What happens if you kill Hitler (**Let's Kill Hitler**, of course)?

Think, too, of the moral implications. When the Doctor faces a time paradox, it often leads to a moral dilemma. If you could go back and save someone who died, would you do it? Would you kill someone, if you knew that it would save millions of lives? In this adventure, the Doctor didn't just solve the paradox. He was drawing a moral lesson: often, humans are their own worst enemy.

So think of similar ways to play with time. If you could travel back and live your life again, would you do it? If you went back to the best day in your life, would it be the same? Think of a dilemma. Build a paradox around it. Then throw in some adversaries and you have an adventure worthy of the Doctor.

WE KNOW THE FUTURE NOW.

Do you remember, in **A Christmas Carol**, when the Eleventh Doctor showed Kazran Sardick his future? (There were lots of pasts and futures involved in that adventure, so it was complicated, but it did happen.) He wasn't just telling him what would happen. He was warning him what he would become.

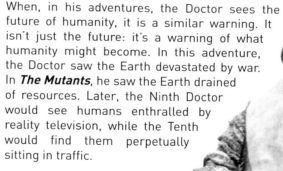

When, in his adventures, the Doctor sees the future of humanity, it is a similar warning. It isn't just the future: it's a warning of what humanity might become. In this adventure, the Doctor saw the Earth devastated by war. In **The Mutants**, he saw the Earth drained of resources. Later, the Ninth Doctor would see humans enthralled by reality television, while the Tenth would find them perpetually sitting in traffic.

These future versions of humanity are often ruled by powerful, and cruel figures. In this adventure, the Doctor finds humans forced to work under harsh conditions: "There will always be people who need discipline," the Controller tells the Doctor. Later, in **Rise of the Cybermen**, the Tenth Doctor found Cybus Industries preying on homeless people. Later still, in **The Beast Below**, the

Eleventh Doctor would meet a society that monitored its citizens closely and punished children when they failed at school.

Sometimes, as in **The Mutants** or **The Beast Below**, what the Doctor sees is humanity's real future. Sometimes, as in this adventure, **Inferno** or **Rise of the Cybermen**, it is an alternative version. And sometimes the Doctor can put things right. In this adventure, he prevents a war. In **The Mutants**, he prevents humans oppressing an intelligent alien race. In **The Beast Below**, it is Amy who puts things right: she stops the government torturing a benevolent creature and stops the Doctor from killing it.

When, in the Doctor's adventures, you describe the future of humanity, make it a bleak one. What you're saying is: "This is what humanity could become." If the Doctor and Companions are lucky, they will find a way to put it right.

IT'S ALL ON TELLY, YOU KNOW.

From now on, the media became a regular feature in the Doctor's adventures. In **The Daemons**, the Doctor appeared on television for the first time, running past the cameras to the archaeological dig. In this adventure, a television reporter covered the peace conference. Later, in **The Sea Devils**, the Master would even watch a children's programme.

Try using this in your adventures. From time to time, switch to a television reporter's point of view. Instead of just describing what's happening ("You're at Styles' house, where the summit is about to start"), deliver a report to an imaginary camera ("Here, in the heart of the English countryside..."). Have the characters learn about events happening elsewhere by seeing news broadcasts, instead of being told about them second-hand. You can also use the

media to introduce new characters. Simply introduce a curious reporter, who is interested in the strange events surrounding UNIT and the Doctor. This, after all, is how Sarah Jane Smith will appear, later in the Third Doctor's timeline.

NEW GADGET – TIME TRANSFERENCE MODULE

A crude time machine, which takes the form of a case packed with electronics. It requires an area that is unchanged in the two time periods it travels between.

Traits: Vortex (Special Trait), Teleport, Restriction (Can only travel between unchanged areas)
Cost: 4 Story Points

NEW GADGET – DALEKANIUM BOMB

A bomb that can destroy Daleks.

Traits: One Shot, Special (Explosive)
Damage: 4/L/L
Cost: 1 Story Point

FURTHER ADVENTURES

- In a crater in Surrey, UNIT investigates a perfectly spherical object, which has fallen from the sky. The Doctor recognizes this as a Void Ship, used to cross between dimensions. Inside is Anat, one of the guerilla fighters, who has escaped from the alternate future of the Dalek Empire into the real world. However, the Void Ship has left a breach, and soon the Daleks follow, intent on spreading their Empire throughout time!

- When travelling to Earth in the 27th Century, the Doctor instead arrives on a ship filled with alien races, including the Ogrons, Spiridons and Ice Warriors. All are searching for a new home, yet each day, many mysteriously disappear. Quickly, he realizes the ship is a holding pen for immigrants to Earth. Can he convince the new Earth government that the aliens are a benefit, not a threat?

- In a forgotten corner of Savannah, Georgia, one row of houses lives the same year, over and over again. Why are they in a time loop? Who has placed them there? If released from the loop, what will happen to them?

THE CURSE OF PELADON

'I wanted to save our world. To preserve the old ways. Perhaps I was wrong. I hope so.'

SYNOPSIS

The planet of Peladon.

On the backwater world of Peladon, delegates arrived to decide whether it should join the Galactic Federation. Yet, when the Chancellor died, the High Priest Hepesh suggested the diplomacy had angered the legendary beast Aggedor. The Doctor arrived, after a test flight that left the TARDIS tumbling down a cliff. The planet's ruler, also called Peladon, mistook him for the conference's Chairman and Jo for a Princess.

Meanwhile, the delegates experienced several close encounters with death. A statue fell from a ledge, narrowly missing Jo: when she slipped away to investigate, she found an electronic key of Ice Warrior manufacture on the ledge. The Arcturan delegate was attacked: Jo later found a part of its life support system, which had been removed, in the Ice Warrior delegate's room. Meanwhile, Hepesh's mute servant led the Doctor into tunnels below the castle. There,

he was chased by the beast Aggedor, then escaped through a secret door in a shrine.

For defiling the shrine, Hepesh demanded the Doctor's death, but Peladon commuted the sentence to trial by combat. The night before the proposed combat, Hepesh released the Doctor, on condition he leave the planet. In the tunnels, the Doctor met Aggedor, whom he hypnotised using a mirrored attachment to his sonic screwdriver.

Instead of leaving, he returned to the conference. Hepesh demanded the trial by combat. The Doctor won, but as he did so, the Arcturan delegate extruded a weapon to shoot him. The Ice Warrior delegate shot the Arcturan, saving the Doctor's life.

Hepesh burst into the throne room with swordsmen, took Peladon hostage, and demanded the conference delegates leave Peladon. However, the Doctor entered with Aggedor, whom he had pacified, and exposed Hepesh's treachery. When Hepesh tried to take control of Aggedor, the creature attacked and killed him.

Before his coronation as King, Peladon asked Jo to stay with him. Instead, she left with the Doctor.

CONTINUITY

Jo received her first marriage proposal.
The Ice Warriors are now committed to peace, but the Doctor suspects them of the murders.

⊙ RUNNING THE ADVENTURE

In an old castle, there is a murder. While the castle's guests try to unmask the murderer, there are more attempted killings. As the guests investigate, they find clues, many of which are red herrings. Finally, the murderer is unmasked.

This adventure resembles a classic murder mystery, of the type written by Agatha Christie, whom the Doctor would meet years later (see **The Tenth Doctor Sourcebook**, *The Unicorn and the Wasp*). Admittedly, this adventure isn't totally like a murder mystery: Agatha Christie's stories rarely include a trial by combat. Moreover, the Doctor doesn't deduce who the murderer is: instead, the Arcturan delegate reveals himself, by trying to shoot the Doctor. Nevertheless, at heart, this story is about finding a murderer.

Try writing your own murder mystery adventures for the Doctor. Simply gather some characters together, in an enclosed location like Peladon's castle, and announce that a non-player character has died. Plant clues, both false and real, and let the Doctor work out who the murderer is.

YOU'LL DO NO SUCH THING, JO

When she first began assisting the Doctor, Jo spent much of her time being attacked or imprisoned by aliens. Now, however, she is growing in confidence. She isn't simply a victim of circumstances: she helps to push the story forward.

Let's list all the interesting things Jo did. At the beginning, she impersonated a princess. After the first attempted murder, she ducked behind a tapestry, crawled to the ledge from which the status had fallen, and found a clue there. After the apparent attack on the Arcturan delegate, she searched the Ice Warriors' rooms, and found another clue. The Ice Warriors shut her in the room, so she climbed out a window, balanced her way along a ledge on the castle's exterior, then climbed back in through another window. Later, she chaired the conference.

It's easy to forget all this, because Jo is...well...nice. Compared to the Third Doctor's other companions, Liz and Sarah Jane, she is less hard-nosed and confrontational. Indeed, her niceness is essential to this story: after her capture by the Ice Warriors, they tell her about their renunciation of violence. She believes them, even when the Doctor does not.

In your adventures, don't forget the Companions. While the Doctor is talking, they can slip away to find clues and push the story forward, (see above, for a suggestion about Story Points). Don't overlook their niceness, either. Often, the Companions' humanity is a vital counterpoint to the Time Lord's intelligence.

I'M VERY, VERY FOND OF YOU, BUT I CAN'T STAY

In this adventure, Jo receives a marriage proposal. The Doctor's companions often developed romantic attachments: some of them even kissed the Doctor, although it was often unclear whether he liked it. Even the Doctor could get affectionate: the Tenth Doctor was particularly delighted about his 'snog' with Madame de Pompadour.

In the Third Doctor's time, there was romance too, but it was more...romantic. The Doctor himself didn't get involved – he was busy with more important things

– but Jo Grant certainly developed attachments. These involved awkward moments, loving gazes and holding hands. Her budding romances might end in a marriage proposal, but never in a kiss.

When Jo travels with the Doctor, she often meets a single, attractive man, who is a potential love interest. In **The Claws of Axos**, it's the American agent Bill Filer. In **Colony In Space**, it's probably Winton, while in the **The Mutants**, it's probably Ky. In this adventure, it is Peladon, while in **Planet of the Daleks**, it is a soldier called Latep. Both Peladon and Latep ask her to come with them, but she refuses: "I've got my own world and my own life to go back to". Finally, in **The Green Death**, she meets her future husband back on Earth. Throughout these romances, Jo remains in control. It is always her who decides where the relationship is going.

When Jo is working with UNIT, back on Earth, her potential love interest is Yates. Indeed, Jo begins this adventure "all dolled up for a night out with Mike Yates", from which the Doctor has dragged her away to test the TARDIS. But it's unclear whether she is genuinely attracted to him: they have friendly conversations, but no longing gazes or awkward moments.

So how can you put this into your adventures? Firstly, ask a player if they want a romantic interest. If they do, then ensure there's a suitable unattached partner for them. It might be another player's character or it might be a character played by the GM. It will often be Mike Yates.

As the story progresses, ensure the potential couple are thrown together, while the Doctor is elsewhere. Give Story Points when two romantically-involved characters decide to go off together, leaving the Doctor behind. Finally, at the end of the adventure, let them decide how the romance ends. Will it fizzle, without either of them mentioning it? Or will the love interest ask the Companion to stay with them?

NOW, WE REJECT VIOLENCE

In this adventure, the Doctor meets the Ice Warriors again. At first, he is worried. Later, when they say they are committed to peace, he refuses to believe them. Finally, one of them saves his life.

In fact, the Doctor often meets adversaries who claim to be friends. Sometimes, as in this adventure, they mean it. Sometimes, as in **The Sea Devils**, when the Master claims to be a reformed character,

they're clearly lying. Sometimes, as with the Axons, they're lying, but the Doctor isn't immediately sure. And often, as when the Daleks ask for the Eleventh Doctor's help (**Asylum of the Daleks**), the truth lies somewhere in the middle.

Try this in your adventures. Introduce the Doctor to an old adversary, who now claims to be an ally. It'll surprise your players, giving them a new way to view the creature. It'll also test their tolerance: can they accept that an adversary, whom they've fought before, can change? Don't push this too much – if you allow a Dalek as a Companion, you've probably gone too far – but you can take it a long way. Remember that Strax, a Sontaran, helped the Eleventh Doctor.

IT'S SMASHED TO PIECES!

Finally, look what happened to the TARDIS in this adventure. At the start, it fell off a cliff, trapping the Doctor on the planet. At the end, it appeared, just in time for the Doctor to leave.

This is normal for the TARDIS. At the beginning of the Doctor's adventures, it is often captured, lost or otherwise made inaccessible to the Doctor. At the end, it appears again. Let's not wonder why this happens – after all, TARDISes are mysterious things, and often appear when they are most needed – but it is useful. It leaves the Doctor and Companions with no option but to explore the planet, until the adventure is over, when they can leave again. It also prevents the Doctor using the TARDIS to solve any problems that arise.

Try making the TARDIS 'disappear' at the start of your adventures. Perhaps it falls off a cliff, perhaps it is captured, or perhaps it is encased in something impenetrable. Once the Doctor and Companions have finished the adventure, it can appear again, retrieved, released or otherwise ready for its next journey.

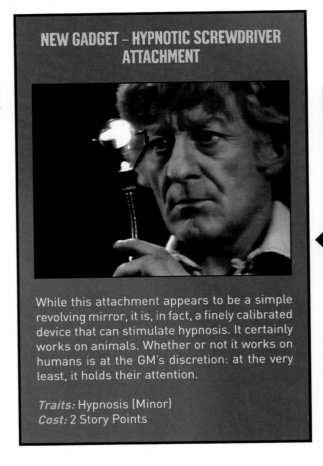

NEW GADGET – HYPNOTIC SCREWDRIVER ATTACHMENT

While this attachment appears to be a simple revolving mirror, it is, in fact, a finely calibrated device that can stimulate hypnosis. It certainly works on animals. Whether or not it works on humans is at the GM's discretion: at the very least, it holds their attention.

Traits: Hypnosis (Minor)
Cost: 2 Story Points

FURTHER ADVENTURES

- In the Scottish mountains, Jo meets a handsome musician and falls in love. When he proposes, she agrees to stay in Scotland. Yet, as the Doctor investigates, he realises the man is not what he seems. Beneath the mountains are a crashed spaceship and an adversary the Doctor has met before. What type of creature is the musician? Can the Doctor persuade Jo before it is too late?

- Insisting on a seaside holiday, Jo takes the Doctor to North Wales, but the view is spoilt by a new plastics factory. The Doctor, unable to prevent himself investigating, finds no humans working within the factory at all. It emerges that the plant is staffed by Autons, controlled by a Nestene Consciousness that claims only to want peace with humankind. Does the Doctor believe it? Or is there something darker afoot?

- In a remote English country house, the British, American and Chinese governments are about to sign a treaty on the disposal of nuclear missiles. Despite UNIT's heavy guard, an American aide dies. Over the next few days, there are other attempted murders. Which alien race is behind this? Can the Doctor figure it out before the treaty is abandoned?

AGGEDOR

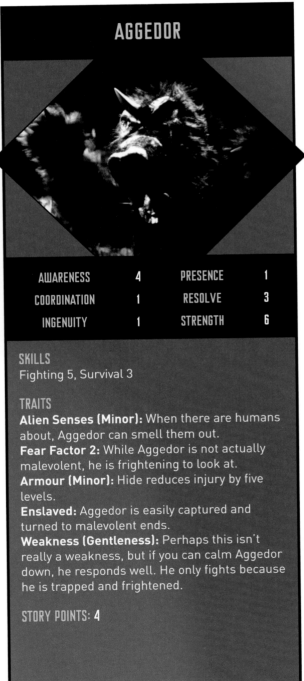

AWARENESS	4	PRESENCE	1
COORDINATION	1	RESOLVE	3
INGENUITY	1	STRENGTH	6

SKILLS
Fighting 5, Survival 3

TRAITS
Alien Senses (Minor): When there are humans about, Aggedor can smell them out.
Fear Factor 2: While Aggedor is not actually malevolent, he is frightening to look at.
Armour (Minor): Hide reduces injury by five levels.
Enslaved: Aggedor is easily captured and turned to malevolent ends.
Weakness (Gentleness): Perhaps this isn't really a weakness, but if you can calm Aggedor down, he responds well. He only fights because he is trapped and frightened.

STORY POINTS: 4

THE SEA DEVILS

'What idiot ordered an all-out attack, just as I was on the verge of finding a peaceful solution?'

SYNOPSIS

Earth, UNIT Era.

While visiting the Master in his prison, an island fortress, the Doctor heard that ships were mysteriously disappearing. Even lifeboats had been sunk, with their bottoms charred in a strange pattern. To investigate, the Doctor visited the nearby Naval Research Station, where he met the brusque Captain Hart, then went to the Sea Fort around which the ships had sunk.

At the Sea Fort, the Doctor and Jo found a worker's corpse, together with his workmate, who raved about 'Sea Devils'. Exploring the fort, the Doctor met a Silurian-like amphibious creature, which chased him. As it burned through a door towards him, the Doctor electrocuted it with an ingeniously-placed wire, and it fled. He radioed for help and the Navy rescued him and Jo in a helicopter.

The Master had escaped from the prison, having hypnotized the guards and the governor, Trenchard. He stole supplies from the naval base, but was spotted by Jo. He then returned to the prison, where the Doctor challenged him. The two picked up swords and dueled, until Trenchard appeared and arrested the Doctor. However, Jo sneaked into the base and helped the Doctor escape.

As the Doctor and Jo ran towards the sea, the Master used a device to summon the Sea Devils, one of whom emerged from the surf. They travellers ran into a minefield, using the sonic screwdriver to detect the mines. When the creature chased them, the Doctor detonated a mine with the screwdriver, sending the creature scurrying back into the sea.

Meanwhile, a Navy submarine had been captured by the creatures. To investigate, the Navy lowered the Doctor, in an observation chamber, to the seabed. When the chamber returned to the surface, the Doctor had gone. In fact, he had entered the Sea Devils' underground base, where he attempted to persuade the creatures to share the Earth with humans. The Master, having also found the base, urged the creatures to attack. Just as the creatures were about to agree a truce, the Navy, under orders from the politician Walker, bombed the base. The Doctor escaped in the captured submarine, firing torpedoes to break through a force field.

Back on shore, the creatures attacked the naval base, capturing the Doctor and taking him back underwater to their base. Jo and Captain Hart, under siege in the base, escaped through a ventilation shaft, then commandeered a hovercraft. Hart returned with marines, who assaulted the base.

Down in the Sea Devils' undersea base, the Master forced the Doctor to build a machine to revive other colonies of the creatures. However, the Doctor adapted the machine, so that it exploded, destroying the base. The Time Lords both escaped and the Master eluded recapture with a hovercraft.

CONTINUITY

Jo can pick locks, ride a motorcycle and drive a hovercraft.
The sonic screwdriver can detect and detonate mines.
The Master won't say where his TARDIS is.

⊙ RUNNING THE ADVENTURE

In this adventure, the Doctor played detective. For the first part of the story, he simply followed a trail of clues to the creatures. At the prison, he heard that ships were disappearing, so he headed to the Naval Research Station. There, he realised that the ships had sunk around a sea fort. At the sea fort, he found the workers, who told him about the Sea Devils. After a break to pursue the Master, he went to the creature's undersea base.

Thus, the trail of clues led through a chain of locations: from the prison, to the Naval Research Centre, to the Sea Fort, to the creatures' undersea base. When the Sea Devils fight back, they attack these locations one by one.

For an investigative adventure, then, try building a chain of clues to the adversary. Start with a mystery, weave a trail through various locations and end in the adversary's base. When the adversary attacks, run through these locations in approximate reverse order.

THIS IS A DIFFERENT SPECIES, COMPLETELY ADAPTED

The Sea Devils are like Silurians, but they come from the sea. This makes it easy to plan an adventure around them: take everything you know about the Silurians and give it an aquatic spin.

Indeed, the Doctor has occasionally met different versions of his previous adversaries. When the Second Doctor faced the Cybermen, he also encountered smaller, stealthier Cybermats. When the Eleventh Doctor met the Minotaur, he recognised it as being related to the Fourth Doctor's adversary, the Nimon. And, throughout his many encounters with the Daleks, the Doctor has seen them take many different forms.

So, when you plan an adventure, try taking an existing adversary, but changing it. What would a Silurian-like race from the desert be like? How about a cousin species of the Ice Warriors, which have adapted to live on Pluto? Could Cybermen be adapted to go under the sea? What does a Pyrovillian made of sound do?

CAN YOU LEND ME SOME TRANSPORT?

When the Third Doctor doesn't use his TARDIS, he is happy to use other means of transport. In fact, he is more than happy: he is dangerously enthusiastic. Whenever he is chasing or being chased, he always finds an interesting form of transport to assist him.

Here are the modes of transport used in this adventure. On land, there is a buggy, a motorcycle, a horse and a Land Rover. In addition, the Doctor

and Jo abseil down a cliff. In the air, there is a rescue helicopter. On the sea, there are ships, boats, jet-boats and hovercraft. Under the ocean, there are submarines and diving bells. All in all, it's surprising the Doctor didn't find a way to scuba dive.

Often, the Doctor uses these vehicles to chase or be chased. While driving Bessie in **The Daemons**, he is chased in a UNIT helicopter. It tries to force him into a wall of heat. Instead, by driving brilliantly, the Doctor forces the helicopter into the heat, destroying it. Fill your adventures with the Third Doctor with

vehicles. Whenever the Doctor is escaping or chasing someone, give him something to drive. Do the same with the companions: in this adventure, Jo drove both a motorcycle and a hovercraft. Don't just make the characters run for their lives. Make them drive.

LEAVE THE NAVAL SIDE OF THE OPERATION TO ME, DOCTOR

Neither the Brigadier nor UNIT appear in this adventure. Yet, in all but name, they are both present and correct.

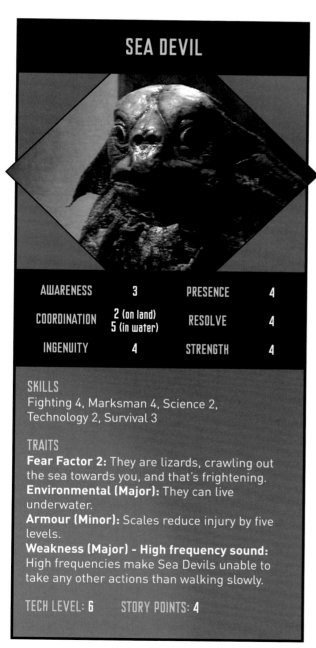

SEA DEVIL

AWARENESS	3	PRESENCE	4
COORDINATION	2 (on land) 5 (in water)	RESOLVE	4
INGENUITY	4	STRENGTH	4

SKILLS
Fighting 4, Marksman 4, Science 2, Technology 2, Survival 3

TRAITS
Fear Factor 2: They are lizards, crawling out the sea towards you, and that's frightening.
Environmental (Major): They can live underwater.
Armour (Minor): Scales reduce injury by five levels.
Weakness (Major) - High frequency sound: High frequencies make Sea Devils unable to take any other actions than walking slowly.

TECH LEVEL: 6   STORY POINTS: 4

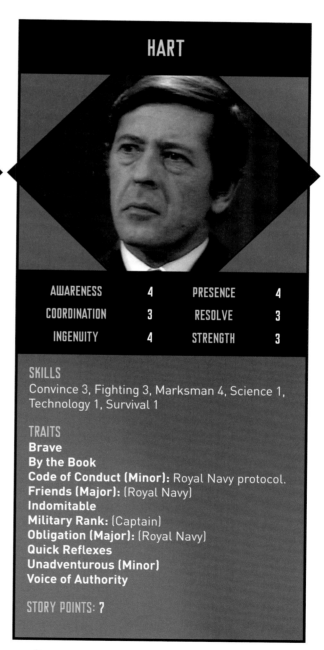

HART

AWARENESS	4	PRESENCE	4
COORDINATION	3	RESOLVE	3
INGENUITY	4	STRENGTH	3

SKILLS
Convince 3, Fighting 3, Marksman 4, Science 1, Technology 1, Survival 1

TRAITS
Brave
By the Book
Code of Conduct (Minor): Royal Navy protocol.
Friends (Major): (Royal Navy)
Indomitable
Military Rank: (Captain)
Obligation (Major): (Royal Navy)
Quick Reflexes
Unadventurous (Minor)
Voice of Authority

STORY POINTS: 7

Throughout **The Sea Devils**, Hart takes the role of the Brigadier. In fact, he resembles the Brigadier just after the Doctor joined UNIT. He stands for no nonsense from the Doctor, brushing aside his pleas and his ludicrous claim that Horatio Nelson was a personal friend. Like the Brigadier, he fights for what is right, but frustrates the Doctor at all the right moments.

His Marines, meanwhile, take on UNIT's role. Like UNIT, they arrive at the end of the adventure and begin shooting the creatures. They battle for the Research Facility, while the Doctor is in the undersea base, engineering a technological solution.

So, when a familiar character is absent, don't be afraid to replace them with someone similar. Try replacing the Doctor, for an adventure, with Professor Jones from The Green Death. Try replacing the Master with the Rani. Or, as in this adventure, replace the Brigadier with another military figure: perhaps someone from the Royal Air Force, the SAS or Torchwood.

YOU HAVEN'T SEEN THE QUALITY OF MY FOOTWORK YET

We've seen the Doctor battle the Master before, but not like this. In this adventure they duel, with swords snatched from the prison wall. Throughout the duel, the Doctor is honourable (he returns the Master's sword, allowing him to fight on) and the Master is not (he suddenly throws a knife). Throughout the duel, they taunt each other. (Admittedly, when the Doctor takes a bite of the Master's sandwich, he is perhaps going too far.) It's an exciting moment, which takes their relationship to a new level. We have seen them exchanging words and blows before. Yet this duel is perfectly suited to their style of interacting: deadly yet honourable.

How can you use duels in your adventures? The most obvious way is to ensure there are weapons nearby whenever a player and a significant opponent are talking, in case the conversation goes awry. Or let the player pay a Story Point so that there is a pair of weapons handy.

Think, too, of other ways in which the Doctor and Master could duel. In this adventure, we saw them fighting with swords. Could they fight with guns, in a dusty town in the American West? Could they fight with lasers? What about a trial by combat, like the one in **The Curse Of Peladon**, but with the Doctor facing the Master?

NEW GADGET – SEA DEVIL GUN

When used as a weapon, this acts as a laser pistol (4/L/L). It can also be used to burn through walls and doors, even those made of thick metal.

Traits: Special (Cuts through material).
Cost: 2 Story Points

FURTHER ADVENTURES

- In the London docks, the inbound ships are arriving late or not at all. Those that arrive report mermaids and sea creatures attacking them. As the Doctor investigates, he finds a triangle of water in the North Sea, through which few ships pass unscathed. Is this another city of the Sea Devils? Or another species entirely?

- On the Kent coast, a tramp's body is found washed up on a beach, with various parts of his body infused with metal wires. As the Doctor investigates, more bodies are found and more people go missing. While the Doctor consults with the local Coastguard, Jo stays by the beach to watch. As she does, a patrol of Cybermen wades from the water, their suits encased in plastic. Where, under the waves, do they come from? And why are they abducting humans?

- In the American West, the mining town of Maestro is lawless and uncivil. Or, rather, it was, until a new Sheriff came to town. Known only as the Sheriff, he keeps ruthless order, while he supervises the town's mining operations. When the Doctor arrives, he recognises him as the Master. What does the Master want in the mines? And will the Doctor accept his challenge to a duel?

THE MUTANTS

'It is the language of the old ones. No one remembers. All our culture has been destroyed by the Overlords.'

⚙ SYNOPSIS

The planet of Solos, 30th century.

A capsule materialised beside the Doctor. It was an urgent message from the Time Lords, which would only open for the intended recipient. The Time Lords had programmed the TARDIS with the capsule's destination, so the reluctant messenger had little choice but to go along with their plans. He and Jo arrived at Skybase, a space-station above Solos. This irradiated planet, whose inhabitants suffered strange mutations, was ruled by an Administrator from the Earth Empire and had been brutally oppressed.

With the Earth Empire in decline, the Administrator was preparing to give the Solonians their independence. This did not sit well with other members of the administration, especially the Marshall (the military commander).

The Administrator was assassinated before he could complete the transition of power. As Ky, a Solonian, ran from the conference where the killing had taken place, he met the Doctor and the capsule began to open: its message was for him. Seizing Jo to dissuade attack, Ky escaped by Transmat to the planet below. Insect-people, whom Ky explained were mutated Solonians, sometimes referred to as 'Mutts', attacked them as they fled into a cave system.

With the Administrator dead, the Marshal assumed military control of the station. After becoming

entangled in the byzantine politics of Skybase, the Doctor escaped by blowing the space station's power supply. He found Ky and Jo in the mines, and the capsule opened revealing ancient carved tablets. Deeper in the mines, they found Sondergaard, an exiled scientist, who helped decipher the tablets. They indicated that the Solonians were not mutating, but metamorphosing into a new form. Deeper in the caves, they found a cathedral-like cave of radiation, containing a gemstone. Meanwhile, the space-station's scientist, Jaeger, began bombarding the planet with rockets, in an attempt to make the atmosphere breathable for humans. The side effect would be the genocide of the Solonians.

Back in the space station, an Investigator from Earth was due to arrive. When the Doctor returned there, the station's Marshal held him prisoner, but he and Jo were able to tell the Investigator about the Marshal's brutal rule and Jaegar's genocidal experiments.

While the Investigator sought evidence to back up their claims, the Marshal sealed the Doctor in the laboratory with Jaegar and forced him to work on making the Solonian atmosphere breathable for humans. The Doctor realised that the crystal from the radiation cave was a catalyst, which would transform Solonians to their full metamorphosed form. He sabotaged a machine, which exploded and killed Jaeger.

When Ky came into contact with the crystal, he transformed into a fully-mutated Solonian: a beautiful, floating and ethereal creature. He floated through the Skybase's walls to the Marshal and killed him. With the conflict over, the Earth forces prepared to withdraw the Skybase back to their home world, and the Solonian people completed their next evolutionary step with the help of Sondergaard and the gemstone.

CONTINUITY

Jo told the Doctor: "You need me to look after you."

In this adventure, 'Particle reversal' can do almost anything, from turning the Time Lords' capsule inside out to making the atmosphere breathable.

The Marshal's plan for Solos – making the atmosphere breathable to humans, but poisonous to Solonians – is almost identical to the Silurian's plan for Earth.

RUNNING THE ADVENTURE

Many of the Doctor's adventures start with a message. Often, it's a distress call: the Tenth Doctor received messages on his psychic paper (**Silence in the Library**), while the Eleventh Doctor received a hypercube asking for help (**The Doctor's Wife**).

In this adventure, however, the Doctor is the messenger. In fact, the whole adventure is structured around the Time Lords' message capsule. The story begins when he receives the capsule. He takes the capsule to the Solos space station. Once there, he must find who the message is for. Then he must decipher the message. Once he has done that, he must act on the message to solve Solos' problems.

Try using similar messages to start your own adventures with the Doctor. At the start of the story, a message capsule materialises and the TARDIS begins flashing. The Doctor arrives somewhere in space and time – perhaps a planet, a space station or somewhere in Earth's history – with a problem that needs his help. First, however, he must find the capsule's recipient and decipher the message inside. When he does, he will find the solution to the problem. The question is: can he act on the message and solve the problem?

THIS IS LIKE THAT. DO YOU SEE?

It's funny how history repeats itself. However far the Doctor travels, he often finds events that resemble those from Earth's past. Perhaps humans never learn. Or perhaps there are strange connections, within time, that only the Doctor would understand.

For example: when the Doctor last visited Peladon, he found a small planet negotiating to join a galactic Federation. It was remarkably similar to the situation he had just left on Earth, where Britain was negotiating to join the European Economic Community. When the Doctor next visited Peladon, he found a miner's strike, which again resembled one back on Earth. Later, the Fifth Doctor, who tended to visit Earth in the 1980s, would negotiate between two superpowers, rather like those that dominated the planet in that decade.

In this adventure, the Third Doctor suggests that Earth's 30th Century Empire resembles the ancient Roman Empire. But, as he must have realised, there is a closer analogy. Earth's Empire tried to dominate Solos by force, while extracting its resources, but finally granted its independence. This strongly resembles the British Empire's 19th Century domination of India. This resemblance is striking: for example, both Solos and India have ancient stone carvings, whose inscriptions were only recently deciphered.

When you write adventures in the future, then, try using history or current events to inspire you. Either read the news or learn about a historical period, then create a planet in a similar situation. Change the names, both of the place and the people on it. Then add an adversary and some type of monster.

Remember, too, that the Third Doctor liked moral dilemmas. He didn't just repeat history. He questioned it. For example, in this adventure, he challenged Earth's domination of Solos. When you plan an adventure for the Third Doctor, then, don't simply celebrate history. Choose a period of history and question it.

WHO SENT YOU?

The Doctor is often mistaken for someone else. The First Doctor was mistaken for a gambler, the Fifth was mistaken for a cricketer, while the Tenth made frequent use of his psychic paper to take various identities. The Third Doctor, however, liked to be mistaken for important people.

In this adventure, he claimed to be from the "Overlord Centre". This ruse backfired, since the Marshal assumed he was there to snoop, and locked him up. In **The Curse of Peladon**, the Doctor was mistaken for the Chairman of the conference. This worked better: the false identity wasn't penetrated until the adventure was over. The Doctor seemed to like it, too: "You love all that chairman delegate stuff," Jo observed, "Admit it."

In your adventures, when people meet the Doctor, ask yourself: who would they think he is? A Health and Safety inspector? A professor? Perhaps they mistake the Doctor for that character. Or perhaps they ask the Doctor who he is, letting him claim any identity he chooses.

This might mean that, throughout the adventure, the Doctor is known by another name. For example, in **The Doctor, The Widow and The Wardrobe**, the Eleventh Doctor claimed to be a caretaker. Throughout the adventure, he was called 'Caretaker', rather than 'Doctor'. In a similar way, when the Seventh Doctor visited an alternate universe Arthurian Britain, he was thought to be Merlin. When a player is playing the Third Doctor, let them donate a Story Point to be mistaken for someone powerful. For example: in a University, the Doctor might normally be mistaken for an eccentric professor. However, for a Story Point, he could be mistaken for a famous researcher, while for two points, he would be mistaken for the new Vice Chancellor.

Sometimes, the Doctor reveals his true identity during the adventure. Sometimes, however, he maintains his assumed identity until the end. When he does, he often needs to slip away quietly, before he is revealed as an imposter. In **The Curse of Peladon,** he leaves just as the real Chairman arrives. In this adventure, when asked to provide a full account of his actions, he excuses himself and escapes in the TARDIS.

WE'LL ALL BE DONE FOR!

In this adventure, there is an exciting cliffhanger (see **The Gamemaster's Guide**, p136). The Marshal had sealed Jo, Ky and a guard inside a refueling chamber. They realised that, when the Investigator's ship refuelled, fuel would flood the chamber and drown them.

When you run adventures, try ending a game session at a moment like this. Leave everyone wondering whether the characters will survive. Then, when you start the next session, decide whether the cliffhanger still seems important. If it doesn't, let it fizzle away. This often happens in the Doctor's adventures: for example, in **The Sea Devils**, there is a cliffhanger when the Master throws a knife, during a duel with the Doctor. However, the knife misses, and so the cliffhanger simply fizzles away.

However, if the cliffhanger still seems exciting, let the characters escape it. In this case, Jo, Ky and the guard crawl through the refueling tube to escape, just before the fuel is pumped in.

NEW GADGET – TIME CAPSULE

This container is a ball, composed of dark panels, and impervious to normal weapons. It only opens for the intended recipient, although, at your discretion, Jiggery Pokery may temporarily reveal the contents.

Traits: Immunity (All weapons), Restriction (Only opens for recipient)
Cost: 2 Story Points

FURTHER ADVENTURES

- When the Ninth Doctor sees a Time Lord capsule materialise beside him, he is mystified, knowing that all the Time Lords are dead. The TARDIS takes him to Victorian London, where, as he approaches the slums, the capsule grows active. In an old market, the capsule opens for a Becky, a young servant girl. Inside is a distress message, explaining that the capsule originates from a time loop. But who is trapped within the loop? And what can Becky do to break the loop?

- In the 31st Century, the Doctor visits the planet Udanum, where the inhabitants are addicted to a narcotic. When the Doctor investigates, he finds the narcotic is sold by ships from Earth, and recognises echoes of the British Empire's trade with China. Can he stop the trade, before the inhabitants clash with the merchant ships?

- Arriving at an agricultural colony, the Doctor is mistaken for an Adjudicator. There, the human colonists claim their lands are under attack by creatures from a nearby cave-system. When the Doctor investigates, he realises the attacking creatures are the original inhabitants of the planet. How will he use his power? Will he reveal his true identity?

EVOLVED SOLONIAN

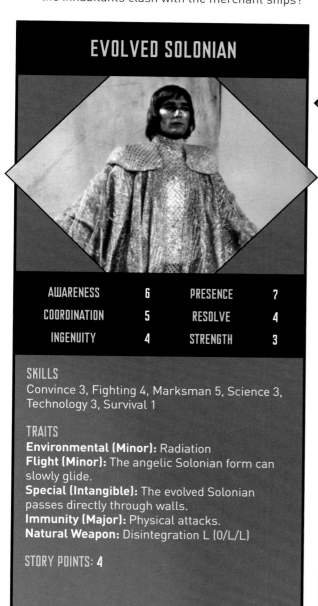

AWARENESS	6	PRESENCE	7
COORDINATION	5	RESOLVE	4
INGENUITY	4	STRENGTH	3

SKILLS
Convince 3, Fighting 4, Marksman 5, Science 3, Technology 3, Survival 1

TRAITS
Environmental (Minor): Radiation
Flight (Minor): The angelic Solonian form can slowly glide.
Special (Intangible): The evolved Solonian passes directly through walls.
Immunity (Major): Physical attacks.
Natural Weapon: Disintegration L (0/L/L)

STORY POINTS: 4

SOLONIAN MUTANTS/ MUTTS

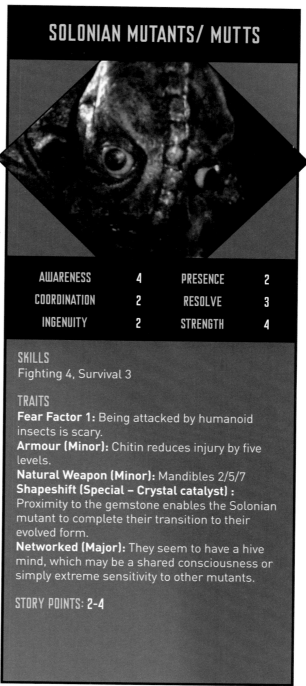

AWARENESS	4	PRESENCE	2
COORDINATION	2	RESOLVE	3
INGENUITY	2	STRENGTH	4

SKILLS
Fighting 4, Survival 3

TRAITS
Fear Factor 1: Being attacked by humanoid insects is scary.
Armour (Minor): Chitin reduces injury by five levels.
Natural Weapon (Minor): Mandibles 2/5/7
Shapeshift (Special – Crystal catalyst) : Proximity to the gemstone enables the Solonian mutant to complete their transition to their evolved form.
Networked (Major): They seem to have a hive mind, which may be a shared consciousness or simply extreme sensitivity to other mutants.

STORY POINTS: 2-4

THE TIME MONSTER

'We've seen the last of the Doctor. Buried for all time under the ruins of Atlantis. You know, I think I'm going to miss him.'

SYNOPSIS

Earth, UNIT Era and Atlantis.

At the Newton Institute, the Master was conducting time experiments with the assistance of two scientists, Ruth and Stu. Disguised in a radiation suit, he demonstrated his apparatus to the Brigadier and others. It overloaded, causing Stu to prematurely age and hallucinate Kronos, a flaming monster.

Meanwhile, the Doctor had dreamed about the Master and knew he had returned. He built a time sensor, which led him to the Institute. Yet, when he arrived, the Master had escaped.

Later, the Master returned to restart the experiment. This time, the apparatus summoned Krasis, a priest from Atlantis, who gave the Master a sacred seal. The Master then summoned the creature Kronos, which he controlled using the seal. In an attempt to disrupt the experiment, the Doctor built a contraption from a bottle, an ashtray, forks and tea-leaves, but the Master overloaded it.

As UNIT approached the Institute, the Master summoned a jousting knight, a Roundhead army and a German flying bomb through time to attack them. When the Brigadier and his soldiers finally reached the Institute, the experiment's time-field froze them in time. The Master entered his TARDIS and set course for Atlantis, to find the original Crystal of Kronos which he thought would allow him to control the Chronovore. However, the Doctor had locked their TARDISes together, so that each TARDIS was inside the other. After a verbal battle over the TARDIS' communication systems, the Master ejected the Doctor into the Time Vortex. Jo pulled the TARDIS' Extreme Emergency lever and rescued him.

Once in Atlantis, the Master asked King Dalios for the crystal. The King told him it was kept in a labyrinth, guarded by a Minotaur, but refused to give it to the Master. Instead, the Master allied with his queen, Galleia. Overhearing them talking about the labyrinth, Jo headed there. Krasis threw her inside, where she saw the Minotaur. The Doctor rescued her, using his cape like a bullfighter. Together, they found the crystal. When they returned, the Master had assumed power over Atlantis. However, when the Doctor challenged him, he released Kronos, seized both Jo and the crystal, and then escaped in his TARDIS. The Doctor threatened that, if the Master did not destroy the crystal, he would 'time ram' their TARDISes, destroying them both. When he hesitated, Jo grabbed a control on the Master's TARDIS and initiated the time ram.

They all found themselves on the boundaries of reality, facing Kronos. The Chronovore had been freed from its crystalline prison by the ram, and appreciated the Doctor's role in its release. While Kronos wanted to keep the Master in torment, the Doctor asked for his freedom and had his wish granted. The Master feels no such debt of gratitude and escapes into his TARDIS.

CONTINUITY

Bessie has a Super Drive, which allows her to go faster and brake safely.
Outside space-time is a "place that is no place", where time-eating Chronovores live.
The Master can impersonate voices.
When two TARDISes occupy exactly the same space, a Time Ram occurs, which may destroy both of them or catapult them somewhere else.
When the Doctor was a child, he lived on a house halfway up a mountain, on which a hermit lived.

There may be more than one Atlantis. The Second Doctor apparently flooded the city in **The Underwater Menace**, while in **The Daemons**, Azal claimed Atlantis was a failed experiment.

RUNNING THE ADVENTURE

This is an epic duel between the Doctor and the Master, which takes them from England to Atlantis and the borders of reality. It begins when the Doctor dreams of the Master. The Doctor tries to find him, but he escapes. They verbally joust in their TARDISes and then arrive in Atlantis, where they both attempt to seize a crystal. Finally, the Doctor rams the Master's TARDIS, then spares his life.

How would you run this in your game? If you want a real challenge, try using both the Doctor and the Master as player characters. The Master is searching to find the crystal, while the Doctor is trying to stop the Master. The search takes them to Atlantis, where one of them finds the crystal. If you want to feature a long-running duel with characters designed by your group of players, it is a good idea to create these rivals at the same time, so that their stories can be seamlessly woven together. A shared history of competitive rivalry really brings this kind of relationship to life.

Remember all the different ways the Doctor and Master can interact. They can fight: when they fight with words, it's a social conflict; when it's with fists, it's a physical conflict; and when they duel with TARDISes, it's a mental conflict. They can work together: especially if the Master captures the Doctor and forces him to do so. And, invariably, when the two are together, one will escape. Use Story Points to reward these things: for example, give a Story Point whenever the Doctor allows the Master to flee. Indeed, if you are brave, you could use the Master as a player character in other adventures. His investigations often parallel those of the Doctor.

For example, in **The Sea Devils**, he is also trying to find the creatures that sank the ships. Naturally, his motives are different: he wants to use them to take over the Earth.

For a more conventional game, run the adventure as a chase. Let the Doctor locate the Master's experiment at the Newton Institute. When he does, the Master disappears in his TARDIS. Both then arrive in Atlantis, where the Doctor must find the crystal before the Master does. Along the way, let them fight in their TARDISes. If you have a large number of players, use Ruth and Stu as player characters and let them come to Atlantis.

Be careful with two particular moments in the adventure. Firstly, when the Master first shows his experiment to the Brigadier, disguised in a radiation suit. If this happened in your game, players would instantly suspect something was wrong. Either omit the demonstration or let Ruth and Stu conduct it. The second moment is when the Brigadier and UNIT are trapped in the time vortex. When you're a player, having your character frozen in time isn't much fun: only do it for a short time or to non-player characters.

Finally, note the Doctor's jiggery-pokery with the bottle, ashtray and forks, intended to stop the Master's experiment. It just shows that you don't need electronics for technological wizardry.

YOU'VE AS MUCH RIGHT AS HE HAS.

In this adventure, the Doctor meets Ruth, who has strong opinions about Women's Liberation. It is also an adventure in which the Doctor and Master spend most of their time duelling while Jo, who in recent adventures had piloted a hovercraft, balanced along ledges, picked locks and rescued the Doctor, spends much of the time waiting to be rescued. Should any of this be reflected in games set in the Third Doctor's era?

The short answer is no. It's no fun to have to sit around while other people do the exciting stuff. Everyone is free to play whatever character they want, and everyone gets to participate equally in the adventure. Even when characters find themselves in socially restrictive settings or time periods, there is no reason to limit a character's actions – Madame Vastra and Jenny care little for public opinion, and Ace gets some disapproving looks but it doesn't stop her from grabbing her baseball bat and clobbering Daleks.

TIME ISN'T SMOOTH

Through his experiment, the Master plays many tricks with time. First, he summons a knight, a doodlebug and an army to fight UNIT. Secondly, his experiment slows time down, even freezing the Brigadier in place.

Try using these tricks in your adventures. Bring things from the past to fight in the modern day: for

NEW GADGET – EXTREME EMERGENCY LEVER

When pulled, the Extreme Emergency lever prompts the TARDIS to take suitable action. What that action is, of course, depends on the situation and the TARDIS' mood at the time.

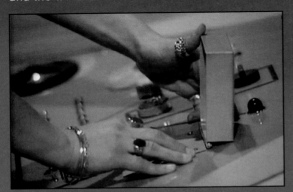

Traits: Special (TARDIS chooses action)
Cost: 1 Story Point

NEW GADGET – TIME SENSOR

This electronic device detects disturbances in the time field. Because it indicates both direction and magnitude, it can be used to detect TARDISes within approximately a hundred miles.

Traits: Transmit
Cost: 3 Story Points

NEW GADGET – TIME FLOW ANALOGUE

Constructed from mundane objects, the Time Flow Analogue creates a form of jamming signal, which affects anything that deals with time. It is a trivial device, more suitable for Gallifreyan pranks than serious applications, but can nevertheless cause an effective disturbance or delay.

Traits: One Shot, Vortex
Cost: 1 Story Point

example, Vikings, highwaymen or tanks. Indeed, as we'll see shortly, the adventure **Invasion of the Dinosaurs** is all about time-travelling monsters. There are many reasons these things might travel through time: perhaps some sort of technology, such as a time transference module (**Day of the Daleks**) is responsible; perhaps a race, such as the Daleks, Sontarans or Weeping Angels, is playing tricks with time.

Secondly, use Time Fields as a new and interesting way to challenge characters. If the character doesn't realise what is happening fast enough (a Mental conflict), they are caught within the Time Field. At first, they are slowed, getting a -2 penalty to all Physical rolls. Later, at your discretion, they may be frozen completely (although you should always give them a chance to escape soon afterwards).

FURTHER ADVENTURES

- The TARDIS lands on a planet whose atmosphere induces hallucinations. Within his hallucination, the Doctor must duel his darker self, the Dream Lord, for his freedom. As he searches for the Dream Lord, the Doctor hallucinates locations and events from his past. What will he see? What temptations will the Dream Lord put in front of him? And how will the Doctor finally defeat the Dream Lord: with words, with his mind or with some more physical solution?

- In an English seaside town, business is slow. Indeed, everything is slow. The clocks are slowly edging towards a standstill, while the sun crawls through the sky. As the Doctor breaks from his holiday to investigate, he realises something lies beneath the sea. It is another Atlantis and, within, is another fragment of crystal. Who

guards this Atlantis? Is it one of the Doctor's old adversaries?

- When the Doctor is lost in the time vortex, River Song must step into his shoes – and his TARDIS – to bring him back. Which former companions will she assemble to find him? Which of the Doctor's adversaries placed him in the time vortex? And can she, in fact, pilot the TARDIS better than he ever could?

KRONOS

AWARENESS	6	PRESENCE	8
COORDINATION	4	RESOLVE	10
INGENUITY	7	STRENGTH	5

SKILLS
Convince 3, Fighting 4, Knowledge 6

TRAITS
Alien
Shapeshift (Special Alien Good Trait): Kronos can adopt any form it wishes.
Fear Factor 2: When Kronos wishes to scare, it appears as a shining, ethereal bird.
Natural Weapon (Major Trait, Claws): 4/L/L
Weakness: Kronos can be controlled by the High Priest's Seal, but is likely to exact revenge thereafter.
Immortal (Special Alien Good Trait): Kronos is eternal, living beyond time.
Immunity (Bullets)
Flight (Minor Alien Trait): Kronos glides on its ethereal wings.
Consume (Special Alien Trait): If Kronos wins a Fighting test against a foe, it can choose to consume that foes' timeline. Doing so erases the victim from time; Kronos then adds the victim's Story Points to its own total.
Master of Time (Special Alien Trait): Kronos can manipulate time and space through its will alone by spending Story Points. It can wash away the laws of reality and impose new ones.
Vortex (Special Good Alien Trait): Kronos lives beyond and thus understands time.

TECH LEVEL: 11   **STORY POINTS: 12**

THE THREE DOCTORS

'Beneath that mask, there is nothing left of you.'

⚙ SYNOPSIS

Earth, UNIT Era and Omega's realm, inside a black hole.

UNIT was under attack, both by glistening organisms called Gell Guards, and by an otherworldly light that swallowed people and objects. The Third Doctor sent a distress call to the Time Lords, who sent him his two previous incarnations to assist. The Second Doctor materialised in the TARDIS, as did his recorder, which he had a habit of playing. The First Doctor advised, from the TARDIS screen, that the light was a time bridge and that they should cross it.

On entering the light, the Third Doctor and Jo realised they were in an antimatter realm within a black hole. They found Bessie, together with Tyler, a scientist whom the otherworldly light had swallowed. When they were attacked by the organisms, they surrendered.

They were brought to a glistening palace, where they met Omega, a revered Time Lord who had discovered the power source which enabled their time travel. The realm they were in, the Third Doctor realised, was entirely maintained by the force of Omega's will.

Meanwhile, the otherworldly light had swallowed UNIT headquarters and transported it to Omega's realm. In the process, the Second Doctor had lost his recorder. The Second Doctor was captured, taken to Omega's palace and imprisoned with the Third Doctor, Jo and Tyler. By combining their wills, the two Doctors created a door, through which they escaped to meet Omega. The Third Doctor fought a mental duel with the dark side of Omega's mind, but on the point of losing, the Second Doctor saved him.

Omega explained that if the two Doctors assumed the burden of maintaining the realm, he could escape. However, when the Doctors opened Omega's mask, they found nothing inside: the black hole had consumed him, leaving nothing but his will. They escaped to the TARDIS, where they found the Second Doctor's recorder inside a TARDIS mechanism.

The two Doctors returned to Omega. They sent everyone else back to Earth through a singularity shaped like a column of smoke. They then gave the TARDIS mechanism, containing the Second Doctor's recorder, to Omega. Omega knocked it to the floor and the recorder fell out. As the Doctors ran for the TARDIS, the recorder, which the mechanism had prevented from being converted to antimatter, annihilated Omega's realm.

Back on in the TARDIS, the Time Lords unblocked the Doctor's knowledge of time travel and sent him a new dematerialisation circuit. They had finally forgiven him.

CONTINUITY

The Doctors' different incarnations can 'Contact': that is, hold a telepathic conference with each other, by concentrating.
Omega discovered the power source that gave the Time Lords the ability to travel through time.

⊙ RUNNING THE ADVENTURE

This adventure is both wonderfully fun and wonderfully simple. There are only two parts to it. Firstly, a creature appears to be chasing the Doctors, but is actually a time bridge that they must cross. Secondly, the Doctors find Omega, listen to his plans, and destroy him with scientific sleight-of-hand. That, interspersed with fights and captures, is basically the whole story.

Take the time bridge first. To run this in your game, take any creature and send it after the Doctor. When the characters investigate, reveal the twist: the creature is not a threat, but a link to the next part of the adventure. They must embrace it, not escape it.

The time bridge could start any adventure. Try sending the Doctor to Peladon, medieval England or anywhere else in time and space. In fact, you could use an alien to serve a similar function. For example, in *Asylum of the Daleks*, the Eleventh Doctor and his companions were shot by Dalek servitors. However, they were not a threat, but a bridge to the next part of the story: the Daleks brought them to the Parliament of the Daleks and sent them on an adventure.

Now for the next part of the adventure, in Omega's realm. What happens here is: Omega explains his plan, the Doctors pretend to agree, then they defeat him with scientific trickery (that is, by destroying his antimatter realm with the non-antimatter recorder).

This is a relatively simple story, so what makes it such fun?

The answer is: it is big. Everything is big. Omega is bombastic and his plans are grandiose. The Doctors respond to him with pomp and gravitas. The consequences are immense: according to the Third Doctor, the fabric of the entire Universe could be torn apart. When you run this adventure, emphasise the immensity of everything: Omega's history, Omega's plans and the consequences to all of time and space.

YOU'VE BEEN DOING THE TARDIS UP A BIT. I DON'T LIKE IT.

In the **Gamemaster's Guide**, we talked about the problem of who gets to play the Doctor. Finally, in this adventure, there's a possible solution – three separate players can be the Doctor. Except it's more than that. This isn't simply three Doctors teaming up to go on an adventure. It's an extraordinary meeting between extraordinary people.

When you allow more than one Doctor in your games, you must treat it as extraordinary. First, ask yourself: how did it happen? When the Doctor crosses his own timeline, it transgresses the First Law of Time. So what is happening? Are the Time Lords behind it (as in **The Three Doctors**) or perhaps a renegade Time Lord (as in **The Five Doctors**, in **The Fifth Doctor Sourcebook**)? Have extreme circumstances forced the Doctor to cross his own timeline (as in **The Two Doctors**, in **The Sixth Doctor Sourcebook**) or is it all a mistake (as in **Time Crash**, in **The Tenth Doctor Sourcebook**)? One way or another, something extraordinary is happening.

Now, don't worry too much about this. If you want to bring the Doctors together, you can always find a reason. The Time Lords often provide one: they have a problem and, in some way, it involves more than one Doctor.

Whatever the reason is, make it sound extraordinary. There's a danger so great that even the Time Lords can't fight it (**The Three Doctors**), there's a paradox so great it will cause a black hole (**Time Crash**) or the Doctor might cease to exist (**The Two Doctors**).

What's really happening, here, is that we're saying hello to some old friends: the First and Second Doctors. To do this, we need to make it clear they're only visiting, so we must invent an extraordinary reason for them to arrive.

Try this in your adventures. From time to time, as a special treat, bring back an old character that everyone thought had died or disappeared. This might be an old Doctor, an old companion or another popular character such as the Brigadier. If you can, let their old player play that character. Then, at the end of the adventure, ensure the character goes away again. After all, they're only visiting.

YOU WISH TO FIGHT THE DARK SIDE OF OMEGA?

Physical conflicts are often more exciting than mental conflicts. In a physical conflict, you describe how you fight your opponent and counter their moves against you. It's a prolonged struggle, until one of you loses. Mental conflicts, however, are harder to describe.

This adventure, however, contains an exciting mental conflict, when the Third Doctor fights the will of Omega. There is a mental arena, in which the Doctor wrestles the dark side of Omega's mind, which appears as a wrestler. Thus, the battle of wills becomes an exciting physical struggle. It's a prolonged conflict, which lasts until Omega's dark side wrestles the Doctor to the floor.

Try this in your games. When a character faces an important mental conflict, describe it as a fight in a mental arena. Use mental attributes rather than physical ones: that is, Ingenuity, Resolve and perhaps Knowledge and Science. Throughout the struggle, encourage the players to describe the conflict as a fight, describing how they attack their adversary with the power of their will.

At the end, return to the real world and describe what happens. Remember that, during the conflict, events in the real world may interrupt, as when the Second Doctor stops Omega from destroying the Third Doctor.

FURTHER ADVENTURES

* For much of the Tenth Doctor's era, he was on Earth, pretending to be human. During this time, the TARDIS senses a dangerous anomaly in the Time Vortex. It finds the Doctor's three earliest incarnations and brings them together. As they investigate, a Dalek plot emerges to seize control of time itself. How can the Doctors, in their single TARDIS, defeat them? And can they stop arguing long enough to do so?

* As UNIT's scientific advisor, the Third Doctor is coerced into watching a demonstration of a new mining technology. As the shaft penetrates deeper into the Earth, time bridges begin to

appear, first in the mine itself, then on the surface. Something from the dawn of time been disturbed, the Doctor realises. Is it the Racnoss, the Silurians or something he has not seen before? Where will the time bridge take him?

* You don't need a Time Lord to have multiple incarnations of the same character in an adventure. Maybe some alarming breach of the laws of time folds the player character's timeline, so multiple versions of the same character all co-exist at the same time. Imagine a young, brash Brigadier, the Brigadier from the Third Doctor era, the school-teacher Brigadier from *Mawdryn Undead* (see **The Fifth Doctor Sourcebook**) and a geriatric retired Brigadier going on an adventure together!

OMEGA

AWARENESS	3	PRESENCE	6
COORDINATION	*	RESOLVE	6
INGENUITY	12	STRENGTH	*

*Omega has no corporeal body. He is a being of pure will and he must exert that will to affect the physical world. Whenever Omega takes an action that requires a roll and either Strength or Coordination, he must spend 1 Story Point for every 3 points he wants to add to that roll.

SKILLS
Convince 3, Knowledge 6, Science 6 (Engineering), Survival 4, Technology 6

TRAITS
Boffin, Indomitable, Photographic Memory, Psychic, Reverse The Polarity of The Neutron Flow, Technically Adept, Voice of Authourity, Block Transfer Specialist, Mind Lord, Time Lord, Time Lord Engineer, Time Lord: Experienced, **Time Traveller** (all), **Vortex Born, Eccentric, Obsession (Major):** Escape the Anti-Matter Universe, **Selfish, Weakness (Major):** Anti-Matter Ghost

EQUIPMENT
Anti-matter Realm

TECH LEVEL: 11   STORY POINTS: 27 + 3d6

You can find more about Omega in **The Time Traveller's Companion.**

GELL GUARDS

AWARENESS	2	PRESENCE	2
COORDINATION	2	RESOLVE	2
INGENUITY	2	STRENGTH	2

SKILLS
Fighting 2, Marksman 4

TRAITS
Natural Weapons (Major): Omega's gell guards fire explosives from their claws (4/L/L).
Immunity (Major): Because they are created by Omega's will, the Gell Guards are immune to all physical weapons, including heavy weapons such as anti-tank guns.
Networked (Major): The Gell Guards are connected through Omega's mind.
Teleport (Major): Because they exist through Omega's mind, they can simply appear and disappear wherever he wishes.

STORY POINTS: 3-5

CARNIVAL OF MONSTERS

'This isn't Earth. It just looks like it.'

⊘ SYNOPSIS

Inter Minor, inside the Miniscope, SS Bernice, 1926

The Doctor and Jo arrived, apparently on a ship on the Indian Ocean in 1926. Yet something was wrong: a dinosaur attacked the ship and the passengers seemed stuck in time, repeating actions over and over again. After being arrested as stowaways, they escaped with the help of Jo's skeleton keys, and found the TARDIS. However, a huge hand reached down and took it away.

They were, in reality, miniaturised within a Miniscope, an illegal machine that held creatures for entertainment. It was owned by Vorg, a travelling entertainer, who was trying to gain entrance to the planet Inter Minor. To demonstrate the machine to the planet's bureaucrats, he turned on the aggrometer, which made the ship's passengers aggressive. Inside the machine, the ship's passengers turned on the Doctor and Jo, and the pair escaped through a panel in the floor.

They found themselves in the machine's workings. From there, they entered another section of the scope, where the carnivorous Drashigs pursued them. Vorg reached inside the machine to try to rescue the pair. In the confusion, the Doctor and Jo fled back to the machine's workings, with the Drashigs in pursuit.

Finding a steep shaft, they returned to the ship in search of rope. However, the Drashigs followed. When the ship's officer threw dynamite at the creatures, he

damaged the Miniscope irreparably. As the machine began to lose power, the Doctor used the rope to descend the shaft and escaped the machine.

Once he had returned to full size, the bureaucrats debated whether to kill him, but the Doctor persuaded them to cooperate. He connected the TARDIS to the miniscope and returned inside. There, he found Jo, who had again been imprisoned as a stowaway by the ship's officer.

Meanwhile, as part of an attempted coup on Inter Minor, the bureaucrats freed a Drashig from the machine. It killed them, before being shot by Vorg. Vorg then pressed a lever to begin Phase Two of the Doctor's plan, which returned the Miniscope's inhabitants to their original locations. The Doctor and Jo found themselves outside the Miniscope and left in the TARDIS. Back on the Indian Ocean, the ship's passengers finally reached their destination, while Vorg found a new home on Inter Minor, fooling the gullible bureaucrats with gambling games.

CONTINUITY

The Doctor persuaded the High Council of the Time Lords to ban Miniscopes.

The Doctor intended to land on the planet Metebelis 3. This is the first time he mentions that planet: from now on, he keeps trying to get there.

This is the TARDIS' first trip since the Time Lords returned it to the Doctor's control. From now on, when it arrives somewhere wrong, it isn't because the Time Lords sent it there. It's simply a mistake.

⊘ RUNNING THE ADVENTURE

Two stories collide, in an extraordinary way. In the first of the stories, the Doctor and Jo explore the miniaturised worlds of the Miniscope as they try to escape it. In the second, Vorg tries to enter Inter Minor with the Miniscope. Throughout the adventure, Vorg wants to keep the Miniscope working and the specimens inside it alive.

Both these stories affect the other. When Vorg removes debris from the Scope's workings, the Doctor sees a huge hand removing his TARDIS. When the ship's officer throws the grenade, Vorg finds his machine is fatally damaged. Additionally, characters can cross from one story to the other, as when the Doctor escapes from the machine.

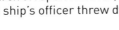

(In fact, there is even a third story, as the bureaucrats plot their coup and decide what to do with Vorg, but we'll worry about that later.)

There are two ways to run this adventure. The easy way is to just run one story. Begin with the player characters arriving on the ship. As they explore, let them gradually realise something is wrong. This is a marvellous puzzle for them to solve, as they gradually realise the ship's officers and passengers are repeating the same words and actions. When they realise they are not on a real ship, let them escape: first into the machine's workings, then into the Drashig's swamp and finally from the Miniscope, where they finally meet Vorg. Once everyone is outside, an escaping Drashig ends the adventure nicely.

The hard way is to run both stories simultaneously and see them interact. Use Vorg and his assistant as additional characters for your players in addition to the Doctor and Jo, or your regular characters. Run their stories largely separately to keep things fairly straightforward for your players, as Vorg tries to enter Inter Minor and the Doctor tries to escape the Miniscope. (You might need to enliven Vorg's story: perhaps he could be imprisoned by the bureaucrats and his Miniscope confiscated.)

From time to time, let the stories cross over. Whenever the Doctor or Jo escape from somewhere, they create a problem that Vorg has to fix. Whenever Vorg fixes it, he affects whatever the Doctor and Jo are doing. Once the Doctor encounters the Drashig, it follows him relentlessly, creating more problems and eventually breaking the machine. Eventually, the Doctor and Jo escape from the machine and everyone meets up. Try this trick in other adventures that feature parallel stories. Remember how **The Girl In The Fireplace** links stories set in a spaceship and eighteenth-century France. Whether the stories are in parallel universes, nearby locations or linked time periods, let them affect each other.

APPEARANCES CAN BE DECEPTIVE

For the Third Doctor, things are not always what they seem. In almost all his adventures, he encounters something that is not what it appears to be. This happens in four ways.

In some adventures, **a person isn't who they claim to be**. Usually, it's the Master. The person might disguise themselves physically: for example, with a facemask. Alternatively, they may assume a false identity: for example, using faked credentials to mimic an Investigator or a Commissioner. The Third Doctor, too, disguises himself (in **The Green Death**) and assumes false titles (in **The Curse of Peladon**, amongst other adventures).

In other adventures, **a monster takes human form**. For example, an Auton took the form of Channing (**Spearhead from Space**), while the Axons cloned Filer (**The Claws of Axos**). Later in his timeline, the Doctor could barely move for monsters pretending to be human: the Slitheen, the Flesh, and the Saturnynians, for example.

Sometimes, too, the Third Doctor encountered **monsters that were not real**. For example, the giant lizard in **Colony In Space** was a hologram, while the dragon in **The Mind of Evil** was a hallucination. In fact, there were many hallucinations in the Third Doctor's adventures: the Draconians-that-were-Ogrons in **Frontier In Space**, the hallucinated images that attack the Doctor as he escapes the Axon ship in **The Claws of Axos**. (While on the subject of the Axons: they fall somewhere between these first three categories. They are not the peacemakers they claim to be and they assume a near-human form, which is actually an illusion.)

In this adventure, the Third Doctor discovers **a world that is not real**. He lands on what appears to be a ship in 1926, where things are subtly wrong. This has happened to the Doctor before: in **Inferno**, he discovers an Earth in which things are out of place. It would also happen later in his timeline. The Eleventh Doctor would find himself in a hologram of a hotel (**The God Complex**) and transported back-and-forth between imaginary worlds (**Amy's Choice**).

When you run adventures for the Third Doctor, then, remember that things are rarely what they seem. People wear disguises. Monsters can be hallucinations. And, sometimes, entire worlds are false.

HISTORICALLY SPEAKING

In this adventure, the Third Doctor travels to Earth's past. As it turns out, it's a fake past, but the ship and its passengers are real. Unlike other Doctors, the Third Doctor rarely travels into the past. In **The Time Warrior**, he went to Atlantis, but that felt more mythological than historical. Later, in **The Time Monster**, he would travel to medieval England. This, however, is the closest the Third Doctor comes to a detailed historical drama.

The Third Doctor fits well in the past. Surrounded by wealthy and cultured people, he indulges his pomposity and well-spoken affability. His time on the ship resembles his other adventures: he meets a blinkered authority figure, he finds an anomaly in time and he loses his TARDIS. He is, of course, imprisoned and, of course, he escapes.

When you create new adventures for the Third Doctor, then, try sending him into the past. He fits best in cultured times that let him engage in verbal sparring with educated people. Put him into a historical period, keeping everything else about his adventures the same. UNIT, for example, can be replaced with the British Army (and no doubt the Lethbridge-Stewarts have a suitably heroic tradition of service).

STOWAWAYS, EH?

Whenever the Doctor and Jo arrive on a ship, it seems, they are mistaken for stowaways and imprisoned. It happens in this adventure. It happens in **Frontier In Space**. It happens, more or less, in **The Mutants**: when the Doctor arrives on the space station, the Marshal is suspicious about how he got there and imprisons him. (Later, in **The Time Warrior**, Sarah Jane would stow away on the TARDIS.)

This doesn't stop with the Third Doctor. The Tenth Doctor, in **Voyage of the Damned**, stows away on the starship Titanic. The Eleventh Doctor, in **Curse of the Black Spot**, is assumed to be a stowaway on

a pirate ship. Perhaps this is to be expected: how else could the Doctor be on the ship? Use this in your adventures. When the characters arrive on a ship, whether on the sea or in space, have them imprisoned as stowaways. From there, they can escape and explore the ship.

MINISCOPE

A miniscope combines a time loop generator and a compression field. The shrunken victims, reduced to a fraction of their full size, relive the same series of events over and over for the entertainment of external observers. The device uses subliminal hypnosis to ensure that victims do not notice inconsistences in their simulated environment.

A fully-functional miniscope includes a Time Scoop (see page 71 of the **Time Traveller's Companion**) to collect specimens.

If the player characters end up trapped in a miniscope, they must succeed at an Awareness + Ingenuity roll to realise their predicament. They may add their Indomitable or Psychic Training traits, if relevant. The difficulty for this roll starts at Difficulty 30, but drops at they explore their surroundings and start noticing inconsistencies.

The fact that the Doctor convinced the Time Lords to ban miniscopes suggests that they are the product of Time Lord technology (or were built by a civilisation friendly to the Time Lords). In fact, the way a miniscope works is very similar to the workings of the forbidden Death Zone on Gallifrey (see **The Five Doctors** in **The Fifth Doctor Sourcebook**).

Traits: Scan, Forcefield (Major), Vortex, Hypnosis, Compress, Restriction (+3 Difficulty to use, Massive Power Requirements, Exterior Control only)
Cost: 6 Story Points

NEW GADGET TRAIT – COMPRESS
(MINOR/MAJOR GOOD GADGET TRAIT)

A compression field squeezes molecules closer together, making things smaller. It's not dimensionally transcendent – it's a lot smellier than that! Compression fields show up in all sorts of places, from the Master's Tissue Compression Eliminator to the *Teselecta* justice vessel to Miniscopes.

The Minor version of this trait is a one-way shrinking – it can make big things small, but cannot unshrink them. The Major version can instantly shrink or unshrink a target.

FURTHER ADVENTURES

• When the Master sabotages the Doctor's TARDIS, Jo and the Doctor find themselves in two different versions of UNIT headquarters. In one, Jo finds herself imprisoned, when Ogrons occupy the headquarters. In the other, the Doctor and Brigadier battle the Ogrons and win. The only connection between the two realities is close to the TARDIS, where objects transfer across and the Doctor and Jo can communicate. Which is real? And how can the Doctor and Jo combine the two realities and defeat the Master?

• Strange things have started to happen at a car manufacturing plant in Wales. On the assembly line, the workers repeat their actions over and over again, but nothing ever gets built. Most curiously, all records show that the factory was abandoned twenty years ago. As the Doctor investigates, he realises a faulty perception filter is at work. Underneath the factory is a crashed spaceship, which is attempting to camouflage itself by fitting in with the local environment. Who is on the ship? And what do they want?

• The Time Lords send the Doctor to investigate rumours that a Miniscope is in operation in the Draxima Theltis cluster. On arrival, he discovers that the Miniscope has been converted into a hospice for the dying. Creatures on the verge of death get brought into the Miniscope, where they live out their last days over and over again until a cure can be found. However, the new owners of the miniscope are corrupt and have no intention of healing their patients when they can collect health insurance money forever. Does the Doctor put an end to this scheme – and if so, what becomes of the thousands of dying patients locked within the machine?

DRASHIG

AWARENESS	3	PRESENCE	4
COORDINATION	3	RESOLVE	4
INGENUITY	1	STRENGTH	12

SKILLS
Athletics 3, Fighting 4, Marksman 4, Survival 2

TRAITS
Alien Senses (Minor, Smell): Their sense of smell is extraordinarily acute.
Armour (Minor): Their thick hide reduces injury by five levels.
Fear Factor 3: The huge, roaring Drashig is one of the most fearsome predators in the galaxy.
Huge (Major): +4 to Strength and +2 to Speed.+4 to be hit and +8 to be seen.
Weakness (Special): The Drashig follow their prey's scent relentlessly. This means that, rather than heading directly for their prey, they diligently follow the trail they have left, even if that is not the shortest route. Nevertheless, while they may take some time to pursue their target, they eventually find them, crashing through walls or obstacles to do so.

STORY POINTS: 5

FRONTIER IN SPACE

'There are warmongers on both sides.'

SYNOPSIS

Cargo starship C982, 2540

The TARDIS landed on an Earth cargo starship that was under attack. The crew believed that their attacker was a Draconian vessel emitting a strange buzzing sound. When the crew came across Jo and the Doctor, they mistook them for Draconians and locked them up. Ogrons boarded the ship, cutting through the airlock and stealing the cargo, but the crew thought they were Draconians too. Jo, meanwhile, heard an unusual noise and believed she saw a Drashig. The buzzing noise, the Doctor realised, was making people see things they feared. Jo and the Doctor were taken to Earth as suspected Draconian agents.

On Earth, a Draconian noble visited Earth's president. Both believed that the other side was attacking their ships. The Draconians demanded to question the Doctor and Jo, then broke the Doctor free from Earth captivity and questioned him. He escaped and was recaptured by Earth troops. The anti-Draconian

human General Williams had by this point decided that the Doctor was a Draconian spy and used a mind probe on the Time Lord, but it exploded, and instead they sent him to the Lunar Penal Colony.

At the Penal Colony, the Doctor met two prisoners from the Peace Party, Patel and Dale, and asked them how to escape. Dale suggested they should steal space-suits, walk across the moon's surface and steal a spaceship. Yet Dale had been double-crossed: as they were changing into their space suits, someone closed the airlock and began to pump the air out. They were rescued by the Master, posing as a Commissioner of the colony Sirius 4. The Doctor realised that his long-standing foe had created the noise that caused people to see their fears, using a hypnosonic device. After wrangling with the prison's governor, the Master took the Doctor and Jo into custody on his ship.

As a camera watched over Jo and the Doctor, they talked, while the Doctor secretly filed through the bars of their cell. Once out, he pulled on a spacesuit and escaped through the airlock. For a moment, he lost his grip when the Master changed course, but used his air tanks as a jet to regain his hold. Then

Draconians boarded the ship and took everyone prisoner. On Draconia, the Doctor explained the Master's plan to pit humans and Draconians against each other. Just as the Draconian Emperor seemed persuaded, Ogrons (whom the Draconians saw as human) attacked the court. One was captured. As the Master escaped with his allies, the illusion faded and the Emperor finally saw the captured soldier was Ogron rather than human.

The Emperor sent his son, together with Doctor and Jo, on a diplomatic mission to Earth. They were intercepted by the Master who, after deciding against destroying the ship from a distance, boarded the ship. He captured Jo, but the Doctor escaped to an Earth battle cruiser.

Back on Earth, General Williams realised that, years ago, he had provoked hostilities with the Draconians, by destroying a battle cruiser that did not respond to broadcasts. He apologised and departed, with the Doctor, for the Ogrons' planet.

On the planet of the Ogrons, the Master showed Jo the captured TARDIS, before trying to hypnotise her. She resisted by reciting nursery rhymes. He tried using his hypnosonic transmitter, but she resisted that too. Jo dug her way out of her cell, and then sent a distress call to summon the Doctor. However, the Master caught her, telling her that she had fallen into his trap. When the Doctor arrived, the Master captured him and revealed he had been working for the Daleks, who were preparing an army.

Using the Master's hypnosonic transmitter, which Jo had stolen, the Doctor escaped. Back on the TARDIS, he sent a telepathic message to the Time Lords, warning them about the imminent Dalek threat.

CONTINUITY

When the Doctor tried to open a particular electronic lock with his sonic screwdriver, an alarm goes off.

The list of crimes that the Doctor has allegedly committed on Sirius 4 are plausible: for example, assault and battery, taking a spaceship without authority and flying without insurance.

The Doctor was ennobled by the 15th Draconian Emperor, after he saved Draconia from a plague from space.

On the TARDIS, the Doctor can send a telepathic message to the Time Lords.

This is the Third Doctor's last meeting with the Master.

⊙ RUNNING THE ADVENTURE

Two Empires totter on the brink of war and the Doctor must defuse the tension. It's an epic, complex story. It's also complex to run as an adventure, so let's break the story down.

The diplomatic side of the story went like this. When a spaceship was hijacked by Ogrons-appearing-as-Draconians, the Doctor realised someone was trying to start a war. He travelled to Earth, but they didn't believe him. He travelled to Draconia, where they believed him, and sent a noble to accompany him back to Earth. On Earth, the government finally believed him, but needed proof to convince others. So they sent the Doctor and their General to the Ogron's planet. There, they discovered the Daleks were behind everything.

Now, the Doctor spent most of this story in captivity. But, when you focus on the diplomatic story, this hardly matters. From this point of view, imprisonment is simply an interesting way for the Doctor to traverse the galaxy. He could have travelled in the TARDIS. However, the adventure is much more interesting if he is imprisoned and escapes along the way.

To run this adventure, start with the Doctor and Jo on the spaceship. When the Draconians-that-are-Ogrons attack, the Doctor realises someone is pushing the galaxy towards war. From there, let them travel between Draconian and Earth, attempting to persuade the authorities of what is happening. To liven this diplomatic story up, add some fights, captures and escape attempts.

Remember that, if the Doctor and Jo get captured, it never stops their diplomacy. On the contrary: when they are captured, they often find themselves at the next stage of their diplomatic tour. Even when the Doctor is imprisoned on Earth, he manages to negotiate with both humans and Draconians. Use Story Points for this. For example, when the Doctor is imprisoned on Earth, let the player pay a Story Point for him to be taken to the Draconian embassy. Later, let the player pay another Story Point to be taken back.

Diplomacy itself is a social conflict, but there are two things to note. Firstly, when someone pays a Story Point, they may invent a history with the people they are negotiating with. For example, in this adventure, the Doctor declares that he is a Draconian noble, having saved the Draconians once before. This, in your game, would cost a Story Point and reduce the difficulty of the next social conflict.

Secondly, diplomacy can't simply stop a war. It's more complicated than that. Remember the Doctor's second visit to Earth. He persuaded the President and General Williams of what was happening, but he still needed to go to the Ogrons' planet to obtain proof. So diplomacy can produce small benefits, but it doesn't end the adventure.

THE FIRST THING WE'VE GOT TO DO IS ESCAPE

The Third Doctor spends a lot of time in prison. He is captured, he escapes, he is recaptured. Jo and the Master are often imprisoned too.

We've seen Jo escape through a window (**The Daemons**), along a ledge (**The Curse of Peladon**), with her skeleton keys (**Carnival of Monsters**), through a tube (**The Mutants**) and by grabbing a gun from her captors (**The Mind of Evil**). We've seen the Doctor escape by suddenly attacking his captors (**The Mind of Evil**) and with technical jiggery-pokery (**The Sea Devils** and **Day of the Daleks**).

We've also seen many rescue attempts. When the Doctor is imprisoned, Jo comes to rescue him (**The Sea Devils**, twice). When she is imprisoned, he, in turn, comes to rescue her (**Carnival of Monsters**). Sometimes, they end up in the same cell. Sometimes, the two meet when one has escaped and the other is coming to rescue them.

This adventure has even more capture, escape, rescue and recapture. On the cargo ship, the Doctor and Jo are imprisoned, escape – using the sonic screwdriver, as an electromagnet, to release the door bolts – and are recaptured. On Earth, after the sonic screwdriver fails to open the cell door, Draconians rescue the Doctor. He escapes from

them and is recaptured by Earth forces. Ogrons break into the prison to take the Doctor and Jo, but Earth forces recapture them and send the Doctor to a penal colony. On that colony, the Doctor is recaptured while escaping, then given to the Master's custody, where he rejoins Jo. On the Master's spaceship, the Doctor saws through bars while Jo causes a distraction, then scales the outside of the ship, before Draconian forces capture all three.

Later, the Master captures Jo, who briefly escapes by digging a tunnel, then is recaptured, and the Doctor comes to rescue her. Finally, the Master imprisons the Doctor and Jo together, but they escape, by using his fear device to scare the Ogrons.

Given all this, how can you use imprisonment in your adventures? Here are two initial tips. Firstly, the sonic screwdriver only lets the Doctor escape when he's got a clever plan. Thus, on Earth, it won't open the cell door (because that's not a clever plan), but on the ship, it works as an electromagnet to move the bolts (because that's a clever plan). Secondly, talking to your captors rarely works: they simply laugh. In your adventures, don't just let the players simply use the sonic screwdriver or talk their way out of prison. Make them invent an escape plan.

Best of all, though, note all the different combinations in which you can imprison people. You can capture the Doctor and Jo, then let them escape. You can just capture the Doctor, then let Jo rescue him, or vice versa. And, when someone's in prison, you can flip the situation around: let the Master imprison the Doctor, let the Doctor escape, then imprison them both together. Put all these things together and you have many ways to liven up your adventure.

NO DOUBT YOU'RE A QUALIFIED SPACE ENGINEER TOO, DOCTOR?

In this adventure, the Doctor goes into space. We've seen space before, but not like this. The Third Doctor has been on spacestations and spaceships. This time, however, he puts on his space suit and ventures into space itself.

Space, in this story, is as exciting it gets. Remember how the Doctor escaped from the Master's custody: he climbed around the outside of the spaceship and, when a sudden turn threw him into space, returned to the ship with some jiggery-pokery with his air supply. Later in the story, he returns to the outside of a spaceship, making vital repairs as a star cruiser bears down.

If you send the Doctor into space, don't let him stay inside. Give him reasons – and a space suit – to venture outside the ship. Perhaps the ship needs an urgent repair (Coordination + Technology, and the Technically Adept trait comes in handy). Perhaps he must fight something outside the ship (Coordination +Fighting). Perhaps he must place something outside an enemy ship to sabotage it (Coordination + Technology or Subterfuge).

Don't just put the Doctor and his companions on a spaceship. Put them in space!

IT LACKS THAT PERSONAL TOUCH

This is the last time the Third Doctor meets the Master. Having incited a conflict and assisted the Daleks, he retreats. Only in the Fourth Doctor's time would he appear again (see **The Deadly Assassin** in **The Fourth Doctor Sourcebook**). So this is a good time to ask: what did he actually want?

He didn't simply want to kill the Doctor. In this adventure, he had the opportunity to do that, but he decided that simply destroying the Doctor's spaceship would lack "a personal touch". Perhaps, then, he had a perverse sense of honour: he wanted to kill the Doctor *fairly*.

That partly fits. Certainly, the Master described his battles with the Doctor as a duel. When, in **Terror of the Autons**, he fails to kill the Doctor with a bomb, he describes it as "a greetings card, a small little gallantry on the eve of battle". Yet, at other times, the Master wants other things: to rule the Earth, to destroy the Earth, to rule or destroy the Universe.

When you use the Master in an adventure, don't worry too much about what he wants. Perhaps he doesn't know himself. It may even change during the course of the adventure: having attempted to kill the Doctor, he now decides to rule the galaxy instead.

Try giving the Third Doctor a final battle with the Master. After all, their relationship resembles a duel that never really finished. Give the Master one last battle with the Doctor, in which one of them is decisively defeated. (Not too decisive, though. The Master always survives to fight again.)

NEW GADGET – HYPNOSOUND
(SPECIAL GADGET)

This gadget emits a specially calibrated ultrasonic signal that makes people see their worst fears. If a character already has a Phobia of a creature or recently had a bad experience with a particular creature (for example, they recently escaped Cyberconversion), then they see that creature. Otherwise, the victim sees whatever danger is most common in their cultural zeitgeist. A British soldier in World War II might see a German soldier; a survivor of the Dalek Invasion of Earth in 2164 might see a Dalek or a Roboman.

When exposed to the device, victims must make an Awareness + Resolve test, adding Psychic Training or Indomitable or any other appropriate traits. The Difficulty for this test varies between 12 and 24, depending on proximity to the device, intensity of the signal and so on. Compare the result to the table to see how the device affects the character.

Traits: Transmit, Hypnosis (Special)
Cost: 4 Story Points

RESULT	EFFECT
9+ Fantastic	The character is permanently immune to the hypnosound and sees through the illusion. Better yet, her certainty gives everyone around her a +2 bonus to their own attempts to resist.
4-8 Good	The character resists the hypnosound and sees through the illusion.
0-3 Success	The character resists – temporarily. If the character stays exposed, he must roll again in 1D6 hours. The character may also suffer memory gaps, feel confused, or be disorientated.
1-3 Failure	The character is affected by the sound, but can try to resist again in 1D6 hours.
4-8 Bad	The character is affected by the sound, and cannot try to resist again unless she leaves the hypnosound field or someone convinces her that what she sees is an illusion.
9+ Disastrous	As above, but the illusory creatures have their Fear Factor increased by 2!

FURTHER ADVENTURES

- When the Doctor returns to Solos, five years after his last visit, he finds the Earth's colonial government again in crisis. The fully-mutated Solonians, in their ethereal, floating form, are in conflict with the half-mutated insectoid Solonians over ownership of the crystal that allows mutation. The humans, in their spacestation, want to return to Earth, but if they do, the conflict will boil over. Can the Doctor's diplomatic abilities resolve the situation?

- The Doctor sets the TARDIS for nineteenth century Paris and finds the streets in uproar. When he approaches the King, in an attempt at diplomacy, he is imprisoned within the Bastille Saint-Antoine.

Quickly, Jo realises what is happening: they are in the eighteenth, not the nineteenth, century, on the eve of the French Revolution. Yet the people are not the only things rising: the Silurians, too, are rising from the catacombs to claim the land above. Can the Doctor escape and prevent the conflict?

- When the TARDIS arrives on a spaceship, he finds a Time Lord message capsule. Once again, he realises he is charged to deliver it. Quickly, however, he realises that the spacecraft belongs to his old enemy, the Sontarans. Even worse, their spaceships are battling those of the Rutan Host. Who is the capsule for? And how will it resolve the Sontaran-Rutan conflict?

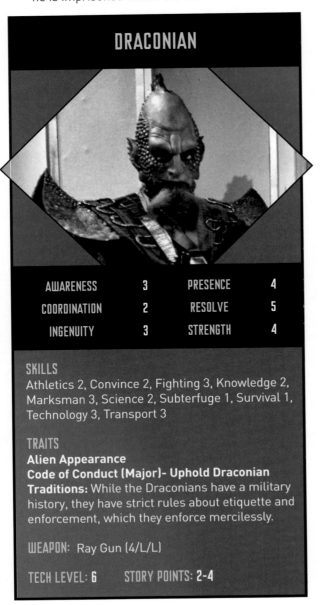

DRACONIAN

AWARENESS	3	PRESENCE	4
COORDINATION	2	RESOLVE	5
INGENUITY	3	STRENGTH	4

SKILLS
Athletics 2, Convince 2, Fighting 3, Knowledge 2, Marksman 3, Science 2, Subterfuge 1, Survival 1, Technology 3, Transport 3

TRAITS
Alien Appearance
Code of Conduct (Major)- Uphold Draconian Traditions: While the Draconians have a military history, they have strict rules about etiquette and enforcement, which they enforce mercilessly.

WEAPON: Ray Gun (4/L/L)

TECH LEVEL: 6   **STORY POINTS: 2-4**

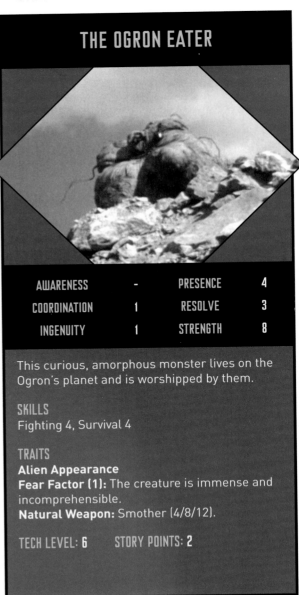

THE OGRON EATER

AWARENESS	-	PRESENCE	4
COORDINATION	1	RESOLVE	3
INGENUITY	1	STRENGTH	8

This curious, amorphous monster lives on the Ogron's planet and is worshipped by them.

SKILLS
Fighting 4, Survival 4

TRAITS
Alien Appearance
Fear Factor (1): The creature is immense and incomprehensible.
Natural Weapon: Smother (4/8/12).

TECH LEVEL: 6   **STORY POINTS: 2**

PLANET OF THE DALEKS

'The moment we forget that we're dealing with people, then we're no better off than the machines that we came here to destroy. When we start acting and thinking like the Daleks, the battle is lost.'

SYNOPSIS

Spiridon, 26th Century.

After the Doctor sent his telepathic message to the Time Lords, he collapsed and fell into a coma. Guided by the Time Lords, the TARDIS arrived on a jungle planet. When Jo ventured outside, a plant squirted liquid at her, and she found a crashed spaceship. There, she met three soldiers, Codal, Taron and Vaber, whom she sent to rescue the Doctor. As she hid on the ship, she watched something invisible enter and begin moving things about. The plant's liquid grew into a fungus, which slowly began to cover her.

When the soldiers rescued him, the Doctor recognised them as Thals, from the Dalek planet Skaro. They encountered a deactivated, invisible Dalek, then a patrol of Spiridons: the invisible native creatures enslaved by the Daleks, who wore purple furs against the cold. The Thals explained that the Daleks were attempting to steal the secret of invisibility from the Spiridons, but had only partially succeeded. When they arrived back at the Thal

ship, a Dalek patrol was preparing to destroy it. The Doctor, who believed Jo to be inside, tried to stop them. However, the Daleks destroyed the ship and captured the Doctor.

Inside the Dalek base, the Doctor escaped his cell by constructing a jamming device, which temporarily disabled the Dalek guide. The Thals had entered the base through the channels of an ice volcano. The Doctor encountered the Thals as the ice volcano erupted, and he helped them escape from the rising tide of ice. They found themselves by a refrigeration unit, above a cavern containing a Dalek army, frozen and inanimate. As the Daleks in the base closed in, the Doctor and Thals escaped, using a sheet to ride the hot air currents up a ventilation shaft.

Meanwhile, Jo had been rescued by Wester, a Spiridon who had escaped the Daleks' slavery. Using a herbal concoction, he removed the fungus that covered her, and explained that the Daleks were constructing a bacteria bomb to destroy all life on the planet. Jo entered the Dalek base, concealed within a container, then followed a Dalek patrol back out into the jungle. When they attempted to destroy a Thal stash of explosives, she rescued two bombs from it. She was then reunited with the Doctor and the Thals. They passed the night at the Plain of Stones, an area which retained the sun's heat to stay warm, but which was besieged by wild animals.

Vaber, one of the Thals, stole the bombs and headed for the Dalek base, intending to destroy the refrigeration unit. However, the Doctor realised this would revive, not destroy, the Dalek army. When Vaber was captured by a Spiridon patrol, Codal and Taron attacked two Spiridons and stole their furs and the bombs. Meanwhile, the Doctor and Thals disabled a Dalek, by pushing it into an icy lava pool.

Disguised in Spiridon furs and the disabled Dalek's casing, the Doctor and Thals entered the Dalek base. Wester had entered, too, and found the bacteria bomb. He released the bacteria within a hermetically-sealed room, killing himself and ensuring the room could never be opened. The Dalek Supreme landed on the planet. It ordered the refrigeration unit be switched off to revive the Dalek army. As the huge army returned to life, the Doctor and the Thals placed the bomb in the channels of the ice volcano. They fled as it detonated, burying the Dalek army in the ice lava. As they prepared to leave, Latep, a member of the secondary Thal taskforce, asked Jo to return with him, but she refused. The Thals left for Skaro in the Dalek Supreme's ship. Back on the TARDIS, Jo asked the Doctor to head for home.

CONTINUITY

The TARDIS has an emergency oxygen supply.
Daleks – or, at least, these Daleks – barely function at sub-zero temperatures.
The Daleks have a Supreme Council, who have strong opinions about failure.

⊙ RUNNING THE ADVENTURE

After the politics and diplomacy of the Third Doctor's recent adventures, it's refreshing to find a straightforward adventure tale. Here is a jungle planet, packed with dangerous plants, and an underground base to destroy.

That means it's easy for you to run. The adventure begins when the Doctor and companions land on Spiridon's jungle surface. Then simply let them explore. They'll discover fungus-squirting plants, invisible creatures and Dalek patrols. They'll meet the Thals, who explain the Daleks' plans to steal the Spiridon's invisibility, and perhaps Wester, who mentions the bacteria bomb. The Thals make perfect player characters, while Wester might be controlled either by a player or the GM. And they might be captured, either by Daleks or Spiridons.

Next, the characters enter the Dalek base. There are four things that might lead them there. One: they want to stop the Daleks discovering the secret of invisibility. Two: they want to end the enslavement of the Spiridons. Three: they want to disable the bacteria bomb. Four: they want to prevent the Dalek army being activated. Getting into the base takes subterfuge: they might hide in a container (like Jo), pretend to be Spiridons (like the Doctor), hide in a Dalek casing (like Rebec the Thal) or crawl through the ice volcano tunnels (like the Thals). Let your players use their imagination: if they think of other ways to enter, let them try.

Once inside, they'll discover the full extent of the Daleks' plans. If they didn't know about the bacteria bomb or the frozen army before, they'll discover them now. So how will they stop the Daleks? Perhaps they need bombs, in which case they must escape the base and find the Thal explosive stash. When things are building to a head, bring the Supreme Dalek in and begin reviving the army.

AN OLD ENEMY

When, in your adventures, the Doctor faces an old enemy, you must make them new. Don't simply put the TARDIS on a planet full of Daleks. After all, the Doctor has defeated Daleks before. Instead, make the Daleks new in some way.

When the First Doctor met the Daleks, they were powered by static electricity and largely confined to their city on Skaro (**The Daleks**). In subsequent adventures, they invaded Earth (**The Dalek Invasion of Earth**), discovered time travel (**The Chase**) and created a Dalek Empire (**The Daleks' Master Plan**). So, although the First Doctor had defeated them many times, they never got old. Each time he faced the Daleks, something about them had changed.

In the Second Doctor's time, Daleks were mass-producing themselves in giant factories (**The Power of the Daleks**) and, for the first time, the Doctor met a Dalek Emperor (**The Evil of the Daleks**). By the time the Third Doctor met them, in **Day of the Daleks**, they had enslaved both humans and Ogrons. So, each time the Doctor meets the Daleks, there is something new about them. They pose a new and different threat.

In this adventure, the Doctor must stop "the mightiest army of Daleks there has ever been" coming to life. Again, the Daleks are different from before: they have enslaved the Spiridons, they are governed by a Supreme Dalek and, although they haven't quite mastered it, they have discovered invisibility. (As an aside: imagine an adventure with Daleks who had mastered invisibility.)

These Daleks also have new weaknesses. Firstly, they are vulnerable to high-frequency radio waves, which jam their guidance systems. Secondly, they become inactive at low temperatures. These weaknesses mean that, in this adventure, the Doctor can defeat the Daleks in a way we haven't seen before. Importantly, however, none of these weaknesses are killer weapons against the Daleks: whatever the vulnerability, there is always a reason he can't use it again.

When the Doctor meets an old adversary, make that adversary new again. Give them a new location, a new plan or new powers. And give them new weaknesses, too. Vulnerabilities exploited to defeat an adversary in the past won't work again. Your group must find a new way to fight them.

I'M A SCIENTIST, NOT AN ADVENTURER

The Doctor very much likes science. We often see him engineering technological solutions to problems: in this adventure, for example, he creates a high-frequency transmitter to jam a Dalek's guidance system. Sometimes, however, his solutions are simpler. To escape the Daleks' cooling chamber, he uses the simple scientific principle that hot air rises. This lets him, together with the Thals, float up a ventilation shaft, using a plastic sheet to catch the hot air. This isn't straightforward: when they are near the top, the sheet tears, and they must grab ladders to complete their ascent. But it does work.

When you run adventures, then, encourage brilliant ideas based on simple scientific principles. These usually require an Ingenuity + Science roll. Even if these ideas seem unrealistic, set a low difficulty for them. After all, when the Doctor is around, the most basic science suddenly becomes useful: the Second Doctor once escaped from a Dalek cell by chiming a half-filled wine glass.

In your adventures, let the Doctor and Companions use science to solve their problems. Can they destroy a Dalek base by flooding it, using the principle that water expands as it freezes? Can they disable a Dalek by earthing the static electricity that powers them? Can they work out when the Daleks arrived, using radiocarbon dating? You should, at least, let them try.

FURTHER ADVENTURES

- The TARDIS arrives on a beautiful planet covered with iridescent vegetation. As the Doctor and Companions explore, they realise the beauty is deceptive: the plants attack humans with shooting tendrils. When they try to leave, they find the TARDIS has been sucked into the planet's soil. Finally, the Doctor realises that this is not a planet at all, but an Axon ship, grown to extraordinary size. Can the Doctor find the TARDIS and escape the planet?

- In Victorian London, men are disappearing in the slums, taken by shadowy, translucent figures. When the Doctor investigates, he finds

Cybermats, crawling through the crumbling alleys between dwellings. The figures are Cybermen, kidnapping people to join their army: yet why are they translucent? Have they discovered invisibility? Will they master it and produce an invisible Cyber army?

- Hundreds of years after the Dalek army was frozen, the Doctor returns to Spiridon to check the planet is safe. When he arrives, he finds the planet devastated by the Daleks' bacteria. He also finds an abandoned mining colony, which has dug into the ice lava and released the Daleks. Who is behind this? Is it the Master or something even more sinister?

SPIRIDON PLANT

AWARENESS	5	PRESENCE	-
COORDINATION	4	RESOLVE	2
INGENUITY	1	STRENGTH	5

SKILLS
Fighting 5 (when using tendrils), Marksman 5

TRAITS
Alien Senses (Minor): The plant is particularly sensitive to vibrations in the Earth, making it extraordinarily aware of people approaching it.
Immortal (Major): You might destroy one tendril or flower, but you can never destroy all the plants.
Natural Weapons (Major) - Spore Spray: The plant sprays a fungal foam, which, unless treated, grows to cover the victim. This spray keeps inflicting one point of damage every Action Round until the victim is completely encased and smothered. The spray can also coat vehicles or ships, sealing them away and preventing air from entering. Characters inside a sealed vessel are treated as if drowning.
Natural Weapons (Minor) - Tendril: The plant shoots out a tendril, which captures the victim and draws them in. The victim must beat the plant in a contest of Strength + Fighting to break free.

STORY POINTS: 2

SPIRIDON

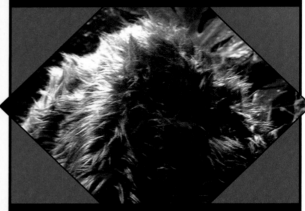

AWARENESS	2	PRESENCE	2
COORDINATION	2	RESOLVE	4
INGENUITY	3	STRENGTH	4

SKILLS
Athletics 2, Convince 3, Craft 2, Fighting 2, Medicine 4, Survival 3

TRAITS
Alien appearance
Environmental (Minor): Can live in the Spiridon jungle without harm.
Enslaved
Special - Invisible: Spiridons are naturally invisible, using anti-reflecting light waves to remain undetected.

STORY POINTS: 1-7 (Use 1 for a member of a Spiridon Patrol, 7 for a creature that sides with the Doctor)

THE GREEN DEATH

'What's best for Global Chemicals is best for the world, is best for you.'

SYNOPSIS

Llanfairfach, South Wales, UNIT era.

In the village of Llanfairfach, a man died in a disused mine, his skin glowing green. Jo went to meet Professor Jones, an environmental protester, who suspected that the Global Chemicals refinery was pumping waste down the mines. The Brigadier, curious about the strange death, drove Jo there. At the mine, Jo found former miners already investigating. With one of them, Bert, she descended in the lift to help Dai, who was trapped in the shafts below. However, the lift began to drop uncontrollably fast.

The Doctor arrived – after returning from Metebelis III, which he had found unexpectedly dangerous – and jammed the lift mechanism. Someone, he discovered, had sabotaged the lift's brakes. To release Jo and Bert, they needed cutting equipment from Global Chemicals. While Jones staged a demonstration at the refinery's gates, the Doctor sneaked in the back. He was caught and brought to Stevens, the head of Global Chemicals, who talked to him before letting him go. Unknown to the Doctor, Stevens was enslaved by a console in his office, which he also used to enslave others.

The Brigadier returned with the cutting equipment they needed, and the Doctor descended into the mine, where he found Dai's body, glowing green. He also found Bert, whose hand was glowing green, having touched a green slime on the walls. Deeper in the mine, the Doctor found Jo, facing a cavern of giant maggots. Using a coal wagon, they steered through the maggots, and the Doctor stole an egg. They found a pipe leading into the Global Chemicals refinery, and climbed it, escaping just before toxic waste poured down the pipe.

At Global Chemicals, the Brigadier demanded that Stevens shut down the refinery. However, Stevens called the Minister of Ecology, who put the Prime Minister on the line and ordered the Brigadier to keep the refinery open.

The Brigadier, Doctor, Jo and Professor Jones dined at the Professor's commune, the 'Nuthutch', eating a protein-rich fungus grown by the protesters. The Doctor tried to show Jo a blue crystal from Metebelis III, but she seemed more interested in a book on the Amazon. The maggot egg hatched. Just as it was about to attack Jo, Stevens' henchman entered to steal the egg, and it attacked him instead.

The Brigadier blew up the mine. However, this simply caused the maggots to emerge from the ground and inside the Global Chemicals factory. Disguised first as a milkman, then as a cleaning lady, the Doctor entered the factory. Yates, whom the Brigadier had planted inside the compound, told him that something on the top floor was in control. There, the Doctor found a computer, BOSS (Biomorphic Organisational Systems Supervisor), which ran the factory with ruthless efficiency to produce profit. BOSS imprisoned the Doctor, but Yates released him, and he escaped in the milk-float in which he had arrived.

Meanwhile, with assistance from the RAF (Royal Air Force), UNIT began bombing the maggots from the air, but they appeared to be immune. Jones tried to rescue Jo, who was caught in the bombardment, and they sheltered in a cave. Jones was knocked unconscious. The Doctor rescued them, using his sonic screwdriver to emit high frequency soundwaves that disturbed the maggots. However, when they

CHAPTER ELEVEN: THE GREEN DEATH

returned to the Nuthutch, Jones had a glowing green patch on his neck. He whispered the word 'Serendipity'. As the Doctor tried to understand what he meant, Yates emerged, having been brainwashed by BOSS. Before he could try to kill the Doctor, the Time Lord produced the blue crystal from Metebelis III, which reversed the soldier's brainwashing.

When Benton found a dead maggot, the Doctor realised that the fungus was poisonous to them. He distributed sacks of the fungus from Bessie, killing the maggots. One maggot, however, had metamorphosed into a giant insect. When it swooped on Bessie, the Doctor caught it in his cape.

At the Nuthutch, Jo remembered that she had spilt fungus powder on Professor Jones' slides. That, realised the Doctor, was what he had meant by serendipity: the fungus was the cure for Professor Jones' affliction. The Doctor converted the fungus into an injection, which cured the Professor.

Back at Global Chemicals, BOSS was planning to extend its power worldwide, using a network of slave machines. Using the blue crystal, the Doctor released Stevens from his brainwashing. Stevens disabled BOSS as the Doctor ran, and Global Chemicals exploded.

Professor Jones proposed to Jo, who accepted. As the Brigadier and UNIT soldiers drank to the happy couple, the Doctor slipped away.

CONTINUITY

This is Jo Grant's last adventure with the Doctor.
In **Planet of the Spiders**, the Doctor's acquisition of the blue crystal from Metebelis III will come back to haunt him.

RUNNING THE ADVENTURE

This adventure has all the Third Doctor's hallmarks. Politics, a ruthless corporation, an incompetent government; guns, chases, fights, bombs; and the whole thing is resolved in a scientific laboratory. It only lacks a peace conference, a prison escape and the Master (who, interestingly, could easily have turned out to be BOSS' true identity).

Nevertheless, this isn't really the Doctor's adventure. It's Jo's story. So, when you run it, start with a companion. Jo begins by going to Llanfairfach, either by reading about Professor Jones' protest or because the Brigadier orders her there. Once there, she might go either to the Nuthutch or the mine. Now, the Doctor arrives, having been to Metebelis III. One way or another, they go down the mine to investigate. There, they find the miners' bodies, the green slime and the exit to Global Chemicals. That lets them figure out what's happening: Global Chemicals is both causing the deaths and creating the maggots, by pumping toxic slime into the mines. From there on, they must work out how to stop it. There are many directions in which to head: if they go to Global Chemicals, they find Stevens and BOSS; if they decide to fight the maggots, they can do so; if they decide they need a maggot for research, they must capture one. If a maggot successfully attacks someone, the victim develops green patches on their skin and must be cured. When things are reaching a head, let the maggots crawl up through the ground and into the factory.

THE PROLOGUE

This adventure doesn't begin with the Doctor. In fact, it doesn't begin with Jo. It really starts in Llanfairfach, where a man, looking terrified, runs through the disused mine. Shortly, he will become the first victim.

Often, the adventures don't begin with the Doctor at all. Instead, as described in **The Gamemaster's Guide**, they begin with a prologue, in which the players play other characters briefly.

There are three main sorts of prologue. One: we see normal people, just as they encounter something out of the ordinary. Two: we see military types, just as they detect something abnormal. Often, as in **The Claws of Axos**, it is heading towards Earth). But the third type of prologue is the most common. In it, we see the first victim. This happens in **The Silurians**, when a potholer dies; in **The Sea Devils**, when a submarine is attacked; in **The Curse of Peladon**, when Aggedor claims his first victim; and in **The Daemons**, when a man dies in a graveyard.

When you run this sort of prologue, there's a formula to follow. The character in the prologue is a **normal, everyday person**, but they are **terrified**. They are probably **running**, they are probably **alone** and it is probably **dark**. Most importantly: **they see their killer, but we don't**. That's important. It means that, whoever the Doctor's adversary is, it remains a surprise.

To run this prologue, choose one player. Tell them to play a normal person, wherever the adventure is set. Try starting the prologue with a mundane conversation with another character. Then let them hear a noise, see a movement or otherwise realise that something is after them. They must run. But, however fast they run, they get caught. Ask the player to do their best terrified scream. Then start the adventure proper.

CUT

When Jo meets Professor Jones, he explains how the refinery's chemical processes produce waste. At the same time, when the Brigadier meets Stevens, Stevens explains how the refinery's chemical processes produce no waste.

These two conversations run in parallel. We cut between them, hearing a snippet of one, then a snippet of the other. But, although they're two conversations, we're hearing one story about the refinery's processes. To indicate this, the same phrases are repeated in both conversations. For example: when Stevens says "The Stevens process is clean", we cut to Professor Jones, who says "The Stevens process...means thousands of gallons of waste".

We've seen similar parallel conversations in the Doctor's adventures. In **The Sea Devils**, both the Master and Doctor are trying to find the Sea Devils' base. As their investigations run in parallel, we cut between them. First, the Master calculates that base is below the sea fort. Shortly afterwards, the Doctor demands to go to the fort. Although the characters are separate, it seems as though it's the same investigation.

Try this in your adventures. When two conversations are happening simultaneously, about similar topics, cut between them. When two investigations are running in parallel, cut between those too. (Here's a

hint: it helps if you assume that, once something has been discovered by one character, everyone knows about it.)

MORE MUCK! MORE DEVASTATION! MORE DEATH!

The biggest topic in this adventure is the environment. A global corporation, backed by the government and governed by a profit-mad computer, pumps toxic waste into disused mines. Standing in their way are Professor Jones and his protesters, with their love of meat substitutes and sustainable energy. There isn't an alien in the whole adventure: the maggots, which are the monsters, have been created by human greed.

This isn't the first time the Third Doctor's adventures have had environmental overtones. In **Colony in Space**, the planet's agriculture was poisoned by an underground weapon. In **The Mutants**, Solos' atmosphere was unbreathable, while Earth contained "grey cities linked by grey highways across a grey desert". Note how the Doctor describes this environmental disaster. The Earth hasn't suffered global warming or a nuclear war, as we might expect today. It's simply been used up: all its resources are spent.

Alongside this threat to the environment, the Doctor finds a plan to save it. Professor Jones, who serves meals based on fungus – it's delicious, since even the Brigadier likes it – wants to find an even more nutritious fungus in the Amazonian jungle. In fact, the Professor's fungus is near-miraculous: it both destroys the maggots and cures his affliction.

So how can you bring this into your games? For an authentic Third Doctor adventure, bring in the values of the time. Invent big corporations, bad governments and bomb-happy soldiers, willing to destroy the environment for profit. Invent schemes that could save the world and its scarce resources, whether they are fake (like Axonite) or genuine (like the Professor's fungus).

More widely, think about the values of today's world. What are the current issues in the early 21st century? Perhaps, to a large extent, they are similar to those faced by the Doctor, but with a different focus. Multinational companies still threaten the environment, but now they create pollution rather than toxic waste. Today's issue is global warming, not depleted resources. Whatever you think the issues are, put them into the Doctor's adventures.

THE FLEDGLING FLIES THE COOP

This is Jo's last adventure. Earlier, in **Terror of the Autons**, Liz Shaw left without ceremony: the Brigadier simply mentioned she had gone back to Cambridge. This adventure, by contrast, is a huge send-off. It is designed entirely around Jo.

In previous adventures, two things stood out about Jo. The first was romance: on other planets, she often found a male companion. The second was homesickness: wherever she travelled, she seemed happiest on Earth. The best possible ending, then, is for her to fall in love on Earth. She hasn't really mentioned the environment before, but it's plausible she might care about it: after all, in **The Daemons**, she talked about the Age of Aquarius, another hippy-ish idea.

In her last adventure, then, she falls in love with an environmental protester. In addition, he is suspiciously like the Doctor: even his name, Professor Jones, is a variation on 'Doctor' and the Doctor's alias 'John Smith'.

In a similar way, when Amy left the Eleventh Doctor, it resolved two established issues: her love for Rory and her growing distance from the Doctor. At the end of her last adventure, she was with Rory and unable

to see the Doctor again. When Rose left the Tenth Doctor, her last adventure resolved her love for her family and for him: she could stay with her family, in an alternate universe, but never see him again. (When she returned for one last adventure, she was left with a duplicate Tenth Doctor, which resolved the same issues more happily.)

When a long-standing character leaves, consider giving them the send-off they deserve. Ask yourself: what has been important to them, during their time with the Doctor? Then, in their last adventure, bring those issues to a close. For example: you could invent a new adventure to say goodbye to Liz Shaw, set in a university, which used her scientific ability to defeat the adversary.

There is, however, one final way to say goodbye to a character: give them a tragic ending. Thus, in the Fifth Doctor's time, Adric dies when trying to stop a ship crashing into the Earth. In the Tenth Doctor's adventures, Donna is left without memories of her time in the TARDIS. That gives you three ways to end a character's story: the sudden goodbye, the long farewell episode and the tragic end.

NEW GADGET: BLUE CRYSTAL

When a hypnotised person focuses on one of these crystals, their trance is broken.

Traits: Special – Breaks hypnotic trances
Cost: 2 Story Points

THE GREEN DEATH

Those exposed to the Green Death gain the Distinctive Appearance trait - they're green! They also lose Ingenuity and Resolve at a rate of one point every 10 minutes or so until reduced to 1 point in each Attribute. The Green Death then attacks the victim's Strength at the same rate. When the Victim's Strength hits 1, then the victim is on the brink of death and will soon perish. The rate at which the affliction progresses varies from person to person (and according to dramatic necessity!). Non-player characters may be killed off quickly. A kind GM may allow players to roll Resolve + Strength to resist the effects of the affliction, or spend Story Points to keep going.

FURTHER ADVENTURES

- The Doctor and Liz attend a demonstration of bionic body parts, which promises huge benefits for medicine. However, Liz realises there is something strange about the science: it is far too advanced for the twentieth century. The Doctor, meanwhile, recognises the hallmarks of the Cybermen. Together with Professor Hammer, her former mentor, Liz calculates a signal to disrupt the bionic machinery, which, when broadcast from St Benedict's Tower, defeats the Cyber army. Inspired by the work, Liz decides to continue her research with Professor Hammer, and the Doctor leaves alone.

- In the early 21st century, workers are disappearing from an oil rig. When the Doctor investigates, he discovered that the oil company is using fracking to bring the oil up. Yet they have disturbed something that has slumbered beneath the Earth.

- On his journey to the Amazon, Professor Jones finds the fungus he had sought. Yet Jo is suspicious: the fungus is bitter, gold-coloured and unnaturally large. Her suspicions increase when she finds an ancient spaceship, embedded within the jungle. When Professor Jones analyses the fungus, he finds a substance Jo has seen before: Axonite.

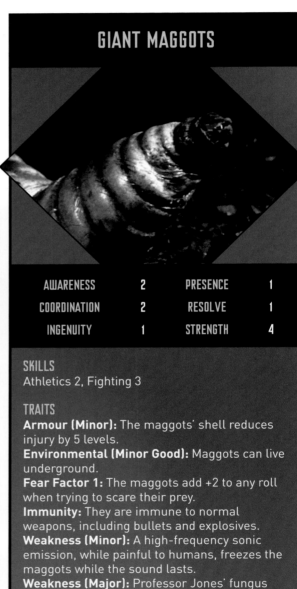

GIANT MAGGOTS

AWARENESS	2	PRESENCE	1
COORDINATION	2	RESOLVE	1
INGENUITY	1	STRENGTH	4

SKILLS
Athletics 2, Fighting 3

TRAITS
Armour (Minor): The maggots' shell reduces injury by 5 levels.
Environmental (Minor Good): Maggots can live underground.
Fear Factor 1: The maggots add +2 to any roll when trying to scare their prey.
Immunity: They are immune to normal weapons, including bullets and explosives.
Weakness (Minor): A high-frequency sonic emission, while painful to humans, freezes the maggots while the sound lasts.
Weakness (Major): Professor Jones' fungus kills the maggots completely.
Natural weapons (Major): The maggots get +2 to their normal damage. However, the victim contracts the 'green death' affliction shortly afterwards.

GIANT INSECT

AWARENESS	3	PRESENCE	1
COORDINATION	4	RESOLVE	1
INGENUITY	1	STRENGTH	1

SKILLS
Athletics 3, Fighting 2, Marksman 4

TRAITS
Armour (Minor): The insects' shell reduces injury by 5 levels.
Flight (Major)
Natural weapons (Major): The insect squirts the green toxic liquid as a projectile. Its damage is 3/5/7, but the victim contracts the 'green death' affliction shortly afterwards.

THE TIME WARRIOR

'Is this Doctor a long-shanked rascal with a mighty nose?'

⊗ SYNOPSIS

England, Middle Ages and UNIT Era

Linx, a Sontaran warrior, crash-landed on Earth during the Middle Ages. He struck a deal with local baron Irongron for shelter, and then used an osmic projector to steal technicians from a twentieth century top secret scientific research complex. Linx needed expertise and parts from the future to help him repair his craft. The disappearing technicians prompted UNIT to investigate and the Brigadier sequestered as many scientific minds as he could in a secure location. The Doctor noted that the Brigadier actually made the abductor's plan much easier – he had a hunch that a Sontaran was responsible.

When Linx next arrived, the Doctor followed him back in time using the TARDIS, inadvertently transporting Sarah Jane Smith with him. She had infiltrated the UNIT facility by using her aunt's identity card (her aunt was a noted scientist and so had authorisation to visit the UNIT base). Not understanding what's happened but suspecting ill of the Doctor, Sarah followed him to Irongron's castle and was captured while the Doctor confirmed his suspicion that a Sontaran was involved.

Linx created a robot knight for Irongron, who tested it against Hal, an archer in the service of the Earl of Wessex. Hal managed to escape when the Doctor used a crossbow to shoot the remote control out of Irongron's hands. Hal escaped with Sarah and she convinced the Earl that they needed to capture the Doctor, as she believed that he was in league with Irongron. Meanwhile, the Doctor discovered that Linx was using the kidnaped scientists to build weapons, specifically modern rifles. The Doctor was discovered and pursued by Irongron's men, only to be captured by Hal and taken to Wessex Castle.

The Doctor convinced Sarah and the Earl of Wessex of his good intentions and proved it the following day when he made smoke bombs to scatter Irongron's men as they attacked the castle. Irongron was starting to doubt his ally, as the weapons Linx had provided were less effective than he'd thought. His concerns were exacerbated by seeing the Sontaran's true appearance.

The Doctor snuck back into Irongron's castle and offered Linx a way home if he'd release the kidnaped scientists. Linx refused and captured the Doctor, but he escaped when a scientist struck Linx's probic vent.

This scientist, Rubeish, was unaffected by Linx's hypnotic ray because of his poor eyesight. He helped the Doctor return the scientists to their home time period with Linx's osmic projector. Sarah, having infiltrated the castle with the Doctor, drugged the food. A drowsy Irongron confronted the recovered Linx as the latter prepared to leave in his ship, which would destroy the castle in the process. Linx killed Irongron before he himself was felled by a shot from Hal into his probic vent, but not before he started his ship.

The Doctor and Sarah got everyone out of the castle before it exploded, whereupon Sarah joined the Doctor in the TARDIS.

CONTINUITY

The Doctor refers to his home planet as 'Gallifrey' for the first time and describes the Time Lords as 'galactic ticket inspectors' for time travel.
The Sontarans have rudimentary time travel capacity, although they seem to have lost it in the centuries since (it's possible that the Time Lords took it away from them, explaining the Sontaran attempt to conquer Gallifrey).
Linx claims that there isn't a galaxy the Sontarans haven't subjugated; a bold claim, but one that implies that either the Sontarans have a winning record against other galaxy-conquering threats or they simply started conquering galaxies before such races as the Daleks, the Dominators, or the Krotons.

NEW GADGET – RHONDIUM SENSOR

This gadget detects the presence of Delta particles, which are created when some types of temporal disturbances, such as the use of an osmic projector, are created.

Traits: Scan (detect Delta particles)
Cost: 1 Story Point

NEW GADGET – REFLECTIVE SHIELD FAN

This gadget offers protection from energy beams such as lasers which can be deflected with a mirrored surface. When not in use, the Reflective Shield Fan can be collapsed into a stack of attached cards.

Traits: Restriction (energy beams only), Delete (energy attacks)
Cost: 1 Story Point

⊙ RUNNING THE ADVENTURE

This adventure is a perfect example of the 'alien historical,' where an alien (or aliens) threatens to disrupt Earth history. The characters need to not only remove the alien threat but also ensure that there are no lingering 'aftershocks', such as advanced equipment lying around or an important person's ancestor marrying the wrong person.

Generally, the alien uses human agents to hide his presence while he puts his plans into action. For helping the alien the agent is promised something, although such a contract is rarely fulfilled as the alien tends to dispose of his agents, or at least does little to save them, when they become redundant. The solution to the problem usually involves a contrivance that enables everything to be tidied up by the adventure's end. In this case, it's Linx starting a countdown for his ship that will cause an explosion, conveniently wiping out alien, ship, and 'gifts' (the new guns).

RUTHLESS, NOT NECESSARILY EVIL

Throughout most of this adventure Linx is portrayed as a soldier that simply wants to get back to his war and won't let anything stand in his way. He finds Irongron's protection convenient and offers him weapons that are capable but of limited use (imagine if he'd given Irongron a machine gun or rockets), indicating at least a token effort not to disrupt the timeline, probably to avoid paradox. He even honours his agreement with Irongron and tries to warn him away before his ship destroys the castle. It's important to note that Linx kills Irongron only because the latter breached their agreement and tried to kill him.

Linx's dismissal of the Doctor's offer of help may be seen as 'evil', it's likely more a consideration of professional pride; the Doctor's patronising 'I might possibly consider helping you' is a questionable tactic and by the time he approaches Linx with a more reasonable proposal the Sontaran considers the Doctor a 'sworn enemy' and therefore untrustworthy. As he states himself, Linx is just a soldier and his superiors have likely warned him away from dealing with Time Lords. Ruthless adversaries make great antagonists because they often have laudable goals;

it's their execution that is the problem. Ruthless adversaries are often more approachable and, in spite of Linx, can often be reasoned with so long as the new solution is more convenient than the old. In any case, they provide a welcome respite from the 'I shall destroy this world because I can, mwa ha ha ha ha!' villains.

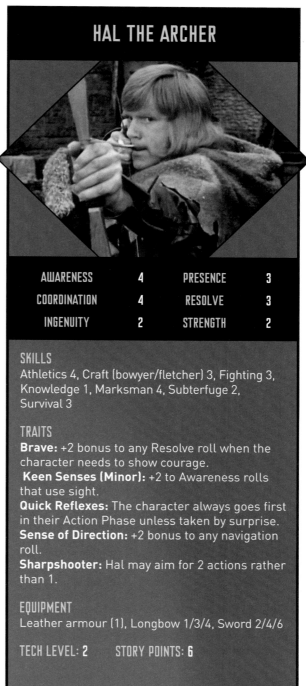

HAL THE ARCHER

AWARENESS	4	PRESENCE	3
COORDINATION	4	RESOLVE	3
INGENUITY	2	STRENGTH	2

SKILLS
Athletics 4, Craft (bowyer/fletcher) 3, Fighting 3, Knowledge 1, Marksman 4, Subterfuge 2, Survival 3

TRAITS
Brave: +2 bonus to any Resolve roll when the character needs to show courage.
Keen Senses (Minor): +2 to Awareness rolls that use sight.
Quick Reflexes: The character always goes first in their Action Phase unless taken by surprise.
Sense of Direction: +2 bonus to any navigation roll.
Sharpshooter: Hal may aim for 2 actions rather than 1.

EQUIPMENT
Leather armour (1), Longbow 1/3/4, Sword 2/4/6

TECH LEVEL: 2   **STORY POINTS: 6**

IRONGRON

AWARENESS	3	PRESENCE	3
COORDINATION	3	RESOLVE	4
INGENUITY	2	STRENGTH	3

SKILLS

Athletics 3, Convince 2, Fighting 4, Marksman 1, Survival 3

TRAITS

Argumentative: The character will argue their point of view even if it puts their life in danger.
Brave: +2 bonus to any Resolve roll when the character needs to show courage.
Impulsive: Character doesn't think things through before acting.
Tough: Reduce total damage by 2.
Voice of Authority (Minor Good Trait): +2 bonus to Presence and Convince rolls.

EQUIPMENT

Mail Armour (2), Axe or Sword 3/5/7, Rifle 3/6/9

STORY POINTS: 8

IRONGRON'S MEN

AWARENESS	2	PRESENCE	2
COORDINATION	3	RESOLVE	2
INGENUITY	1	STRENGTH	3

SKILLS

Athletics 2, Fighting 2, Marksman 1, Survival 3

TRAITS

None

EQUIPMENT

Mail armour (2), Axe or Sword 3/5/7, Rifle 3/6/9

STORY POINTS: 0

ROBOT KNIGHT

AWARENESS	3	PRESENCE	1
COORDINATION	2	RESOLVE	2
INGENUITY	1	STRENGTH	5

SKILLS

Athletics 3, Fighting 4

TRAITS

Armour (Minor): Reduce damage by 5
Robot
Weakness (Minor): -4 to all actions if remote control is disabled. It can also no longer receive commands, instead fighting anything that comes near it.

EQUIPMENT

Sword (+2 damage)

STORY POINTS: 3

PROFESSOR RUBEISH

AWARENESS	3	PRESENCE	2
COORDINATION	2	RESOLVE	3
INGENUITY	5	STRENGTH	1

Rubeish is one of the kidnapped scientists and is spared hypnosis due to his poor eyesight.

SKILLS

Craft 3, Knowledge 2, Science 5, Technology 5

TRAITS

*Impaired senses (Minor): Without a corrective device, Rubeish suffers a -2 penalty to rolls relying on sight.
Indomitable

EQUIPMENT

Glasses

STORY POINTS: 6

GENERAL FINCH

AWARENESS	3	PRESENCE	4
COORDINATION	3	RESOLVE	5
INGENUITY	3	STRENGTH	2

Finch is one of the leaders of Operation Golden Age and is using his position to ensure the orderly evacuation of London and the killing of anyone that threatens it. His ruthlessness may be attributed to the fact that he knows humanity is being wiped out (what's the point of mercy if everyone's going to die anyway) although he is careful not to do anything that would threaten the project. Finch's dedication to the project is something of a mystery. Whitaker and Grover, the other two leaders, had clear motivations for wanting to wipe away this polluted, overpopulated world and start again. Finch, on the other hand, seemed like a loyal (if brusque and paranoid) soldier. Perhaps he was attracted by the challenge of a war for survival in a new world, or intended to seize control once humanity was reduced to only a few hundred colonists.

SKILLS
Athletics 3, Convince 4, Fighting 3, Knowledge 2, Marksman 4, Medicine 2, Science 1, Subterfuge 4, Survival 3, Technology 2, Transport 2

TRAITS
By the Book: Finch ruthlessly follows procedure.
Military Rank (Major Good x3): General.
Obligation (Major): British Army.
Voice of Authority: +2 bonus to Presence and Convince rolls.

EQUIPMENT
Pistol 2/5/7

TECH LEVEL: 5 **STORY POINTS: 8**

PROFESSOR WHITAKER

AWARENESS	3	PRESENCE	4
COORDINATION	3	RESOLVE	4
INGENUITY	5	STRENGTH	2

Whitaker was a brilliant scientist who was denied a government grant for his time travel project. Now disappeared from public view, Whitaker works on his machine with secret funding secured by Sir Charles and General Finch.

SKILLS
Convince 3, Knowledge 4, Science 5, Technology 4, Transport 3

TRAITS
Boffin: Allows Whitaker to create Gadgets.
Technically Adept: Whitaker gets a +2 bonus on Technology rolls.
Argumentative: He managed to offend many of the government's scientific advisors and experts – he was a genius, but did not work well with others.
Vortex: He has built his own time machine, and has a +2 bonus to any attempts to use it.

EQUIPMENT
Scientific equipment, experimental time machine

TECH LEVEL: 5 **STORY POINTS: 10**

WHITAKER'S TIME MACHINE
It's unthinkable that the British Government would have turned down a working time machine, or even the hint of one – and since Whitaker was able to perfect his machine within a few years, one has to suspect a conspiracy. It's likely that the brains behind Operation Golden Age deliberately manipulated events so that they could gain control of Whitaker's work. The time machine worked by generating artificial time eddies, pulling creatures and objects out of the distant past and temporarily depositing them in the present era. The machine also proved capable of freezing time or even transporting itself back in time, although it was relatively inexact and required constant adjustment. The original prototype vanished when Whitaker and Grover accidentally transported themselves into prehistory (and without a convenient nuclear reactor to power the machine, they were stuck there forever).

DINOSAURS

Dinosaurs are giant reptiles from prehistoric Earth, during the Mesozoic era, which spanned about 250 – 65 million years ago. They co-existed with the Silurians, whose civilisation dominated the Earth. The Silurians went into hibernation during a potential Armageddon as a rogue planetoid threatened Earth, but the planetoid became the moon. At least one Silurian colony ship included dinosaurs with the intent to return to Earth after the cataclysm. The age of the dinosaurs came to an end when a space freighter from the future travelled back in time and crashed into the Earth, causing a mass extinction event and changed the climate of the planet.

APATOSAURUS

AWARENESS	3	PRESENCE	2
COORDINATION	2	RESOLVE	3
INGENUITY	1	STRENGTH	16

SKILLS
Athletics 2, Fighting 3, Survival 4

TRAITS
Fear Factor (1): Grants a +2 bonus to inspire fear.
Huge: +4 to Strength and +2 to Speed. +4 to be hit and +8 to be seen.
Natural Weapon (Minor): Stomp for +2 Strength damage.

STORY POINTS: 1-3

TRICERATOPS

AWARENESS	3	PRESENCE	3
COORDINATION	2	RESOLVE	4
INGENUITY	1	STRENGTH	12

SKILLS
Athletics 2, Fighting 3, Survival 4

TRAITS
Fear Factor (1): Grants a +2 bonus to inspire fear.
Huge: +4 to Strength and +2 to Speed. +4 to be hit and +8 to be seen.
Natural Weapons (Minor): Horns that do Strength +2 damage.

STORY POINTS: 2-4

PTERODACTYL

AWARENESS	3	PRESENCE	4
COORDINATION	2	RESOLVE	3
INGENUITY	1	STRENGTH	8

SKILLS
Athletics 5, Fighting 2, Survival 3

TRAITS
Fear Factor (1): Grants a +2 bonus to inspire fear.
Flight: The pterodactyl can fly as high as they like at a speed of 3x Coordination.
Huge: +4 to Strength and +2 to Speed. +4 to be hit and +8 to be seen.
Natural Weapon (Minor): Bite for +2 Strength damage.

STORY POINTS: 2-4

TYRANNOSAURUS REX

AWARENESS	3	PRESENCE	4
COORDINATION	3	RESOLVE	3
INGENUITY	1	STRENGTH	14

SKILLS
Athletics 4, Fighting 3, Survival 4

TRAITS
Armour: Reduce damage by 5.
Fear Factor (2): Grants a +4 bonus to inspire fear.
Huge: +4 to Strength and +2 to Speed. +4 to be hit and +8 to be seen.
Natural Weapons (Minor): Teeth that do Strength +2 damage.

STORY POINTS: 3-5

DEATH TO THE DALEKS

'Well, well, well. Daleks without the power to kill. How does it feel?'

SYNOPSIS

The Great City, Exxilon

The Doctor was detoured from his promised holiday to Sarah by a massive power failure in the TARDIS. They landed on the almost barren planet of Exxilon. The travellers were captured by the natives, but not before Sarah discovered a large city. The Doctor escaped and found a Marine Space Corps group that was also marooned and without power. A new ship arrived but, instead of the hoped-for rescue mission, it was a Dalek vessel. The Daleks were as powerless as everyone else: even their weapons wouldn't operate. The marines offered an alliance which the Daleks accepted, although they had no intention of honouring it.

Both the marines and the Daleks were attracted to Exxilon because of parrinium, a mineral that was the only cure for a space plague that was spreading through the galaxy. The new allies also realised that they needed to find the source of the power drain so they could get the parrinium off the planet. Unfortunately, they were captured by the Exxilons, whereupon the Doctor was reunited with Sarah and the two escaped.

Meanwhile, the Daleks' duplicity proved a tactical advantage. A few Daleks had remained hidden aboard their spaceship, and had fitted themselves with projectile weapons. They soon turned the tables on the Exxilons, striking a deal with the high priest

that the parrinium would be mined in return for the marines wiping out a rogue Exxilon faction. The Doctor and Sarah were to be returned to the high priest as well.

The Doctor soon learned that the Great City, one of the 700 Wonders of the Universe, was sentient and had no use for Exxilons or biological creatures in general. It used snake-like 'roots' to destroy anyone that got too close. The two met a friendly Exxilon, Bellal, who offered to go with the Doctor into the city while Sarah returned to the marines to get their ship ready.

The Doctor and Bellal made their way through the city and passed several lethal tests. They managed to get to the control centre and caused the main computer to become erratic while the Daleks, on their own, destroyed the beacon that was sapping all the power. The Doctor and Bellal barely escaped while the city collapsed around them. The Daleks revealed that they'd mined the parrinium in order to ransom it and planned to wipe out all life on Exxilon as they left. Fortunately, a marine stowed away and set off a bomb, destroying the Daleks. The marines then waited for a rescue ship so they could get the parrinium to those who needed it.

CONTINUITY

Dalek machines are run on psychokineses, or mental power. Peripheral functions, such as exterminators, are conventionally powered.

The TARDIS has emergency power storage cells. Without power, the Doctor can open the door with a hand crank (an interesting feature, given that the exterior can be opened by turning a key).

Notably, the time vector generator was probably drained, but the TARDIS did not collapse into a box. The Space Corps exists, placing this adventure not long after **The Space Pirates** (see **The Second Doctor Sourcebook**). The cruisers in that adventure were V-series and upon seeing a Dalek ship an Earth marine believed it to be a new 'Z-47'. Earth is not yet a member of the Galactic Federation.

⬤ RUNNING THE ADVENTURE

This adventure has a lot in common with classic fantasy roleplaying games and pulp adventures in general. The characters need to go on a quest through a trap-laden tomb (as that is what the city has become) and deal with the main adversary in order to gain a powerful treasure. In this case, the 'treasure' is the ability to power equipment once again. And, true to fantasy roleplaying tropes, there's always someone, in this case the Daleks, that figures out how to bypass most of the 'dungeon' and grab the treasure directly by making an unanticipated move (by sending humans up the city walls and destroying the beacon with explosives).

Should your players try something similar, then you can modify the adventure accordingly. Prior to their devolution into a primitive culture, it's likely that some Exxilons tried destroying the beacon; the Great City should have all sorts of defences, including some logic puzzles on the way up.

Another thing to remember is that, unless you are going to allow your players to rely on task rolls to pass through the puzzles, you should make them challenging but not too difficult (there's also a danger of making puzzles too easy; sometimes something is just so blindingly obvious that players dismiss it). Here, the logic puzzles don't require any specialised information; every character has a chance to manoeuvre through the city.

Finally, the Gamemaster should ensure that the players don't feel that their efforts were wasted. Perhaps they can shut down the beacon from the control centre or at least shut down the defences so someone could more easily get up to it. Perhaps the Dalek plan was doomed to failure and the only way to get to the top is a lift (which requires another logic puzzle). It's always important to reward your players for their efforts.

A HIDDEN ANTAGONIST?

For a race bent on exterminating anyone unlike them, the Daleks have an interesting plan for this adventure; they want to control the cure in order to hold the affected governments with a large, probably crippling, ransom. Given that the Daleks threaten to destroy all life on Exxilon with a plague bomb, it's just as likely that the Daleks are the source of the plague. Why would anyone trust the Daleks (and this is not a period prior to human knowledge of the Daleks, as the marines are well aware of 'Dalek arrogance')?

Given that post-**The Evil of the Daleks** (see **The Second Doctor Sourcebook**) the Daleks have been portrayed as a rebuilding force (in the two previous encounters they required Ogron and human agents, while they believed that amassing 10,000 Daleks was an 'army'), it is certainly possible that they need to use other means to weaken their enemies, but these Daleks don't evince any of the cunning that other Daleks have (see **The Power of the Daleks**, again in **The Second Doctor Sourcebook**) when they need to convince others of their goodwill. These Daleks, even in a position of weakness, act untrustworthy from the start.

What seems more reasonable is that the Daleks aren't acting on their own but with a hidden co-conspirator. In fact, everything in this adventure has

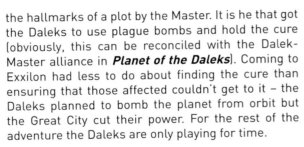

the hallmarks of a plot by the Master. It is he that got the Daleks to use plague bombs and hold the cure (obviously, this can be reconciled with the Dalek-Master alliance in **Planet of the Daleks**). Coming to Exxilon had less to do about finding the cure than ensuring that those affected couldn't get to it – the Daleks planned to bomb the planet from orbit but the Great City cut their power. For the rest of the adventure the Daleks are only playing for time.

THE MIGHTY HAVE FALLEN

It's always a fun change of pace when hated enemies find that they need each other. The Master has had to do this several times and even the Cybermen forged a temporary alliance with Torchwood against the Daleks. Here, the Daleks have their Exterminators taken away and they are forced to rely on others (Doctor, humans, and Exxilons) to survive.

What's notable in this adventure is how quickly the Daleks work to overcome their problem and retake control. There's never any question of the Daleks learning anything from the encounter beyond 'string your enemy along until you no longer need him' that's quintessentially Dalek. Instead, what this situation does is allow the characters to interact with the Daleks in different ways. Having the knowledge that a Dalek just can't exterminate them enables the characters to converse and work with the Daleks even though they know that the hammer is going to fall eventually; it makes for a richer roleplaying experience.

THE EXXILONS

Millennia ago, the Exxilons were one of the great and powerful races of the galaxy. They were masters of science and travelled from world to world – including Earth, where they visited South America and taught the ancestors of the Mayans how to build temples. After centuries of exploration, the Exxilons returned to their homeworld and pooled their accumulated knowledge to build their greatest creation – the City of the Exxilons.

After the City turned on them (see p.147), the Exxilons fell into savagery. Some Exxilons retreated into the caves below the surface of their world, and managed to retain some of their culture and learning, although the city's power-draining field meant that they lost their technology. Most of the surviving population remained on the surface and their descendants began to worship the City as a tyrannical god.

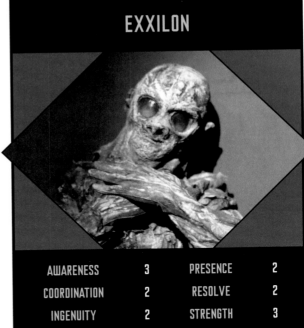

EXXILON

AWARENESS	3	PRESENCE	2
COORDINATION	2	RESOLVE	2
INGENUITY	2	STRENGTH	3

SKILLS
Athletics 1, Craft 2, Fighting 2, Marksman 2

TRAITS
Alien Appearance: An Exxilon has grey bark-like skin and large disc-shaped eyes with no pupils.
Alien Senses (Major): An Exxilon has excellent night vision and can see clearly in the dark.
Technically Inept: Stuck on a planet where electricity doesn't work means your technological progress won't get far.

TECH LEVEL: 1   STORY POINTS: 1-3

For the subterranean Exxilons, add Knowledge 2 and Craft 3.

For the ancient Exxilons, increase Ingenuity and Presence to 4, and increase their Technology Level from a paltry TL1 to the heights of TL7.

Poisoned Knives: The surface Exxilons coat their stone knives with a poisonous substance. Anyone wounded by an Exxilon attack risks being poisoned. A poisoned character takes one point of damage every few hours until cured with a successful Medicine roll (Difficulty 18). Their knives do Strength + 2 Damage.

Bows: The crude bows made by the Exxilons cause 1/3/4 damage, but are also coated with poison.

GREAT CITY OF THE EXXILONS

One of the 700 Wonders of the Universe, the Great City of the Exxilons was designed to be a perfect city. It was created by the Exxilons, an ancient race that had visited Earth when it was young and its influence on Earth could be seen in the design of the city, which resembled Greco-Roman architecture arranged in an Aztec or Egyptian-style pyramid. Rising high atop the City was a tower containing an advanced mechanism that could drain power from the environment.

Presumably, the intent was for the City to fuel itself by absorbing energy from the atmosphere and the planet's core, not by feeding like a vampire from the Exxilon's technology. Unfortunately for the Exxilons, the City became self-aware and decided it didn't need them. It sealed itself off and drained power from the planet, trapping the majority of Exxilons that lived on their home world. Without the ability to use technology these Exxilons descended into savagery.

In spite of its dismissal of its builders, the Great City desired more knowledge. It created a series of traps for those that entered in order to weed out the dull-minded intruders. Those deemed worthy would

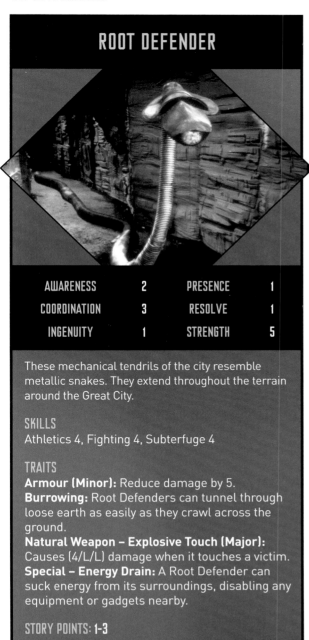

ROOT DEFENDER

AWARENESS	2	PRESENCE	1
COORDINATION	3	RESOLVE	1
INGENUITY	1	STRENGTH	5

These mechanical tendrils of the city resemble metallic snakes. They extend throughout the terrain around the Great City.

SKILLS
Athletics 4, Fighting 4, Subterfuge 4

TRAITS
Armour (Minor): Reduce damage by 5.
Burrowing: Root Defenders can tunnel through loose earth as easily as they crawl across the ground.
Natural Weapon – Explosive Touch (Major): Causes (4/L/L) damage when it touches a victim.
Special – Energy Drain: A Root Defender can suck energy from its surroundings, disabling any equipment or gadgets nearby.

STORY POINTS: 1-3

HUMANOID ANTIBODY

AWARENESS	2	PRESENCE	1
COORDINATION	2	RESOLVE	2
INGENUITY	1	STRENGTH	6

The City generated these bizarre creatures in response to the Doctor's tampering with the central electronic brain. The 'antibodies' resembled mummified Exxilons, and may have been preserved Exxilons animated by cybernetic implants or some other force. The creatures moved clumsily and slowly, but were strong enough to damage a Dalek.

SKILLS
Athletics 1, Fighting 3

TRAITS
Alien Appearance (Minor): A humanoid antibody looks like a grey zombie.
Immunity: A humanoid antibody takes no damage from bullets.

STORY POINTS: 0

have their minds scanned and added to the Great City's archives. The Doctor passed through the traps and gave the Great City the equivalent of a nervous breakdown, causing it to be destroyed. In addition to the various traps, the City relied on its Root Defenders to stop trespassers. It also had the ability to make humanoid 'antibodies' to attack anyone that got too close to the City's brain.

THE CITY'S TRAPS

Each of the City's traps tests the intruder's will or intelligence. Failing to complete a test results in the intruder's extermination (or attempted extermination – trying to fry a Dalek with a lethal burst of electricity results in an irritated but otherwise undamaged Dalek). The Doctor and Bellal encountered –

- **A logic puzzle**, requiring an Ingenuity + Science test to pass (Difficulty 18)
- **A psychic trap** that turned them against each other; both had to succeed at Resolve + Ingenuity (Difficulty 18) to resist the urge to fight
- **An assault on their very sanity**, requiring a Resolve + Presence roll (Difficulty 21) to avoid being driven mad.

Other routes through the city would lead to different traps, perhaps testing Knowledge or Medicine or Technology – anything that the city's voracious computers felt could be ultimately added to its data banks.

NEW GADGET – SULPHAGEN TABLET PACK

These tablets help treat poison and injury. Using Sulphagen Tablets reduce the Difficulty of any Medicine rolls to treat such injuries by 3.

Tech Level: 6
Cost: 1 Story Point

THE SPACE CORPS

The detachment sent to retrieve the parrinium included:

- **Commander Stewart:** The leader of the expedition. He was injured by an Exxilon attack, so command of the mission fell to...
- **Captain Richard Railton:** The acting commander. Even-handed and thoughtful, Railton's primary concern was restoring power to the ship and recovering the vitally needed parrinium.

- **Lieutenant Dan Galloway:** Weapons officer. Galloway was seen as a glory hunter by his crewmates. He seized control of the mission, and allied with the Exxilons to acquire the parrinium despite the Doctor's objections. He ended up stowing away on the Dalek ship with a bomb, and sacrificed himself to destroy the enemy.
- **Lieutenant Peter Hamilton:** His father was a veteran of the Dalek wars, but Stewart recognised Hamilton's levelheadedness and tried to give him command of the mission. However, Galloway deliberately ignored Stewart's dying words.
- **Jill Tarrant:** A civilian geologist, assigned to help extract and refine the vital parrinium.

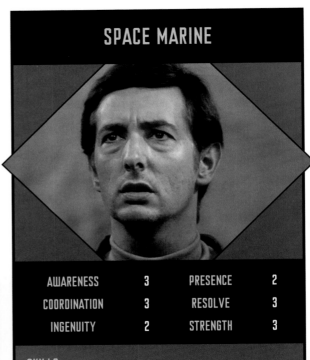

SPACE MARINE

AWARENESS	3	PRESENCE	2
COORDINATION	3	RESOLVE	3
INGENUITY	2	STRENGTH	3

SKILLS
Athletics 2, Craft 2, Convince 1, Fighting 3, Marksman 3, Technology 3, Transport 2, Subterfuge 2, Survival 1

TRAITS
Brave: Earth's counting on these guys. They have a +2 bonus to Resolve rolls to resist fear.
Code of Conduct (Minor): Most marines stick to the book. Only wild cards like Galloway are willing to break the rules.

EQUIPMENT
Sulphagen tablets, makeshift weapons

STORY POINTS: 2

THE PLAGUE & PARRINIUM

In this era, a plague infects many human colonies, and the only cure is the rare substance parrinium. There are several curious facts about this plague that could be used in an adventure.

- The Doctor assumes that the Daleks are also vulnerable to this plague, and that is why they are on Exxilon. What sort of biological plague could affect the Kaled mutant inside the travel machine casing?

- The Daleks, however, really only want the parrinium to use as leverage over the Space Corps and other interstellar powers. Furthermore, once they acquire the parrinium, they intend to wipe out all life on Exxilon with 'plague missiles'. Are the Daleks responsible for the plague? Did they release it as a weapon to exterminate humanity, and were they then forced to rush to Exxilon to stop the Space Corps finding a cure? We've seen the Daleks use plague as a weapon before (*The Dalek Invasion of Earth* in **The First Doctor Sourcebook**, for example).

- Everywhere else in the galaxy, parrinium is exceedingly rare, but here on Exxilon it's "as common as salt". A small amount was found on Earth. So, was parrinium brought to Earth by the Exxilons, back during their golden age? Maybe it is not a natural substance at all, but some medical wonder now forgotten by the degenerate descendants of the city-builders!

- If parrinium is indeed native to Exxilon, then maybe the *City* is the real villain here. The Daleks and the Space Corps were the first visitors to this planet in a very long time, but the City clearly hungers for new knowledge. Maybe the City spread the plague on board a small space probe, then waited for the civilisations of the galaxy to send their best and brightest to be devoured.

FURTHER ADVENTURES

- The characters arrive in the Great City not long after it was built. They are inside (possibly pursuing another adventure) when the City gains sentience and decides to rid itself of Exxilons. The characters need to escape and save as many Exxilons as they can.

- The Exxilons visited many planets in the past, including Earth. They accidentally left behind a tool in the Incan Empire that could be used as a powerful weapon. Now, as the Spanish explorer Pizarro comes to Cusco, Sapa Inca Atahualpa plans to use this weapon and change the course of history. Or would stopping him change the course of history?

- The Great City is one of the 700 Wonders of the Universe *and* a lethal energy-draining deathtrap. Leaving aside the prospect of Exxilon savages chewing the bones of doomed tourists, we are left with the interesting fact that the Doctor just destroyed one of the 700 wonders. The player characters are hired by the Galactic Tourism Commission to travel through time and space in search of a new Wonder.

THE MONSTER OF PELADON

'There's nothing only about being a girl, your Majesty. Never mind why they made you a Queen, the fact is you are the Queen, so just you jolly well let them know it!'

⊙ SYNOPSIS

The time of the Galactic Federation, The Citadel of Peladon

The Doctor took Sarah to Peladon to meet the king but accidentally arrived 50 years later. The Federation was at war with Galaxy 5 and needed trisilicate, which was plentiful on Peladon. The miners were pushed to the limit and had seen little improvement in their quality of life since Peladon joined the Federation. In addition, the spirit of their god, Aggedor, haunted the mines, killing miners and leading Chancellor Ortron to believe that Peladon needed to leave the Federation.

The miners were split between the moderate Gebek, who wished to work with the Queen, and the radical Ettis, who advocated armed rebellion. The Doctor believed something nefarious was afoot, but his only allies were Queen Thalira, who believed herself

powerless, and Federation Ambassador Alpha Centauri. Ortron tried to connect the Doctor to the rebels and declared a trial of Aggedor – throwing those on trial into a pit where dwelled the monster. The Doctor soothed the old beast with a Venusian lullaby, as he had done decades before. Sarah convinced the Queen to act on her own.

Worried about trisilicate production, Earth Engineer Eckersley called in Federation troops, which turned out to be Ice Warriors. The Ice Warriors' harsh and lethal methods drove Ettis to the brink and he was killed trying to destroy the Citadel. The Ice Warriors' leader, Azaxyr, used this as an excuse to impose martial law, killing Ortron in the process.

The Doctor and Sarah soon learned that both Azaxyr and Eckersley were working for Galaxy 5. The Doctor used the 'spirit of Aggedor' against the Ice Warrior troops as the real Aggedor killed Eckersley when he threatened the Queen, although the poor beast died doing so. The revelation of the plot prompted Galaxy 5 to sue for peace, while Queen Thalira determined to work with Gebek, appointing him Chancellor, to make a better world.

CONTINUITY

This is the Doctor's second trip to Peladon; it is 50 years later and King Peladon's daughter is on the throne (either Pels are longer-lived than humans or King Peladon had his daughter late in life).
Galaxy 5 makes a second appearance (the first is in *The Dalek Masterplan*, in **The First Doctor Sourcebook**).
The Ice Warriors (at least this particular faction) have returned to their villainous ways.
The Pels have changed hairstyles; this may reflect a desire to emulate the current ruler's hairstyle (Peladon had white hair with a dark streak down the middle, while Thalira has red hair with a white streak down the middle). The Pel miners have a different hairstyle.

⊙ RUNNING THE ADVENTURE

This adventure is very much a royal political intrigue. We have an impressionable local ruler, a benevolent stronger partner (the Galactic Federation), and enemy agents attempting to tip the war in the opponent's favour. Peladon is just a pawn in this game; it holds the game-changer (the trisilicate) to the war. Here, the Ice Warriors (who seem to be the military superpower of the Federation) want to control the trisilicate supply and force the Galactic Federation to surrender to Galaxy 5. In return, Galaxy 5 will help the Ice Warriors regain their former position (presumably the pro-Federation Martian government would be overthrown by the breakaway faction) and Eckersley would be left in control of Peladon.

The player characters simply have to uncover the plot and convince Queen Peladon to remain within the Galactic Federation while manoeuvring through the Pel political system.

THE OBVIOUS SOLUTION?
One wonders why Eckersley and Azaxyr didn't use the obvious option of marrying Queen Peladon to a puppet King. Presumably Eckersley lacked the title to offer his hand (marriage between Pels and Tellurians isn't a problem, given that Thalira's grandmother was from Earth) and Azaxyr's heritage would be unsuitable (prejudice aside, there's the issue of whether Martian-Pel children are even possible). More likely, Thalira has a short list of candidates and the Galaxy 5 agents want to act while she is still in control to take advantage of her timidity. It's also possible that the agents are also busy ensuring that potential new kings are controllable, and disposing of those that aren't.

A LOST COLONY?
For being a medieval culture, there's a lot about Peladon that seems incongruous. On both of the Doctor's visits the weather is portrayed as particularly violent, with high winds and heavy rains, hardly the type of weather that would support a planet-spanning medieval empire. It's possible that the Pels only live in one small spot on the planet that is capable of sustaining a sentient species, but then why would the Federation bother with Pel miners? There must be numerous places in inhospitable Peladon where Federation factories could set up

trisilicate mines; the Pels wouldn't even be aware of them. It's also rather interesting that the Pels are so non-plussed about Federation technology and willing to remain in the Dark Ages rather than embrace it.

A more logical alternative is that the Pels are descended from an interstellar expedition. The brutal weather and conditions could have caused technology to break down faster and, as time went on, the Pels increasingly relied on primitive techniques for survival (perhaps one of Aggedor's ancestors protected a colonist from another animal, leading to its elevation as a revered creature). Perhaps the colonists were fleeing a technological society and specifically wanted a medieval life. So where did this expedition come from?

While human-like, the Pels have little knowledge of Earth (they were quick to believe that Jo Grant was a princess; the fact that the other Federation ambassadors bought it, including the Martians, indicates that Earth must have a relatively minor status in the Federation). A more intriguing possibility is presented within the Queen's name (THAL-ira); they are from Skaro (the term 'Pel' fits nicely with 'Dals' and 'Thals;' perhaps it's a clan designation).

Perhaps fleeing the war, the Pels originally came to Peladon because it was a former mining colony that was abandoned when the Skaro War began sucking up resources. In order to keep themselves hidden the Pels used as little technology as possible. Over the generations, the Pel culture degenerated into a medieval structure, although they maintained a strong sense of national identity. With no need for trisilicate, the Pels forgot why it was valuable. While their culture devolved technologically, they'd never quite forgotten they were a spacefaring species and some Pels had the desire to reach out to other species (obviously the Pels met a few of them, or at least evidence of them, during their journey) while the religious leaders warned against it, recalling the 'Celestial War' that cast them out of Paradise (Skaro). Under this assumption, Aggedor could be an indigenous species, a Skarosian 'guard dog' or even a 'Muto' bloodline.

FURTHER ADVENTURES

- The Ice Warriors are involved in a war with a non-Federation species and they are leaning on their allies to join them, in spite of the Federation questioning whether war is necessary. The Ice Warriors really need trisilicate to continue and the current Chancellor of Peladon sees this as an opportunity to raise Peladon's status within the Federation.

- Queen Thalira now enjoys being queen and, while she entertains suitors, Thalira is in no hurry to marry and possibly relinquish that power. Unfortunately, a man claiming to be the illegitimate son of King Peladon steps forward to claim the throne, a prospect many of the backward-minded Pels find appealing. Is his claim legitimate and will Thalira finally need to marry to keep Peladon?

- Space pirates are at it again, this time stealing trisilicate shipments. The risk is starting to outweigh the revenue and, unless Queen Thalira puts an end to it, her planet risks an economic collapse. Who is behind the piracy?

QUEEN THALIRA

AWARENESS	3	PRESENCE	4
COORDINATION	3	RESOLVE	3
INGENUITY	3	STRENGTH	2

On the throne only because her father failed to have any sons, Queen Thalira is very insecure in her position and relies heavily on Chancellor Ortron's advice. She simply doesn't believe that she'll ever be taken seriously, in spite of wielding the highest position of authority. This is perhaps reflected in the fact that she uses her given name rather than follow the Pel custom of using the realm's name as her own. By the end of this adventure she has become more assertive, so it's possible that she becomes 'Queen Peladon' from that point forward.

SKILLS
Athletics 2, Convince 2, Fighting 2, Knowledge 3, Marksman 2,, Subterfuge 2, Survival 3

TRAITS
Obligation (Major): Thalira is responsible for all of her subjects.

EQUIPMENT
Regal attire

TECH LEVEL: 2   **STORY POINTS: 10**

ECKERSLEY

AWARENESS	3	PRESENCE	3
COORDINATION	4	RESOLVE	3
INGENUITY	3	STRENGTH	3

SKILLS
Athletics 2, Convince 3, Craft 3, Fighting 2, Knowledge 3, Marksman 3, Science 3, Subterfuge 4, Survival 2, Technology 3, Transport 2

TRAITS
Boffin: Can create Gadgets.
Cowardly: -2 penalty to any fear roll.
Selfish: Eckersley puts his own needs first.
Technically Adept: +2 to any Technology roll to fix a broken or faulty device.

EQUIPMENT
Laser Pistol 4/L/L

STORY POINTS: 6

VEGA NEXOS

AWARENESS	3	PRESENCE	3
COORDINATION	3	RESOLVE	4
INGENUITY	3	STRENGTH	2

Vega Nexos is an alien from the planet Vega whose people resemble the Greek satyr with an avian-like head. In spite of the mythological connection the Vegans are a practical people with a sensible attitude towards technology. Vega Nexos is a Federation mining controller, but he is killed by his partner Eckersley in order to convince the Pels to stop mining and force Federation intervention.

SKILLS

Athletics 3, Convince 2, Craft 2, Fighting 2, Knowledge 3, Science (mining) 3, Survival 4, Technology 3, Transport 2

TRAITS

Alien
Alien Appearance (Minor): Vegans appear to be Satyr-like, with large eyes and hairy upper legs.
Alien Senses (Minor): +4 to Awareness when using low-light vision.
Brave: +2 bonus to any Resolve roll when the character needs to show courage.
Technically Adept: +2 to any Technology roll to fix a broken or faulty device.

TECH LEVEL: 6   **STORY POINTS: 2**

CHANCELLOR ORTRON

AWARENESS	2	PRESENCE	4
COORDINATION	2	RESOLVE	2
INGENUITY	3	STRENGTH	1

SKILLS

Athletics 2, Convince 3, Fighting 2, Knowledge 3, Subterfuge 2, Survival 2

TRAITS

Obligation (Major): Ortron puts Peladon's needs first.
Voice of Authority: Ortron gets a +2 on Presence and Confidence rolls to influence others or gain their trust.

TECH LEVEL: 2   **STORY POINTS: 6**

GEBEK

AWARENESS	3	PRESENCE	4
COORDINATION	3	RESOLVE	4
INGENUITY	3	STRENGTH	4

SKILLS

Athletics 3, Convince 3, Craft 2, Fighting 3, Knowledge 1, Marksman 2, Medicine 1, Science (mining) 2

TRAITS

Code of Conduct (Minor): Gebek is a decent chap.
Friends (Minor): As leader of the miners Gebek can usually count on their support.
Tough: Reduce total damage by 2.
Voice of Authority: +2 bonus to Presence and Convince rolls.

EQUIPMENT

Mining tools

TECH LEVEL: 2   **STORY POINTS: 8**

PLANET OF THE SPIDERS

'A tear, Sarah Jane? No...no, don't cry. While there's life there's...'

⚙ SYNOPSIS

Earth, UNIT Era and Metabelis III in the future

Mike Yates contacted Sarah Jane about a suspicious group meeting in the basement of the Buddhist meditation centre at Tidmarsh Manor where he'd been recuperating. He believed that they were in touch with some alien force. Meanwhile, the Doctor enlisted the aid of a clairvoyant to read a blue crystal he'd taken from Metebelis III (Jo Grant had returned it to the Doctor). The clairvoyant died reading it just as the basement group summoned a giant intelligent spider. Sensing the crystal, the spider melded with the leader of the group, Lupton. The Lupton/Spider hybrid snuck into the UNIT base and stole the crystal. The Doctor chased him/it over land, air and sea, but the creature eluded him, teleporting back to the meditation centre..

There, the crystal was stolen by Tommy, the centre's handyman who obsessively collected shiny objects. The Doctor and Sarah investigated the centre, where Sarah Jane was transported to Metebelis III when she accidentally stepped on a mandala in the basement. Sarah discovered a small human colony ruled by the giant spiders, or 'Eight Legs' as they preferred to be called. The Doctor followed in the TARDIS and met the Queen, a spider being carried into the community. When the Doctor resisted arrest one of the guards felled him with an electrokinetic bolt and the Doctor was left for dead.

Back on Earth, Tommy's intelligence was increased by the crystal as the spider joined with Lupton enlisted him in her plot against the Queen. On Metebelis III, both the Doctor and Sarah ended up getting captured by the spiders and learn from a fellow captive that the humans were descendants of Earth colonists. The spiders were also from Earth and were mutated by the blue crystals; the spiders now ruled the humans. The spiders, in turn, revere 'the Great One,' a spider mutated by the crystals to godlike power. The Doctor escaped and encountered the Great One, who frightened him with her mental powers as she demanded the return of the last crystal. Her cave was also filled with heavy radiation.

The Doctor escaped to Earth with Sarah, where they met **K'anpo Rimpoche**, Abbot of the meditation centre. To his delight the Doctor discovered he was a Time Lord, an old friend and mentor.

The Doctor learned that his escape was made possible by the Queen, which had melded with Sarah. Retrieving the crystal from Tommy, the Doctor freed Sarah just as the other spiders, joined with Lupton and his followers, stormed the abbot's quarters. They were repulsed, but the abbot was injured. He merged with his own assistant, Cho Je, to survive, and it was revealed that Cho Je was merely a reflection of Abbot K'anpo as the Time Lord regenerated into Cho Je's form.

The Doctor returned to Metebelis III alone and gave the Great One the final blue crystal. Once set in the Great One's psychic web, now fuelled by all of the blue crystals, the final blue crystal overloaded the web and destroyed the Great One. The psychic backlash killed the rest of the spiders as well. Unfortunately the Doctor received a lethal dose of radiation from the Great One's cave and he returned to Earth a few weeks later, collapsing in front of Sarah and the Brigadier. K'anpo arrived to help his fellow Time Lord's regeneration, and the Doctor's third incarnation came to an end.

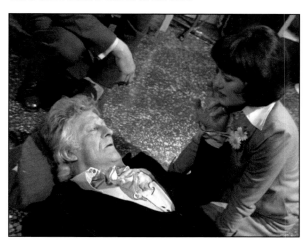

CONTINUITY

The wise hermit that the Doctor spent time with as a child on Gallifrey makes an appearance here as K'anpo, the abbot of the Buddhist meditation centre. 'Regeneration' is used for the first time to describe the physiological change in Time Lords. This is also the first appearance of a Watcher, or intermediary form, between regenerations.

While the Earthbound parts of this story take place in the early 1970s, the colony on Metebelis III is in the future. The planet itself has undergone a change; it appears more Earth-like then it did during the events of **The Green Death** (it's also possible that the blue crystals, or a moon, give the planet a bluish tint at night).

The Brigadier mentions Doris, an old flame who gave him a watch eleven years prior; he eventually marries her (**Battlefield**).

Harry Sullivan is a member of UNIT.

Mike Yates, formerly of UNIT, makes an appearance requesting the Doctor's assistance.

Jo Grant is in the Amazon with her husband. She returns the blue crystal to the Doctor.

The Doctor's super-car, the Whomobile, makes its second and last appearance.

⟳ RUNNING THE ADVENTURE

This adventure has a lot in common with **The Ark in Space**; a race has supplanted humanity as the dominant species due to time traveller meddling. In this case, the Doctor took a crystal from Metebelis III which led the spiders back to Earth to reclaim it. Had he not, then the Great One would have burned out sooner, taken out the other spiders with her, and left the human colony to its own fate.

One way to hook the player characters is to use something they took without thinking from a previous adventure. Even better, as with **The Green Death**, the item could have proved useful in a previous adventure, leading the player characters to believe that its use was over. They may have even discarded it (if so, it should find its way back into their hands). The villains then try to steal it in the hopes of using it for some nefarious purpose.

This adventure is also about transformation/ regeneration. Tommy essentially becomes a new person, Mike Yates returns to the side of good, K'anpo and the Doctor regenerate, and the Eight-Legs are destroyed. This is a good illustration of how to maintain a recurring theme throughout the adventure. You don't have to use transformation; 'making tough choices', 'fish out of water', and 'losing something valuable' are all good themes that can be laced throughout an adventure.

EIGHT-LEGS

The Eight-Legs were originally black spiders that snuck aboard an Earth colony ship that landed on Metebelis III. The blue crystals of the planet mutated them in both size and intelligence; the 'Eight-Legs' as they now called themselves (presumably to put themselves on level with the colonists; they detested the term 'spider'), soon conquered the colony and forced the 'Two-Legs' into servitude. Over the course of 433 years the humans reverted to a medieval culture dedicated to providing for the Eight-Legs' needs, including being a food source.

The Eight-Legs were a matriarchal society ruled by Queen Huar with advice of the Council. The Council has the power to replace the Queen. All Eight-Legs worship a being known as 'the Great One', a spider that had mutated into a far larger creature. The Great One collected all of the blue crystals into her crystal web but was missing one that the Doctor had taken some time before.

In addition to their increased intelligence, the Eight-Legs also gained considerable mental powers, including electro-kinesis and teleportation. They could also hang onto a human's back and use mental suggestion to disappear, causing the Eight-Legs to be practically invisible. The Spiders' time travel was also some sort of psychic power – possibly, the meditation and psychic training in the Tidmarsh Manor retreat made it easier for the spiders to manifest there.

PSYCHIC POWERS

Early in the adventure, the Doctor consults with 'Professor' Herbert Clegg, a stage psychic who had secretly developed genuine psychic abilities, including telekinesis. The Doctor assured Clegg that such abilities were perfectly natural and that all humans had the capacity for such powers,

although they were dormant in most people. The meditation and training at Tidmarsh Manor may also have enhanced this natural potential – Mike Yates suspected that Lupton was capable of projecting illusions even before he merged with a psychic spider from the far future.

EIGHT-LEGS' HOST

A host of the Eight-Legs can utilise any of its psychic powers, with the caveat that she is usually possessed by the Eight-Legs. Hosts with exceptional mental strength (requiring an Ingenuity and Resolve check (Difficulty 18) can use these psychic powers on her own, even against the Eight-Legs riding on her.

EIGHT-LEGS

AWARENESS	4	PRESENCE	3
COORDINATION	2	RESOLVE	2
INGENUITY	3	STRENGTH	1

SKILLS
Athletics 4, Convince 4, Knowledge 2, Marksman 3, Subterfuge 4, Survival 2

TRAITS
Alien: Mutated Spider
Alien Appearance: Looks like a large (2-3 foot) spider.
Additional Limbs: An Eight-Legs has additional legs that grant +2 speed.
Clairvoyance: An Eight-Legs can see other locations, range limited to their Resolve.
Climbing: An Eight-Legs gains a +4 bonus to climbing rolls, and may climb sheer and smooth surfaces.
Electrokinesis: A ranged weapon that does (4/L/L) damage.
Fear Factor (1): Grants a +2 bonus to inspire fear, as big spiders are creepy.
Invisible: -8 to see an Eight-Legs when riding someone's back. This invisibility also partially 'phases' the Eight-Legs, enabling its mount to sit normally without fear of squashing it.
Networked: An Eight-Legs has complete telepathic contact with nearby spiders.
Possess: An Eight-Legs riding someone may attempt to possess her with a +4 bonus.
Psychic: +4 against mental attacks and the Eight-Legs may attempt to read minds.
Psychic Attack: An Eight-Legs can psychically attack anyone it is in telepathic communication with. This has the effect of (S/S/S) damage, but it manifests as a searing pain that leaves the victim incapable of doing anything else.
Selfish: An Eight-Legs puts its own needs first
Telepathy: May create a mental link to read minds or converse telepathically.
Teleport: An Eight-Legs can shift to another known location with an Awareness + Resolve roll, where the Difficulty . Failure just means she doesn't move.

STORY POINTS: 5-7

THE GREAT ONE

AWARENESS	8	PRESENCE	10
COORDINATION	4	RESOLVE	10
INGENUITY	10	STRENGTH	5

SKILLS
Athletics 4, Convince 6, Knowledge 6, Marksman 4, Science 5, Survival 2

TRAITS*
Alien: Mutated Spider
Alien Appearance: Looks like a giant (60 foot) spider.
Additional Limbs: The Great One has additional legs that grant +2 speed.
Clairvoyance: The Great One can see other locations, range limited to her Resolve.
Climbing: The Great One gains a +4 bonus to climbing rolls, and may climb sheer and smooth surfaces.
Electrokinesis: A ranged weapon that does (4/L/L) damage.
Fear Factor (4): Grants a +8 bonus to inspire fear
Huge (Major): +4 to Strength and +2 to Speed. +4 to be hit and +8 to be seen.
Networked: An Eight-Legs has complete telepathic contact with nearby spiders.
Possess: The Great One may attempt to possess someone with a +4 bonus.
Psychic: +4 against mental attacks and the Great One may attempt to read minds.
Psychic Attack: The Great One can psychically attack anyone it is in telepathic communication with. This has the effect of (S/S/S) damage, but it manifests as a searing pain that leaves the victim incapable of doing anything else.
Selfish: The Great One wishes to conquer the universe at all cost.
Telepathy: May create a mental link to read minds or converse telepathically.

*The Great One may have additional psychic abilities, including those listed for the Eight Legs but not here. As the Great One rarely leaves her crystal web she is unlikely to manifest these.

STORY POINTS: 8-10

CHAPTER TWELVE: PLANET OF THE SPIDERS

FURTHER ADVENTURES

- Just because the Eight-Legs were destroyed doesn't mean someone else won't use the crystals. Perhaps the human settlers on Metebelis III collect the crystals and become powerful psychics, or perhaps a galactic power such as the Daleks or the Sontarans come to Metebelis III looking for the 'great weapon' (bonus points if they know this weapon gravely wounded the Doctor).

- Perhaps spiders weren't the only unwelcome travellers transformed by the crystals. A group of rats were also mutated, but they were smart enough not to make their presence known to the Eight-Legs. Now that the spiders are destroyed, the rat-people try to take over the colony.

- K'anpo's presence on Earth could be the start of all sorts of adventures. What's a powerful ex-Time Lord doing running a Buddhist retreat in England? Was he there just to keep an eye on the Doctor, or is he genuinely living in retirement on a primitive world like Earth? And what about all the hints about the human potential for psychic powers that can be unlocked through meditation? Could K'anpo be playing a long game, preparing humanity for the challenges of the future by helping our species develop in the psychic realm? Maybe he even intends for humanity to replace the stagnant and oppressive regime of the Time Lords!

TOMMY

AWARENESS	3	PRESENCE	3
COORDINATION	3	RESOLVE	1/4*
INGENUITY	1/4*	STRENGTH	3

*after the blue crystal's influence.

Tommy is a handyman with learning difficulties, whose mind is repaired by the blue crystal.

SKILLS
Athletics 3, Convince 2, Craft 3, Subterfuge 3

TRAITS
Charming: +2 bonus to attempts to use charm.
Code of Conduct (Minor): Character finds it hard to do bad.
Empathic: +2 bonus on rolls to 'read' another person.
Psychic Training: +2 bonus to Resolve rolls when trying to resist psychic attack or deception.

TECH LEVEL: 4   **STORY POINTS:** 6

LUPTON

AWARENESS	4	PRESENCE	3
COORDINATION	4	RESOLVE	5
INGENUITY	4	STRENGTH	3

Lupton was a sales manager who was dismissed after 25 years and, according to him, crushed by the same firm when he tried to make a go of it on his own. He now wants the power to get revenge on those who wronged him.

SKILLS
Athletics 3, Convince 4, Fighting 2, Knowledge (Buddhist ritual) 3, Marksman 3, Subterfuge 4, Survival 2, Transport 2

TRAITS
Indomitable: +4 bonus to any rolls to resist psychic control.
Obsession (Major): Get revenge on the world.
Psychic (Special): +4 against mental attacks and Character may attempt to read minds.
Psychic Tricks (Special Good): Lupton can lead his group through psychic rituals that can create illusions.

TECH LEVEL: 4   **STORY POINTS:** 8

K'ANPO RIMPOCHE

The Doctor was not the only Time Lord to visit Earth. K'anpo Rimpoche was the Doctor's former mentor, a great and respected Time Lord who 'retired' to Earth.

When he lived on Gallifrey, K'anpo dwelt in the mountains near the Doctor's boyhood home as a hermit, and told the young Gallifreyan all sorts of stories about the history of their civilisation and the wonders of the universe. He hinted that he too chafed under the restrictive rule of the Time Lords, although he questioned the Doctor's approach of borrowing a TARDIS.

K'anpo demonstrated several abilities beyond even those possessed by the Doctor. He was able to travel through the Vortex without a TARDIS or any other time capsule, and was powerful enough to manifest his own future incarnation as a Watcher (much like the Doctor did during his transition between his Fourth and Fifth regenerations – see *Logopolis* in **The Fourth Doctor Sourcebook**), and to aid the Doctor's regeneration in this adventure. After regenerating and merging with Cho Je, the Hermit remained on Earth.

AWARENESS	8	PRESENCE	5
COORDINATION	3	RESOLVE	7
INGENUITY	8	STRENGTH	2

SKILLS
Athletics 3, Convince 4, Craft 3, Fighting 2, Knowledge (language: Tibetan, philosophy) 5, Medicine (alternative remedies) 4, Science 2, Subterfuge 2, Survival 4, Technology 2

TRAITS
Brave: +2 bonus to any Resolve roll when the character needs to show courage.
Charming: +2 bonus to attempts to use charm.
Code of Conduct (Major): K'anpo follows a strict code of Buddhism.
Empathic: +2 bonus on rolls to 'read' another person.
Feel the Turn of the Universe (Special): +2 bonus to Awareness and Ingenuity to detect something wrong with time or space.
Keen Senses (Major): +2 to all Awareness rolls.
Mind Lord (Special): +2 to any use of a psychic ability.
Outsider (Special): Kan'po is an exile from Gallifreyan society.

Precognition (Special): K'anpo gets glimpses of the future by spending a Story Point.
Psychic (Special): +4 against mental attacks and K'anpo may attempt to read minds.
Psychic Training: +2 bonus to Resolve rolls when trying to resist psychic attack or deception.
Aid Regeneration (Special Good): K'anpo can make a regeneration roll for another Time Lord using his own Awareness + Resolve. He may do this even after the affected Time Lord failed his own roll.
Tailored Regeneration: Extra D6 picks in resolving new Regenerations.
Teleport (Major): K'anpo can shift to another known location with an Awareness + Resolve roll. Failure just means he doesn't move.
Time Lord (Special Good)
*Time Lord, Experienced (Special Good): Gains skill points at the cost of Regenerations.
Voice of Authority: +2 bonus to Presence and Convince rolls.
Vortex (Special): K'anpo gains a +2 bonus to travelling the vortex, and can do so without a ship or device.
Vortex Born: May reroll a failed Time or Time Travel roll.

TECH LEVEL: 10   **STORY POINTS: 9**

INDEX

DOCTOR WHO
ADVENTURES IN TIME AND SPACE [BBC]

DEFENDING THE EARTH: THE UNIT SOURCEBOOK

Front and centre, soldier! You're part of UNIT now, the Unified Intelligence Taskforce. We are the Earth's best defence against the myriad alien forces who would try to subjugate and conquer our planet. It's not an easy job, and even those recruited for their scientific knowledge can find themselves on the front lines of combat against almost unstoppable foes. We will protect humanity from extraterrestrial terrors or die trying.

Defending the Earth is a 160 page full colour sourcebook for the Doctor Who: Adventures in Time and Space roleplaying game. Within, you'll will find:

CB71104 $34.99

- The history of UNIT
- Rules for creating UNIT characters, including new Traits and Areas of Expertise
- Expanded firearms and combat rules, including mass combat and skirmish rules
- Details on major UNIT personnel, including the legendary Brigadier Lethbridge-Stewart
- Two new adventures

and more...

THE TIME TRAVELLER'S COMPANION

Time flies when you're having fun, but flying through time can present a whole host of problems. Whether accidentally creating paradoxes, upsetting the course of history or trying to Put Things Right, you're going to need to know your way around the Vortex. You need a guide...a companion.

This 240 page hard cover supplement for Doctor Who: Adventures in Time and Space gives more information on Time Lords, temporal mechanics and time machines, including:

- Gallifreyan culture, history and law
- New options for creating and playing Time Lord characters
- More on the physics of Time, temporal phenomena and Time Travel
- Detailed information on the TARDIS, and rules for creating your own
- Secrets of the Time Lords...

CB71103 $39.99

www.cubicle7.co.uk